iSeries and AS/400®

APIs at Work

About the *at Work* Series

Developed by Merrikay Lee, the *at Work* series gives working professionals the tools, techniques, and usable code they need to craft streamlined solutions to everyday challenges.

Merrikay Lee is series editor for the MC Press line of professional books, which comprises more than 75 titles. She has spent more than 20 years as a technical professional in the IBM midrange industry and 15 years in the publishing field. She is the author of four books and has worked with numerous IT technical professionals to develop titles for the IBM midrange community of IT professionals. She is president of Lee Publishing Services Inc. in Dallas, Texas, and can be reached at *mlee@leepublishing.com*.

iSeries and AS/400®

APIs at Work

Doug Pence and Ron Hawkins

MIDRANGE
COMPUTING
IIR PUBLICATIONS INC.

First Edition
First Printing—March 2001

© 2001 Midrange Computing
ISBN: 1-58347-022-0

Midrange Computing
5650 El Camino Real, Suite 225
Carlsbad, CA 92008–7147 USA
www.midrangecomputing.com

For information on translations or book distribution outside the USA or to arrange bulk-purchase discounts for sales promotions, premiums, or fund-raisers, please contact Midrange Computing at the above address.

V4R4

ACKNOWLEDGMENTS

If you benefit from this book, your thanks should be directed to Merrikay Lee and Victoria Mack of Midrange Computing. They identified the need and asked us to participate in the project. We hope that the result justifies their faith in us.

We consider this book a tribute to friendship. Anytime you can hang out with someone for 20 years and still enjoy the company, you must be doing something right.

Once again, we would like to thank our coworkers at CPU Medical Management Systems. It is an honor to work with such talented and dedicated individuals.

It is not really possible to extend enough gratification to our immediate families. Your sacrifices are many and we are very appreciative. We promise that we will not take any more of these projects for a while. No, really! This time we are serious! This time we really mean it! Why are you still smiling and shaking your heads?

We would also like to extend thanks to all those dedicated individuals in this business who are so eager to share their knowledge. Attending and participating in COMMON and IBM Technical conferences has been both an honor and a privilege.

CONTENTS

INTRODUCTION

Every man is ignorant, only on different subjects.

—Will Rogers

For over two decades, we have been accumulating knowledge on that mystical language known as RPG. From the System/3 to the iSeries 400, much has changed. One of those changes has been the advent of application program interfaces (APIs).

APIs will get you as close to the metal as you can get. There are hundreds of APIs, and they seem to multiply with each release. They can be used to deliver information to you or do your dirty work for you. They can be as simple as a program call or so complex they can make your head swim.

APIs are the language of communication. If you want to talk to other applications (including IBM's), you do so through APIs. As computers evolve (from System 38 to AS/400 to iSeries 400), one thing is certain: APIs will remain the language of choice for communication with the rest of the world.

API is just a fancy term for a system-provided program. APIs have been around for years, but at first, few programmers were adventurous enough to explore them. Much has changed in recent years. The demands on our industry have increased dramatically. While the Internet is responsible for much of the increased demand, the business world also now realizes the kind of impact information systems can make on productivity.

You are going to need to write Web pages and post your reports on the Internet. You are going to need to use high-level encryption to store sensitive information. You are going to need to write interfaces from Microsoft Windows to your AS/400 RPG applications. Are you alarmed yet? Well, don't be. This book shows you how to use APIs to do all of those things and more. You will greatly enhance your value to your organization, while learning that there is nothing you cannot do with the AS/400 if you know where to look.

This book is chock full of code and examples of APIs, and how you can use them in RPG. It covers most of the more important APIs, and shows you where to go for more information. It begins by covering the basics of API programming. From there, you delve right into the details of list APIs and user spaces, file APIs, command-processing APIs, work-management APIs, message-handling APIs, security APIs, object APIs, socket APIs, and Web APIs. Each chapter of this book is full of business examples designed to work for you, to help you get your work done.

Whether you are looking for your AS/400 to deliver Web pages or to extract information deep within the recesses of your system, APIs are your ticket to the dance. If you work in RPG on the AS/400, make some space for this publication on the shelf of your RPG reference library.

A final note for you to consider is the issue of the name of the IBM midrange box we have all known as the AS/400. Now that IBM has officially rebranded the AS/400 to the eServer iSeries 400, referring to the box can get a little complicated. In the name of simplicity, the familiar term *AS/400* is used throughout this book. Be assured that all of the topics covered here apply to IBM's eServer iSeries as well as the AS/400.

1

API FUNDAMENTALS

All APIs use a set of standards that define how system programs communicate with application programs. While every API communicates different information, they all communicate that information using the same set of standards. Notice that *standards* is plural. Different types of APIs use different ways to pass data. Some use one long variable to pass data back to your program, while others use a user space to do it. (If you are not familiar with this terminology, don't worry. You'll learn the terms as you progress through the book.) You will soon see that once you understand the different formats used, you are well on your way to using any API in the system.

Begin with the Basics

One of the many strengths of the AS/400 is its ability to incorporate new advancements in hardware technology without affecting application programs. This amazing feat is accomplished by *machine interface* (MI). As shown in Figure 1.1, MI is an intermediate software layer between your application programs and the AS/400's hardware. Because your application program doesn't talk directly to the registers in the hardware, the hardware can and does change without any changes to the application software. This special "upward compatibility" is one of the primary reasons that the AS/400 is the best business system available.

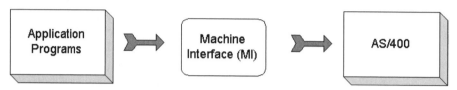

Figure 1.1: MI provides a layer between application programs and the AS/400.

But MI can also be viewed as a liability. When your programs need to get information from the system that's not readily available, your hands are tied because there is simply no way to get around the machine interface. Being the intuitive programmer that you are, you already know where we are going with all of this: APIs are the answer. APIs let you get at system information that you normally cannot access. And best of all, APIs let you get at that information without by-passing the machine interface. This is essential because, when IBM changes the hardware (as it always does), your application will still run.

Furthermore, API standards allow for future enhancements, so that even if IBM changes a particular API in the future, that API will still be compatible with older versions. Of course, you won't be able to take advantage of the new enhancements to the API unless you modify your code, but your existing code will still function just as it did when you wrote it.

Another benefit of APIs is speed. Some CL commands retrieve information about the system into a special kind of file called an *outfile*. You can then process this outfile to get at the information you want. While this method works and is easy to use, it is rather slow because the system has to build the file and then write records to it.

For example, if you specify OUTPUT(*OUTFILE) OUTFILE(SOMENAME) with the Display Object Description (DSPOBJD) command, you can then read the file SOMENAME to get at the information about the object. A much faster way to process this same information, though, is via the Retrieve Object Description API, QUSROBJD. This API returns the same information (if not more) as a parameter when you call it. Because it doesn't have to build and process the file, this method is much faster than using the command.

APIs can perform many different kinds of functions. The Command Line API, QUSCMDLN, brings up a screen that lets you enter commands to the system. Others, like QCMDEXC and QCAPCMD, let you execute commands directly from within application programs. (See chapter 4 for examples of these handy APIs). There are APIs to handle messages, process spool files, and work with any object on the system.

Where to Get Information About APIs from IBM

The best source for information about APIs (with exception of this fine publication, of course) is the IBM manuals: *AS/400 System API Reference* V4R4 (IBM's publication number SC41-5801-03) and *OS/400 Program and CL Command APIs* (SC41-5870-03). If you prefer to access this information online as shown by Figure 1.2, point your browser to:

```
http://publib.boulder.IBM.com/index.html
```

and select Master Catalog.

Figure 1.2: IBM has many publications available online.

From the master catalog, as shown in Figure 1.3, enter either the name of the book or the IBM publication number (SC41-5870-03, in our example), and click the FIND button.

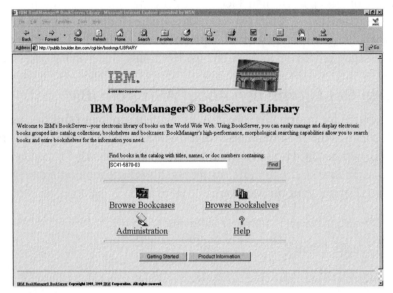

Figure 1.3: IBM's Online Publications Master Catalog will help you locate publications.

Once you have found the book, bookmark the selected page as a "favorite" in your browser. As you start working with APIs, you will refer to the IBM manuals often for parameters and syntax.

As we researched materials for this book, IBM was in the process of moving a lot of this type of information to their new Information Center. It is possible that access to IBM manuals might have been moved or altered by the time you read this. Nevertheless, you should still be able to find your way to the API manuals you need. The following link to the IBM Information Center page should get you started:

```
http://publib.boulder.IBM.com/pubs/html/AS/400/infocenter.html.
```

Information Already on Your System

If you have a library called QSYSINC, you already have a wealth of information about APIs on your system. Every system comes with this library, but you have to install it. This library contains source members that could save you a great deal of time when using APIs.

There are about 20 source files in the QSYSINC library. Most of the files are for using APIs in different languages such as C, COBOL, and RPG. The main file for ILE RPG is QRPGLESRC. Each member in the file contains data structure definitions for an individual API. Usually, the name of the API and the name of the member correspond, but there are some generic members that cross multiple APIs, such as the QUS member, which contains common structures for the user-space APIs.

Try to use these definitions every time you use an API. This provides consistency from program to program. It also reduces problems with erroneous definitions of the data structures. It does not completely eliminate the potential for problems with the definition, though, because some fields are defined as varying in length, where you supply the length of the field. These fields are usually dependent on how much data you want the API to return. Still, using the supplied definitions will save you lots of time overall.

Another benefit of using the data structure definitions found in QSYSINC is that every field is well documented. Pointers to data structures contain text describing the denoted data structure and how to get to the pointer data. The text will tell you the name of the field and what structure points to it. Keep in mind that, if the manuals don't help with a particular problem with an API, sometimes you can browse the corresponding member in QSYSINC for clues on how to proceed.

One drawback to using the members in this library is size. The structures are so well documented (when was the last time you heard *that* about an IBM manual?) that a simple structure can balloon into hundreds of lines of code. It's not uncommon for a 200-line program to expand to 1,000 lines with all of the text describing each field in each structure. Because comments are not pulled into the compiled object, this is not a significant problem.

The sheer volume of documentation with each API caused us a problem in writing this book. While we feel the correct way to use the API is to pull in the complete definition of the structures from QSYSINC, we could not show this with each sample program in this book. If we did, this book would quickly have become encyclopedic. To keep the book to a manageable size, therefore, we haven't included all of the source documentation.

Pass the Data, Please...

To use an API, you simply code a CALL statement. Most APIs pass information back and forth by parameters. It's important to understand how these parameters work.

Usually, when you call APIs, you pass parameters the same way as if you were calling another application program. The appropriate terminology to use when describing this technique is *passing parameters by reference.* When one RPG program calls another, you generally pass parameters by reference. Your program doesn't actually pass the data from program to program (even though you specify a data field as a parameter). Instead, a pointer to that data is passed. This is why a change to the data in the called program is automatically seen in the calling program, even if the calling program ends abnormally. The change to the data occurs immediately, and both programs have pointers that point to the same data.

Some APIs, however, support a different method of passing data. This method is referred to as *passing parameters by value.* Passing by value actually passes the data between the programs. RPG IV, for example, supports this method with the keyword *VALUE. So, if the API you are using has been categorized as pass by value, be sure to use the *VALUE keyword. This method is generally applicable to UNIX-type APIs.

Another thing you will find about APIs is that some parameters are required, while others are optional. If a parameter is optional, all parameters after it are also optional. Conversely, if you leave out one optional parameter, all subsequent parameters must be left out as well.

Some API parameters can be omitted. Omitting parameters is different than dropping an optional parameter. Parameters that follow an omitted parameter can still be used. To pass an omitted parameter, you must pass a null pointer. This is usually accomplished by passing the keyword *OMIT for the parameter.

You will see more about these parameter concepts as you continue your journey into the world of APIs.

Data Types

When APIs deal with numeric values, they predominantly use binary numbers. There are a few nuances to note. The IBM manuals call for a binary field as either BINARY(2) or BINARY(4). If you aren't familiar with binary numbers, you would probably define these with a length of two and four (respectively), and with a type of *B*. This makes complete sense to an RPG programmer. Nevertheless, in the world of APIs, it's completely wrong!

A BINARY(2) field is a 2-byte binary field that can be defined in a data structure with "from" and "to" positions. A BINARY(4) field is a 4-byte binary field that also can be defined in a data structure with "from" position 1 "to" position 4. However, the 4-byte binary field can also be defined as a stand-alone field. If defined as a stand-alone binary type field, it must have a length of between five and nine digits. When a 4-byte binary field is called for, you also can code a 10-digit integer (type I).

A pointer is another data type that is commonly used to process information returned by APIs. Unlike most other data types, a pointer doesn't really describe an element of data. Instead, as its name implies, it points to an address that contains the data you want. As you'll see a little later in this chapter, pointers are very useful when working with user spaces.

All pointers are, by definition, 16-byte fields. They can be defined with a type code of *. Notice we say they "can" be defined that way. In fact, they don't have to be defined at all! If you use a field in such a way that it can only be a pointer, the system will define it for you. Take a look at Figure 1.4 and check out the definition specification for the data structure named DATADS. It has a keyword

BASED(**FieldPtr**). The basing variable, **FieldPtr**, is not defined anywhere in the source code, but the system knows that it is a pointer and will define it as such. Figure 1.4 shows different ways to define these fields.

```
*
*    this is an example of a different data types commonly used
*      by APIs
*
DName+++++++++++ETDsFrom+++To/L+++IDc.Keywords++++++++++++++++++++++++++
D Receiver        DS            320

 * 2-byte binary
D  TwoBytes                1     2B 0

 * 4-byte binaries
D  NbrFormats             62     63B 0
D  DBFileOffS            317    320B 0

 * 4-byte binary
D Bytes4          S              9B 0

 * 4-byte integer
D Integer         S             10i 0

 * Pointer
D ListPtr         S               *

D DataDs          DS                    based(FieldPtr)
D  Field1                         1
```

Figure 1.4: APIs can have different data types.

Telling an API What to Return

One of the primary reasons you would want to use an API is to retrieve and return information to your programs. The Retrieve Object Description (QUSOBJD) API, for example, can be used to return almost anything you would want to know about an object. But, as you will see, APIs are not always restricted to just one flavor. Sometimes, APIs can be called several different ways, depending on exactly what information you are trying to retrieve.

Simple logic would dictate that the more information an API has to gather about an object, the longer it would take the API to run. Why does this matter? Wouldn't you want to gather all of the information about an object each time you ran your API? Aren't APIs really fast? Well, yes, they are, but machine cycles are cumulative. In a time when advances in hardware have far exceeded advances in software, we programmers have a tendency to forget that. The more efficient our code is, the better our system will run. This is the case no matter how fast hardware becomes.

Generally, informational APIs provide you with a couple of methods for filtering your request for information. The most common way to filter API information is through the use of a *record format parameter*. A record format parameter accepts a record format name that describes the format of the returned information. The API record format names are predetermined and available in the documentation for the API. You select the record format name that will return the data you are interested in, and name it on a parameter when you call the API. The record format will determine the data that you get back.

Usually, API record format names end in a sequence number. The Retrieve Object Description (QUSOBJD) API, for example, accepts four record format names. Table 1.1 reflects how the manual describes them. As you have probably already guessed, the smaller the sequence numbers, the faster the response. This is not always true, but it is a good rule of thumb to follow.

Table 1.1: Record Formats for the Retrieve Object Description API (QUSOBJD)	
Format	**Description**
OBJD0100	Basic information (fastest).
OBJD0200	Information similar to that displayed by the programming development manager (PDM).
OBJD0300	Service information.
OBJD0400	Full information (slowest).

Keyed Interface

Another method of controlling what information an API returns is through the use of keys. Each piece of information the API deals with (called a *key*) is assigned a value by the API. You tell the API what piece (or pieces) of information you require by specifying an array of key values.

Keys allow you to filter the information you want the API to return. For instance, suppose you had a program that needed to know the name of the job queue through which it was submitted. You could use the Retrieve Current Attributes (QWCRTVCA) API to get this piece of information. QWCRTVCA returns lots of information about a job, but if you specified key 1004, it would return only the name of the job queue.

You usually pass the key(s) as a parameter (which happens to be a variable-length record). The parameter contains the number of keys being passed, the keys specifying the data being requested, and any data associated with the keys.

Returning Data

Generally, APIs use two methods to return data. The output depends on the amount of data being passed. When a limited amount of information is to be retrieved from an API, the information is retrieved directly into a receiver variable that is defined as a parameter on the call to the API.

Some APIs, such as list APIs, return a lot of information, however. The List Database Fields (QUSLFLD) API, for example, will return a multiple occurring data structure with each occurrence providing information about each field in the file. As you can imagine, if you have a file with very many fields, this API can return a lot of data. Because of the nature of such an API, list APIs return their information into a *user space*.

A user space can be up to 16 megabytes in size. In contrast, the largest size of a receiver variable, otherwise known as a variable field, is 32 kilobytes.

Both retrieval methods basically return the same type of data. In other words, they return a series of data structures. Each structure generally contains some information as well as one or more pointers to other data structures that contain more information. You process the information by accessing the first data structure, then use the correct offset to the next structure, and continue through all structures until you reach the one that contains the data in which you are interested. While this all may seem a little confusing at first glance, it all will begin to make sense when you get to the various code examples.

Receiver Variables

One of the problems with returning data into a variable is that you don't always know the size of the data that will be returned to you. Even if you think you know, IBM might in the future enhance the API to return more data than it was originally coded for.

Most of the data returned by the retrieve APIs begins with two binary fields: the bytes available and the number of bytes returned. The bytes-available field returns the total number of bytes that the API *could* return. The bytes-returned field contains the total number of bytes actually returned with the call to the API. For purposes of this discussion, these fields can be referred to as *spatial requirement fields*.

You can use these spatial requirement fields to ensure that your receiver variable is always defined large enough to contain the data being returned by the API. If you are going to use receiver variables, you will be calling the API twice. The first time, you call it just so that the API will tell you the number of characters it will return. You then allocate that much space to a receiver variable, and call it again with the variable that is now the correct size. As you can imagine, performing the API call twice hampers speed and performance, but it ensures that your program will continue to run even if the API is enhanced with future releases.

Figure 1.5 shows an example of how to use receiver variables. This sample program uses the Retrieve Library Description (QLIRLIBD) API to get the size of a given library (including all of the objects in the library). The first call to the API uses a variable (**Receiver1**) that is defined with a length of 8 bytes. This is just enough to hold the bytes returned (**BytesRtn1**) and the bytes available (**BytesAvl1**) fields. After the first call to the API, the **BytesAvl1** field contains the number of characters that will be returned.

In this example, the next thing we do is allocate the appropriate amount of storage to the actual receiver variable (as determined by the first call to the API) that will be used in the next call to the API. The allocation of storage is done with the ALLOC (allocate) operation code and a basing pointer field. In Figure 1.5, you can see that the result field position of the ALLOC op code contains the field **ReceivePtr**. This field is defined as a pointer via the BASED keyword on the Receiver definition. After executing the ALLOC operation code, the Receiver will have enough storage to hold the results of the second call to the API.

When the API is called a second time, the receiver is used as the return variable. Because enough storage is allocated for the receiver based on the original call to the API, the receiver will be large enough to contain all of the information returned by the API. Figure 1.5 includes the code necessary to process the returned data. This program displays the size and size multiplier of the library passed to it as a parameter. This program is meant to illustrate one of the methods of retrieving data; it's not a tutorial on the Retrieve Library Description (QLIRLIBD) API. This example does not describe this API in detail.

```
DName+++++++++++ETDsFrom+++To/L+++IDc.Keywords+++++++++++++++++++++++++++
D Receiver1       DS
D   BytesRtn1                      10i 0
D   BytesAvl1                      10i 0

D Receiver        DS                        Based(ReceivePtr)
D   BytesRtn                       10i 0
D   BytesAvl                       10i 0
D   NbrRcdsRtn                     10i 0
D   NbrRcdsAvl                     10i 0

D Attributes      DS
D   NbrOfAttrs                     10i 0 inz(1)
D   Key1                           10i 0 inz(6)

D Returned        DS                        Based(ReturnPtr)
D   ReturnLen                      10i 0
D   ReturnKey                      10i 0
D   DataSize                       10i 0
D   LibSiz                         10i 0
D   LibSizMult                     10i 0
D   InfoStatus                      1
```

Figure 1.5: This technique determines the proper size of the receiver variable (part 1 of 2).

```
D  Reserved                        3

D  ErrorDs         DS            116     INZ
D   ErrBytPrv            1         4B 0 inz(116)
D   ErrBytAvl            5         8B 0 inz(0)
D   MessageId            9        15
D   ERR###              16        16
D   MessageDta          17       116

D  Library         S             10
D  ReceiveLen      S             10i 0
D  X               S             10i 0


CLON01Factor1+++++++Opcode&ExtFactor2+++++++Result++++++++Len++D+HiLoEq
C       *entry        Plist
C                     Parm                    Library
 * Retrieve size that receiver variable should be
C                     Call      'QLIRLIBD'
C                     Parm                    Receiver1
C                     Parm      8             ReceiveLen
C                     Parm                    Library
C                     Parm                    Attributes
C                     Parm                    ErrorDs

 * Allocate enough storage for receiver
C                     Alloc     BytesAvl1     ReceivePtr

 * Call the API to get the information you want
C                     Call      'QLIRLIBD'
C                     Parm                    Receiver
C                     Parm      BytesAvl1     ReceiveLen
C                     Parm                    Library
C                     Parm                    Attributes
C                     Parm                    ErrorDs

 * Process the data from the API
C                     Eval      ReturnPtr = ReceivePtr + 16
C                     Do        NbrRcdsRtn    X
C    LibSiz           dsply
C    LibSizMult       dsply
C                     if        NbrRcdsRtn <> X
C                     Eval      ReturnPtr = ReceivePtr + ReturnLen
C                     Endif
C                     Enddo

C                     Eval      *inlr = *on
```

Figure 1.5: This technique determines the proper size of the receiver variable (part 2 of 2).

At the end of the following section on user spaces, there is another method of using receiver variables. This method shows you how to "trick" the API into using a user space instead of a receiver variable. First, however, read the section on user spaces.

APIs and User Spaces

APIs that can potentially return a lot of data usually use a user space. A user space is an object (type *USRSPC) that you can use to hold data. As mentioned earlier, a user space can hold up to 16 megabytes. Furthermore, a user space can increase itself, much like a subfile, so that you don't have to define it as 16 megabytes to begin with. You create the user space at some size that seems reasonable to your needs, and mark it as expandable. If the API returns more data than will fit, it will increase to the size it needs!

You create a user space by calling an API. (You aren't surprised, are you?) You call the Create User Space (QUSCRTUS) API. Figure 1.6 shows the code needed to create a user space. The Create User Space API doesn't return any data; it simply performs a function: to create a user space. Table 1.2 reflects the various parameters for the QUSCRTUS API. The code shown in Figure 1.6 creates a user space named SPACENAME in library QTEMP.

```
DName+++++++++++ETDsFrom+++To/L+++IDc.Keywords+++++++++++++++++++++++++++
D PasSpcName      DS            20
D  SName                 1      10    inz('SPACENAME')
D  SLib                 11      20    inz('QTEMP')
D SpaceAttr       S             10    inz
D SpaceAuth       S             10    INZ('*CHANGE')
D SpaceLen        S            9B 0   INZ(2048)
D SpaceReplc      S             10    INZ('*YES')
D SpaceText       S             50
D SpaceValue      S              1    INZ(x'00')

 * Create the user space
CLON01Factor1+++++++Opcode&ExtFactor2+++++++Result++++++++Len++D+HiLoEq
C                    CALL      'QUSCRTUS'
C                    PARM                    PasSpcName
C                    PARM                    SpaceAttr
C                    PARM                    SpaceLen
```

Figure 1.6: Use the Create User Space (QUSCRTUS) API to create a user space (part 1 of 2).

```
C                    PARM                    SpaceValue
C                    PARM                    SpaceAuth
C                    PARM                    SpaceText
C                    PARM                    SpaceReplc
```

Figure 1.6: Use the Create User Space (QUSCRTUS) API to create a user space (part 2 of 2).

Table 1.2: Parameters for the Create User Space API (QUSCRTUS) (part 1 of 2)

Parameter	Description	Type	Attribute	Size
1	The user space name/library. The first 10 bytes are the name, the second 10 bytes are the library. The library accepts *LIBL and *CURLIB.	Input	Char	20
2	An extended attribute, which must be either a valid name or blank. You can elect to assign an extended attribute to the user space.	Input	Char	10
3	The initial size to make user space, from one to 16,776,704.	Input	Binary	4
4	The initial value for characters in the user space (which should be x'00' for best results).	Input	Char	1
5	The public authority. If the replace parameter is *YES, this entry is ignored. Authorities are copied from the replaced user space. This can be any valid authority entry or an authorization list name.	Input	Char	10
6	Text describing the user space.	Input	Char	50
Optional Group 1				
7	Replace existing user space. This defaults to *NO. If *YES, the old space is destroyed if the system value QALWUSRDMN is not set to *ALL or does not contain library QRPLOBJ, and the user space being replaced is in the user domain.	Input	Char	10
8	An error data structure. See the section on error handling later in this chapter for more information.	In/Out	Char	Variable

Table 1.2: Parameters for the Create User Space API (QUSCRTUS) (part 2 of 2)			
Optional Group 2			
9	The domain, which can be one of the following: • *DEFAULT allows the system to decide the domain. • *SYSTEM puts it in the system domain. If it is in the system domain and the security level is 40 or greater, you cannot use pointers to retrieve information. • *USER attempts to put it in the user domain. If *USER, the library the user space is being created into must be in the QALWUSRDMN system value, or an error occurs. Domains are discussed later in the chapter.	Input Char	10
Optional Group 3			
10	The transfer size request, which is the number of pages to transfer between main storage and auxiliary storage, zero to 32 pages. Zero indicates the default transfer size. Better performance might result with a larger transfer size.	Input Binary	4
11	The optimum space alignment. A zero (the default entry) means do not use optimum space alignment. A one means do use it, which might improve performance but reduces the maximum user space size by one page size (4,096 bytes) minus 512.	Input Char	1

Two Methods to Access Data from a User Space

If you have worked on the AS/400 for more than a day, you know the following axiom to be true: There is always more than one way to get the job done. With user spaces, this means that you can access data using two different methods. Each method has its strengths and weaknesses, which deserve some exploration.

First, consider the "slow" method, which involves the use of the Retrieve User Space (QUSRTVUS) API. You give this API the name, starting position, and length of data to retrieve, and it gets that information and puts it in a variable for you. Since IBM introduced pointer support into RPGLE, this method is generally considered passé. The reason, of course, is speed. Every time you want to extract data from a user space, you have to call the API multiple times. Every call involves some overhead.

A faster method of retrieving data from a user space involves using the Retrieve User Space Pointer (QUSPTRUS) API and pointers. You simply "feed" this API the name of the user space, and it returns a pointer to your program that represents the beginning of the user space. Then, you add "offsets" to this pointer to get at different positions in the user space. Walking through an entire list of fields in a file only requires one call to the Retrieve User Space Pointer (QUSPTRUS) API, versus one call for each field using the Retrieve User Space (QUSRTVUS) API.

At this point, you might be asking yourself, "What is an offset?" An *offset* is simply the number of positions away from a central reference point. Offsets will be returned to you when you call an API. Don't be intimidated by some of the concepts and terminology at this stage. These concepts will be much easier to understand once you get to the actual code examples.

Be aware, as you use the Retrieve User Space (QUSRTVUS) API, that all of the offset values returned in various data structures are relative to position zero of the user space. This means that you must add one to the value to get the correct offset position. If you are using pointer math, however, the offsets are correct and you don't need to add one.

We feel that QUSPTRUS should be the obvious choice of methods to access data in a user space. However, you should be aware that it has a few potential drawbacks:

- If your security level is 40 or greater, you cannot use this API on a user space that exists in the system domain. Prior to V2R3, user spaces could be created only in the system domain. After that release, you can specify either the system domain or the user domain when you create the user space.

- QUSPTRUS does not update the object-usage information. You can access the user space, and the date last used will not be updated. If this is important, use QUSRTVUS or the Change User Space (QUSCHGUS) API, which do update the object-usage information.

- QUSRTVUS gives you access to the user space even if someone else holds an exclusive lock on it.

All that being said, a preferable method of accessing a user space is still by re-trieving a pointer to it and using "pointer math" to access it. Most of the time, when you create a user space, you should put it in library QTEMP, which is a tem-porary place to store information that is unique to each AS/400 session. When used in this manner, none of the limitations of QUSPTRUS are applicable. Figure 1.7 shows the code to call QUSPTRUS. Table 1.3 reflects the parameters for the Retrieve User Space Pointer (QUSPTRUS) API. Figure 1.8 shows the code to call the Retrieve User Space (QUSRTVUS) API. Table 1.4 reflects the parameters for the Retrieve User Space (QUSRTVUS) API.

Table 1.3: The QUSPTRUS Parameters

Parameter	Description	Type	Attribute	Size
1	The user space name. The first 10 bytes are the name, and the second 10 are the library. Library names *LIBL and *CURLIB are acceptable.	Input	Char	20
2	A pointer to the user space. Base a data structure on this pointer to access data.	Output	Space Pointer	*
Optional Group 1				
3	A standard error data structure. See the section on error handling later in this chapter for more information.	In/Out	Char	Variable

```
DName+++++++++++ETDsFrom+++To/L+++IDc.Keywords+++++++++++++++++++++++++++
D PasSpcName      DS           20
D  SName                 1     10     inz('FIG12RG')
D  SLib                 11     20     inz('QTEMP')

D ListPtr         S                *

CLON01Factor1+++++++Opcode&ExtFactor2+++++++Result+++++++++Len++D+HiLoEq
 * Get pointer to user space
C                   Call      'QUSPTRUS'
C                   Parm                   PasSpcName
C                   Parm                   ListPtr
```

Figure 1.7: Use the Retrieve User Space Pointer (QUSPTRUS) API to get a pointer to a user space.

```
DName+++++++++++ETDsFrom+++To/L+++IDc.Keywords+++++++++++++++++++++++++++
D GENDS           DS          140
D  OffsetHdr             117   120B 0
D  SizeHeader            121   124B 0
D  OffsetList            125   128B 0
D  NbrInList             133   136B 0
D  SizeEntry             137   140B 0
D                DS
D  StartPosit            1      4B 0
D  StartLen              5      8B 0

CLON01Factor1+++++++Opcode&ExtExtended-factor2+++++++++++++++++++++++++++
C                   Eval      StartPosit = 1
C                   Eval      StartLen = 140
C                   CALL      'QUSRTVUS'
C                   PARM                   UserSpace
C                   PARM                   StartPosit
C                   PARM                   StartLen
C                   PARM                   GENDS
```

Figure 1.8: Use the Retrieve User Space (QUSRTVUS) API to retrieve data from a user space.

19

Table 1.4: The QUSRTVUS Parameters

Parameter	Description	Type	Size
1	The user space name. The first 10 bytes are the name, and the second 10 are the library. Library names *LIBL and *CURLIB are acceptable.	Input	Char(20)
2	The starting position of the data to be retrieved.	Input	Binary(4)
3	The length of data to return from the user space, which must be greater than zero and less than the declared size of the variable receiving the data.	Input	Binary(4)
4	The variable structure to return the data into. This is usually a data structure.	Output	Char(Varies)
Optional Group 1			
5	An error data structure. See the section on error handling later in this chapter for more information.	In/Out	Char(Varies)

Automatically Extendable User Spaces

Much like a database file, a user space can have the capability to increase the amount of memory it requires. Also like a database file, the user space does not have this capability unless you perform the steps necessary to make it so. If you want a user space to automatically extend itself, you need to set the Change User Space Attribute API (QUSCUSAT) of the user space. You might find that this step is necessary to make your user space big enough to hold the information returned by one of the informational APIs. Figure 1.9 shows some sample code to change the attributes of a user space. Table 1.5 lists the parameters for QUSCUSAT.

```
DName++++++++++ETDsFrom+++To/L+++IDc.Keywords+++++++++++++++++++++++++
D RtnLib            S             10

D                   DS            20
D PasSpcName                      20      inz('SPACENAME QTEMP')
D  SName                          10      overlay(PasSpcName:1)
D  SLib                           10      overlay(PasSpcName:11)

D ChgAttrDs         DS
D  NumberAttr                     9B 0 inz(1)
D  KeyAttr                        9B 0 inz(3)
D  DataSize                       9B 0 inz(1)
```

Figure 1.9: Use the QUSCUSAT API to change the attributes of a user space (part 1 of 2).

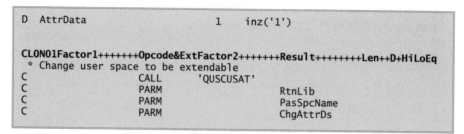

```
D  AttrData                      1    inz('1')


CLON01Factor1+++++++Opcode&ExtFactor2+++++++Result+++++++Len++D+HiLoEq
 * Change user space to be extendable
C                    CALL        'QUSCUSAT'
C                    PARM                      RtnLib
C                    PARM                      PasSpcName
C                    PARM                      ChgAttrDs
```

Figure 1.9: Use the QUSCUSAT API to change the attributes of a user space (part 2 of 2).

Table 1.5: QUSCUSAT Parameters

Parameter	Description	Type	Attribute	Size
1	The library where the user space resides. The API will return the name of the library that contains the user space that it altered.	Output	Char	10
2	The name/library of the user space. The first 10 bytes are the name, and the second 10 are the library. Library names *LIBL and *CURLIB are acceptable.	Input	Char	20
3	The attribute structure.[1] The following repeat for each attribute: <table><tr><td>**Description**</td><td>**Type**</td><td>**Attr**</td><td>**Size**</td></tr><tr><td>Number of times attribute repeats</td><td>Input</td><td>Binary</td><td>4</td></tr><tr><td>Attribute key</td><td>Input</td><td>Binary</td><td>4</td></tr><tr><td>Attribute size</td><td>Input</td><td>Binary</td><td>4</td></tr><tr><td>Attribute data</td><td>Input</td><td>Varies</td><td>Varies</td></tr></table>	Input	Char	
Optional Group 1				
4	An error data structure. See the section on error handling later in this chapter for more information.	In/Out	Char	Variable

1. Parameter notes: The attribute structure consists of a field containing the number of multiple-occuring data structures that follow the field. Each multiple-occuring data structure consists of a key, the size of the data, and the data. Table 1.6 lists valid attribute keys.

Table 1.6: Attribute Keys

Key	Description	Attribute	Size
1	The size of the user space.	Binary	4
2	The initial value.	Char	1
3	An option to automatically extend the user space.	Char	1
4	The size of the transfer request.	Binary	4

Making Receiver-Variable APIs Use a User Space

Now that you know everything there is to know about user spaces, backtrack for a moment to the APIs that return data to a receiver variable. As discussed earlier, you have to jump through some hoops to ensure that you get all of the data available from the API. Well, just to add a little excitement, here's another hoop to jump through, and this one is on fire!

As previously discussed, user spaces have a lot of advantages over receiver variables. One of the biggest advantages is that user spaces can be made to automatically extend themselves to whatever size is necessary. Doesn't it seem that user spaces should be the vehicle of choice for an API to return data? Well, we are going to show you how to take APIs that return information to receiver variables and make them return the data to a user space instead. It's easy too!

Here are the steps necessary to make a receiver-variable API use a user space instead:

1. Create the user space.
2. Get a pointer to the user space.
3. Base your receiver variable on the same pointer to the user space.

Figure 1.10 shows the code necessary to make this technique work. The trick is in the definition of the receiver variable. Notice that the receiver variable is defined as a data structure based on the pointer variable, **ListPtr**. This is the same pointer that the Retrieve User Space Pointer (QUSPTRUS) API returns. In effect, this causes the data structure to overlay the beginning of the user space.

Take a close look at the call to the Retrieve File Description (QDBRTVFD) API. Then, take a *really* close look at the receiver-length parameter. That's not a typo—the length of the receiver is 16 megabytes! This is a neat trick in itself, considering that the maximum length of a field is 32 KB. Because we're pointing to a user space, the variable now assumes the attributes of the user space. And because 16 MB is the maximum size of a user space.... Well, you get the picture. Of course, 16 MB is not actually reserved for the size of the user space. The receiver size will be the same size as the user space (in this example, 2 KB).

```
DName++++++++++ETDsFrom+++To/L+++IDc.Keywords++++++++++++++++++++++++++
 * Main output from QUSRTVFD API
D Receiver        DS                     based(ListPtr)
D  NbrFormats             62     63B 0
D  DBFileOffS            317    320B 0
D  AccessType           337    338
D  LFFileOffS           369    372B 0

D PasSpcName       DS             20
D  SName                   1     10   inz('FIG15RG')
D  SLib                   11     20   inz('QTEMP')

 * Standard error data structure
D ErrorDs          DS                  INZ
D  BytesProvd              1      4B 0 inz(116)
D  BytesAvail              5      8B 0
D  MessageId               9     15
D  Err###                 16     16

D FileFmt          S              8
D FmtType          S             10
D ListPtr          S              *
D OverRide         S              1
D ReceiveLen       S             10i 0
D RecordFmt        S             10
D RFileLib         S             20
D SFileLib         S             20
D SpaceAttr        S             10   inz
D SpaceAuth        S             10   INZ('*CHANGE')
D SpaceLen         S             10i 0 INZ(2048)
D SpaceReplc       S             10   INZ('*YES')
D SpaceText        S             50
```

Figure 1.10: This code shows how to make a "receiver variable API" send data to a user space (part 1 of 2).

```
D SpaceValue      S              1
D System          S             10

CLON01Factor1+++++++Opcode&ExtFactor2+++++++Result++++++++Len++D+HiLoEq
 * Create the user space
C                 Call      'QUSCRTUS'
C                 Parm                    PasSpcName
C                 Parm                    SpaceAttr
C                 Parm                    SpaceLen
C                 Parm                    SpaceValue
C                 Parm                    SpaceAuth
C                 Parm                    SpaceText
C                 Parm      '*YES'        SpaceReplc
C                 Parm                    ErrorDs

 * Get pointer to user space
C                 Call      'QUSPTRUS'
C                 Parm                    PasSpcName
C                 Parm                    ListPtr

 * Since Receiver variable is based on ReceivePtr which is pointing
 * to the beginning of RTVFDSPC user space, the data returned from
 * the API will be found in that user space.
C                 Call      'QDBRTVFD'
C                 Parm                    Receiver
C                 Parm      16776704      ReceiveLen
C                 Parm                    RFileLib
C                 Parm      'FILD0100'    FileFmt
C                 Parm                    SFileLib
C                 Parm                    RecordFmt
C                 Parm      '0'           OverRide
C                 Parm      '*LCL'        System
C                 Parm      '*EXT'        FmtType
C                 Parm                    ErrorDs

C                 eval      *inlr = *on
```

Figure 1.10: This code shows how to make a "receiver variable API" send data to a user space (part 2 of 2).

The Ultimate User Space Procedure

APIs are often used in programs. Three APIs are available to create a useful user space:

- Create User Space (QUSCRTUS)
- Retrieve User Space Pointer (QUSPTRUS)
- Change User Space Attribute (QUSCUSAT)

Repetitive code is bad because it introduces room for errors and creates maintenance headaches. So, rather than including the code necessary to call these APIs into every program that needs a user space, we have created a procedure that does all of the dirty work for you. If you put this procedure in a service program, using a user space becomes a no-brainer. You simply call the procedure, passing it the name of the user space and the library you want the space created in, and it returns a pointer to that space. Figure 1.11 shows this procedure, and Figure 1.12 illustrates the code necessary to call the procedure from another program.

```
HNOMAIN
 *

 *   procedure name:    CrtUsrSpc
 *
 *   procedure function: Create and return a pointer to an extendable
 *                       user space.
 *
DName++++++++++ETDsFrom+++To/L+++IDc.Keywords++++++++++++++++++++++++++
D  CrtUsrSpc      PR                     *
D    CrtSpcName                   20         const

PName+++++++++++..T.................Keywords++++++++++++++++++++++++++
P  CrtUsrSpc       B                         export
DName++++++++++ETDsFrom+++To/L+++IDc.Keywords++++++++++++++++++++++++++
D  CrtUsrSpc      PI                     *
D    CrtSpcName                   20         const

 * Local Variables

D ErrorDs         DS                        INZ
D  BytesProvd                     10i 0  inz(116)
D  BytesAvail                     10i 0
D  MessageId                 9    15
D  Err###                   16    16

D PasSpcName      DS             20
D  SName                     1    10
D  SLib                     11    20

D ChgAttrDs       DS
D  NumberAttr                     9B 0  inz(1)
D  KeyAttr                        9B 0  inz(3)
D  DataSize                       9B 0  inz(1)
```

Figure 1.11: CrtUsrSpc is the ultimate user space procedure (part 1 of 2).

```
D  AttrData                        1    inz('1')

D ListPtr         S                *
D SpaceAttr       S               10    inz
D SpaceAuth       S               10    INZ('*CHANGE')
D SpaceLen        S              9B 0   INZ(2048)
D SpaceReplc      S               10    INZ('*YES')
D SpaceText       S               50
D SpaceValue      S                1    inz(x'00')


CLON01Factor1+++++++Opcode&ExtFactor2+++++++Result++++++++Len++D+HiLoEq
 * Create the user space
C                   Move      CrtSpcName      PasSpcName
C                   Call      'QUSCRTUS'
C                   Parm                      PasSpcName
C                   Parm                      SpaceAttr
C                   Parm                      SpaceLen
C                   Parm                      SpaceValue
C                   Parm                      SpaceAuth
C                   Parm                      SpaceText
C                   Parm      '*YES'          SpaceReplc
C                   Parm                      ErrorDs
 * Get pointer to user space
C                   Call      'QUSPTRUS'
C                   Parm                      PasSpcName
C                   Parm                      ListPtr
 * Change user space to be extendable
C                   Call      'QUSCUSAT'
C                   Parm                      Slib
C                   Parm                      PasSpcName
C                   Parm                      ChgAttrDs
C                   Parm                      ErrorDs

C                   Return    ListPtr
P CrtUsrSpc        E
```

Figure 1.11: CrtUsrSpc is the ultimate user space procedure (part 2 of 2).

In Figure 1.12, the **CrtUsrSpc** procedure has been employed to create a user space named SOMESPACE in the QTEMP temporary library. The attributes for this newly created user space have been modified so that SOMESPACE is "self-extending." In the end, the pointer variable **SpacePtr** will contain the pointer to the newly created user space.

```
DName+++++++++++ETDsFrom+++To/L+++IDc.Keywords+++++++++++++++++++++++++
D  CrtUsrSpc      PR            *
D   CrtSpcName                 20      const
D  SpacePtr       S            *
D  UserSpace      S            20      inz('SOMESPACE QTEMP')

CLON01Factor1+++++++Opcode&ExtExtended-factor2+++++++++++++++++++++++++
C                   Eval       SpacePtr = CrtUsrSpc(UserSpace)
C                   Eval       *inlr = *on
```

Figure 1.12: You can use CrtUsrSpc to call a procedure from another program.

Domains

A domain is a characteristic of an object that controls the capability of programs to access the object. A domain comes in two flavors: *user* or *system*. If you are operating at security level 40 or higher, access to objects in the system domain is restricted to commands and approved APIs only. This means that for user spaces in the system domain, you cannot use the Retrieve User Space Pointer (QUSPTRUS) API to retrieve data; instead, you must use the Retrieve User Space (QUSRTVUS) API .

Most objects are created into the system domain. You can control which libraries are allowed to contain user domain objects. This control is provided via the Allow User Domain system value, QALWUSRDMN. This value ships with the value *ALL, but you can change it to a list of libraries. If security is an issue in your shop (and it should be, if your system is open to the Internet), consult the proper authorities to determine if this system value needs to be modified.

Error Handling

Most APIs accept an optional error-handling data structure (although UNIX-type APIs and high-level, language-independent, ILE CEE-type APIs do not). If you include this structure when you call the API and an error occurs, the system will not generate those ugly error messages for the world to see. Instead, the API will fill in fields in this data structure describing the error that occurred. Your program can then take appropriate actions based on the error.

While the error parameter might, technically, be optional on some APIs, you should not consider it to be optional in your work. If you don't code to handle errors, and an error does occur, IBM's OS/400 has been known to throw up some pretty cryptic error messages—just to confound the user.

Figure 1.13 shows the code necessary for the error-handling data structure. After calling the API (in this case, the Retrieve Object Description API, QUSOBJD), you test the bytes available (**BytesAvl**) field for zeros. If an error occurs, the API fills this field with the number of bytes it returned in the error data structure describing the error. It also fills the **MessageId** field with the CPF message ID, and the **MessageDta** field with the description of the CPF error message. If no error occurred, the **BytesAvl** field will be zero.

```
DName+++++++++++ETDsFrom+++To/L+++IDc.Keywords++++++++++++++++++++++++++++
D ErrorDs          DS               116    INZ
D   BytesPrv                1         4B 0 inz(116)
D   BytesAvl                5         8B 0 inz(0)
D   MessageId               9        15
D   ERR###                 16        16
D   MessageDta             17       116

CLON01Factor1+++++++Opcode&ExtFactor2+++++++Result++++++++Len++D+HiLoEq
 * Attempt to retrieve object description

C                         CALL      'QUSROBJD'
C                         PARM                    ReceiveVar
C                         PARM                    ReceiveLen
C                         PARM                    ObjdFormat
C                         PARM                    ObjectLib
C                         PARM                    ObjectTypF
C                         PARM                    ErrorDs
C                         if        BytesAvl <> 0
 * Error occurred
C                         endif
```

Figure 1.13: You can use the "optional" error data structure with an API.

Table 1.7 reflects the parameters for the "optional" error data structure that is used with many APIs.

Table 1.7: "Optional" Error Data Structure Parameters

Parameter	Description	Type	Attribute	Size
1	The number of bytes you have defined for this structure. This should be the total size of the error data structure.	Input	Binary	4
2	The number of bytes returned by the error. If zero, no error occurred. If greater than zero, an error did occur.	Output	Binary	4
3	The seven-character message ID. This field is not reset if no error occurs because a message ID from prior errors could be present.	Output	Char	6
4	The message description, which is also not cleared if no error occurs because text from prior errors could be present.	Output	Char	Variable

Common Errors to Avoid

APIs can be complicated to code even when things go exactly right the first time. They can be a nightmare to debug when things don't go exactly right. We cannot guarantee you will code bug-free every time you use an API if you adhere to the following guidelines, but we can guarantee that you will have a far better experience with APIs.

No Matter What They Say, Size Does Matter

It is essential to define a receiver variable with the correct length. Be absolutely certain that the receiver variable is not smaller than the length you specify to the API.

Take a look at Figure 1.14. You can see that the receiver variable is defined with a length of 320 bytes. But when the Retrieve Database File Description

(QDBRTVFD) API is called, the parameter **ReceiveLen** is coded to tell the API that the length of the receiver variable is 330. This is not good! It could adversely affect variables that have nothing to do with the API itself. If it can return 330 bytes, it will return 330 bytes, and the extra 10 bytes will overflow into the fields that are defined immediately after the receiver variable. After calling this API, the fields **Afld1**, **Afld2**, and **FileFmt** have unpredictable values.

```
 *
 *   this is an example of a common error that can cause
 *   enormous headaches to debug.
 *
DName++++++++++++ETDsFrom+++To/L+++IDc.Keywords+++++++++++++++++++++++++++
D Receiver        DS            320
D   NbrFormats          62      63B 0
D   DBFileOffS         317     320B 0

D Afld1           S              5
D Afld2           S              3 0
D FileFmt         S              8
D FmtType         S             10
D ListPtr         S              *
D OverRide        S              1
D ReceiveLen      S             10i 0
D RecordFmt       S             10
D RFileLib        S             20
D SFileLib        S             20
D System          S             10

 * Standard error data structure
D ErrorDs         DS                   INZ
D   BytesProvd          1       4B 0 inz(116)
D   BytesAvail          5       8B 0
D   MessageId           9      15
D   Err###             16      16

 *   call the Retrieve File Description API. Notice that
 *   the ReceiveLen parameter has a value of 330 but the
 *   Receiver field is defined with a length of 320. This
 *   will cause lots of weird results when the program runs!
CLON01Factor1+++++++Opcode&ExtFactor2+++++++Result++++++++Len++D+HiLoEq
C                   Call      'QDBRTVFD'
C                   Parm                    Receiver
C                   Parm      330           ReceiveLen
C                   Parm                    RFileLib
```

Figure 1.14: This example shows the common error of defining the receiver variable incorrectly (part 1 of 2).

```
C                    Parm      'FILD0100'   FileFmt
C                    Parm                   SFileLib
C                    Parm                   RecordFmt
C                    Parm      '0'          OverRide
C                    Parm      '*LCL'       System
C                    Parm      '*EXT'       FmtType
C                    Parm                   ErrorDs

C                    eval      *inlr = *on
```

Figure 1.14: This example shows the common error of defining the receiver variable incorrectly (part 2 of 2).

The Only Thing Constant Is Change

It is important that you code your APIs with an eye on the future. IBM will not change the format of the data the API is using, but it might change the content of the data in some future release. New features are continuously being added to the operating system. You cannot assume that the only valid values for a parameter today will be the only ones valid on the next release. So, avoid using global ELSE statements when comparing data elements returned from APIs. Make sure that you code your API with the implicit value with which you are working.

Don't Make Errors with Your Error Handling

Use the error-handling data structure whenever it is available. And obviously, when you use it, check it for results. Don't just code your program so that the API won't blow up when an error occurs. The proper way to check to see if errors occurred is by checking the number-of-bytes-returned field for zeros. If the number of bytes returned by the API is not zero, an error occurred with the execution of that API. Make sure your program is coded to take the appropriate action should an error condition occur.

Another common error is to check the error data structure's message ID or message data fields instead of the number of bytes returned. It would be only natural to presume that an error occurred if these fields are not blank. However, these fields are not reset each time the API runs, while the number-of-bytes-returned field is. If you check the message ID field, have an error, correct the error, and run the API again, it might appear that you still have an error condition when running your API (even when you don't).

Continuation Handles

Some APIs can return large amounts of data. These APIs sometimes have more data than can fit into the variable you have defined to receive the data. "Tricking" these APIs into using a user space instead of a receiver variable is a great technique, but some APIs have a different technique built into them. They use something called *continuation handles*.

A continuation handle is a field in the receiver variable that the API uses internally to keep track of the data it couldn't return to you. If you pass a continuation handle to an API, it knows that this is a continuation of a previous call.

Keep all other parameters as they were the first time you called the API. The API will return the rest of the data that couldn't fit (or it will return as much as it can, and again set the continuation field to indicate that it still has more). Like many of the concepts discussed in this chapter, this technique sounds more complicated than it really is. You will see examples of the various nuances of APIs throughout this book.

Summary

Every release of the operating system provides more and more APIs. They are the best way to get information out of the AS/400 that would otherwise not be readily available. You will find that whenever one of your applications needs to see or do something out of the ordinary, there is probably an API designed to do it. Whether you simply want to list all jobs currently running in a subsystem or communicate with a Microsoft Windows program, you need APIs to do it.

APIs do their job quickly and efficiently. Plus, they're upgradeable. IBM can and will enhance APIs as the OS/400 operating system continues to evolve. If you use the proper coding techniques demonstrated in this chapter, your applications should be more functional, without being more difficult to maintain.

2

LIST APIs

Now that you are familiar with the fundamentals of processing APIs, it is time to take a look at some of the various types of APIs. *List APIs* return a list of data to your programs. Because of the variety of data that can be returned, list APIs can be somewhat unpredictable. The first time you call the API, it might return one item in a list; the next time you call the API, it might return 1,000 items.

As discussed in chapter 1, the type of output from an API depends largely on the volume of data that may be returned. Because list APIs have the potential for returning a tremendous amount of data, most of them use a user space.

List APIs follow their own standard regarding the format of the data returned in the user space. Once you understand this unique standard, you will be able to process any list API. Like all APIs, they return data in the form of data structures, and each data structure can contain pointer fields that point to other data structures.

Open list APIs are a very special kind of list API that don't use a user space to return data. Instead, they use a variable-length field. Open list APIs are asynchronous and blazingly fast. Asynchronous processing is similar to the concept of processing threads. Open list APIs are examined later in this chapter, after the more ubiquitous list APIs.

General Data Structure

The main data structure, common to all list APIs that use a user space, is referred to as the *General data structure*. The General data structure is the first structure returned by any list API and it contains three principal components: a 64-byte user area, the size of the Generic Header data structure, and the Generic Header data structure itself.

Generic Header Data Structure

Depending on which version of RPG you use, there are two possible formats for the Generic Header data structure. Generic Header Format 0100 is for the original program model (OPM), whereas Generic Header Format 0300 is for the Integrated Language Environment (ILE). The two formats are identical except that the ILE version has two additional fields, which are found at the end of the Generic Header data structure.

General Data Structure
64-Byte User Area
Size of Generic Header Data Structure
Generic Header Data Structure

Figure 2.1: The layout of the General data structure is common to all list APIs.

Figure 2.2 shows the complete ILE version of Generic Header Format 0300. Fields QUSEPN and QUSRSV2 are the two fields that differentiate the ILE format from the OPM version. The point to note here, though, is how IBM has added the ILE format to the Generic Header Format, en-suring the backward compatibility that all AS/400 APIs share.

The new fields in the Generic Header Format were required when ILE came along because the size of API names increased dramatically. The OPM version of the General Header data structure contained a field that returns the name of the API used to put information into the user space, but this field is only 10 bytes long. In ILE, names of APIs can be up to 256 bytes. Rather than increase the size of the field, a new field was added to the end of the data structure. And rather than add it to the end of the existing structure, a new structure was provided to ensure that the new capability would not conflict with existing programs. It is good to know that well-written programs will continue to run, even as the system changes around them.

```
 * Generic header data structure common to all list APIs
 *    found in Qsysinc/Qrpglesrc/QUSGEN

DName++++++++++++ETDsFrom+++To/L+++IDc.Keywords++++++++++++++++++++++++++
DQUSH0300         DS
D*                                               Qus Generic Header 0300
D QUSUA00                      1     64
D QUSSGH00                    65     68B 0
D QUSSRL00                    69     72
D QUSFN00                     73     80
D QUSAU00                     81     90
D QUSDTC00                    91    103
D QUSIS00                    104    104
D QUSSUS00                   105    108B 0
D QUSOIP00                   109    112B 0
D QUSSIP00                   113    116B 0
D QUSOHS00                   117    120B 0
D QUSSHS00                   121    124B 0
D QUSOLD00                   125    128B 0
D QUSSLD00                   129    132B 0
D QUSNBRLE00                 133    136B 0
D QUSSEE00                   137    140B 0
D QUSSIDLE00                 141    144B 0
D QUSCID00                   145    146
D QUSLID00                   147    149
D QUSSLI00                   150    150
D QUSRSV1                    151    192
D QUSEPN                     193    448
D QUSRSV2                    449    576
```

Figure 2.2: The Generic Header data structure comes directly from the QRPGLESRC source file in the library QSYSINC on your AS/400.

Generic Header Format 0300's code definition, shown in Figure 2.2, comes directly from the QRPGLESRC source file in the library QSYSINC on your AS/400. The QSYSINC library comes as a non-chargeable feature with every AS/400, but the odds are that you will need to load the feature before you can use it.

In either case, you can use the /COPY statement to bring the code definition into your program. The /COPY statement can save you a lot of time generating programs that use a list API. The only drawback is that sometimes you end up with many field definitions that aren't pertinent to the task you are performing. We didn't use /COPY to prepare the samples in this book because too much unnecessary code would have been included.

The main function of the Generic Header data structure is to provide information about the contents of the rest of the user space. Table 2.1 provides a description of each field in this structure. Obviously, you won't need to process every field, but consider some of the more important ones that you have deal with to process a list API.

Table 2.1: Description of Generic Header Fields (part 1 of 2)	
Field Name	**Description**
QUSUA00	The user area. Put anything you want in this area; you can use it as a scratch pad.
QUSSGH00	The size of the generic header information that follows, not including the 64-byte user area (QUSUS00).
QUSSRL00	The structure's release level, which contains a code indicating one of two different generic header data structure layouts. Code 100 indicates the Original Program Model (OPM) layout. Code 200 indicates Integrated Language (ILE).
QUSFN00	The format name.
QUSAU00	The name of the API used to put information into the user space. If it is an ILE-type API, this field is reserved, and the API-used information can be retrieved from QUSENP00.
QUSDTC00	The date and time when the user space was created.
QUSIS00	The information status, which is a code describing the accuracy of the data in the user space. The possible codes are as follows: C—Complete and accurate. I—Incomplete. P—Partial but accurate.
QUSSUS00	The size of the user space.
QUSOIP00	An offset to the input parameter data structure. (For more details, see "Input Parameter Section" later in this chapter.)
QUSSIP00	The size of the input parameter section to which QUSOIP00 points.

Table 2.1: Description of Generic Header Fields (part 2 of 2)

Field Name	Description
QUSOHS00	An offset to the header section data structure. (For more details, see "Header Section" later in this chapter.)
QUSSHS00	The size of the header section data structure to which QUSOHS00 points.
QUSOLD00	An offset to the list data structure. (For more details, see "List Data Section" later in this chapter.)
QUSSLD00	The size of the list data structure to which QUSOLD00 points.
QUSNBRLE00	The number of entries in the list. This is the number of QUSSLD00 data structures in the user space.
QUSSEE00	The size of each entry in the list.
QUSSIDLE00	The CCSID list entry.
QUSCID00	The country ID.
QUSLID00	The language ID.
QUSSLI00	The subset list indicator.
QUSRSV1	Reserved.
QUSEPN	The entry point name.
QUSRSV2	A second reserved field.

As it pertains to AS/400 APIs, offset is really a "pointer" that tells you where to get something (generally a field or data structure). This "pointer" is in reference to the beginning of the object in question. Because the offset is in relationship to position zero, the trick to using an offset is that you must add one to the offset value before using it.

How can you use data from the Generic Header to process data using a list API? There are only three fields that are pertinent for your initial purposes:

- QUSOLD00—The size of the list data
- QUSNBRLE00—The number of list entries
- QUSSEE00—The size of each entry

37

The offset to list entries (QUSOLD00) gives you a pointer to where the first entry in the list begins. The number of entries in the list (QUSNBRLE00) tells you how many entries you have to process. You can use this number to set up a DO LOOP to process all of the entries in the list. During each iteration, the size of each entry (QUSSEE00) can be added to the QUSOLD00 pointer of the DO LOOP, causing the pointer to point to the next entry in the list. This process is shown in Figure 2.3.

While the DO LOOP process adequately describes the heart of the program, there are a few other pieces of the Generic Header data structure that should be used to ensure your program works right every time. The information status field (QUSIS00) gives a small but important piece of information regarding the results of the call to the API. This small bit of information is a status code that indicates whether the API correctly returned everything you asked for. If the API performed as requested, the code will be *C*. If it did not, the code will be *I*. If the API returned the correct information, but it could not all fit in the user space, the code will be *P*.

You need to test this return code after the call to the API. If it's *C*, everything is fine. Process the user space information. If the return code is *I*, send an error message and get out. If the return code is *P* (and the API makes use of continuation handles), you need to process the user space and then call the API again to get the rest of the information loaded. When you call it a second time, pass the continuation handle as a parameter. This continuation handle is retrieved from the unique header section of the API. Then repeat the processing loop. If the API doesn't use continuation handles, then you need to call the API requesting less information. The Generic Header data structure is common to all APIs that use a user space. However, every API also has its own *Header section* data structure that is unique to that API. Be sure not to confuse the two structures.

Figure 2.3: The processing flow of a list API makes use of information from the Generic Header data structure.

Header Section

The unique Header section is located by using the QUSOHS00 field found in the Generic Header section. This field definition is shown in Figure 2.1 and is defined in Table 2.1. The Header section contains information about the input parameters to the API. If a parameter accepted special values, such as *LIBL or *CURRENT, this section will list to that special value resolved to when it executed.

For instance, one of the parameters of the Retrieve File Description (QDBRTVFD) API is the library and name of the file from which you want to retrieve information. The library portion of the parameter accepts *LIBL, which tells the API to search the jobs library list until it finds a library that contains the file. When this happens, the header section will contain the name of the library in which the API found the file.

Input Parameter Section

Another useful data structure that the Generic Header data structure points to is the *Input Parameter* section. This data structure is located via the QUSOIP00 offset field. This section contains the parameters that you passed to the API when you called it.

The Input Parameter section can also contain a copy of the continuation handle value that you passed as a parameter when you called the API.

List Data Section

The *List Data* section is at the heart of every list API. It is the information you are looking for when you run the API in the first place. It is located by using the offset found in the QUSOLD00 field of the Generic Header section.

The format of the information in the List Data section varies from API to API. Even within an API, the format can vary depending on the amount and type of information you request. You control the format of this data in the format name parameter to the API.

The number of entries in the list is contained in the QUSNBRLE00 field in the Generic Header data structure. The size of each entry is usually contained in the QUSSEE00 field. However, some of the more complicated list APIs might return lists where each entry is of a different size. In these cases, the QUSNBRLE00 field will be zero, and the length of the entry can be found in a field within the format of the returned data.

This all sounds complicated, and it is, but looking at some examples will help you better understand the concepts. Therefore, it is time to see how all of this ties together in a program. The first program example you will see involves a user space accessed using pointers, followed by a variation on this program. The next example uses the Retrieve User Space (QUSRTVUS) API to get the list information from the user space. The differences in the two techniques will become readily apparent as you review these examples.

Program to Find Files with Deleted Records

Every well-written application must be designed to clean up after itself. The odds are that files used within any application will eventually contain some deleted records. Even though they are no longer used by the application, deleted records take up disk space. Therefore, deleted records must be purged from the file in order to regain the space they use up. This is generally done using the Reorganize Physical File (RGZPFM) command.

But "reorganizing" a file can take some time—depending, of course, on the number of records in the file. Logically, you wouldn't want to reorganize every file in the library; you only want to reorganize files containing a given percentage of deleted records.

The program shown in Figure 2.4 looks at all physical files in a particular library and reorganizes the ones containing a certain percentage of deleted records. The percentage used is variable and is passed into the program as a parameter. This sample program also offers the option of just printing a report of the files that should be reorganized, without calling the program to reorganize them. This report shows the amount of disk space that will be saved by reorganizing each file.

We've included all the code to make the program work (even though we're going to concentrate here on the APIs in the program).

The program shown in Figure 2.4 uses five different APIs to accomplish its purpose. Understanding and using this many APIs in a single program is not as hard as it might seem at first. Three of the APIs (QUSCRTUS, QUSCUSAT, and QUSPTRUS) are covered in chapter 1; they simply create and return a pointer to an extendable user space that the List Objects (QUSLOBJ) API can use. These three APIs are all contained in the **CrtUsrSpc** procedure at the end of the program. Because chapter 1 covers these APIs (in the section called "The Ultimate User Space Procedure"), there's no need go over them again here. The data structure definitions were copied from QSYSINC/QRPGLESRC/QUSLOBJ for the List Objects API, and from QSYSINC/QRPGLESRC/QUSRMBRD for the Retrieve Member Description API.

As shown in Figure 2.4, the first thing the program does is call the **CrtUsrSpc** procedure to create the user space and retrieve a pointer to it. The program then calls the List Objects (QUSLOBJ) API, which populates the user space with a list of all files in the requested library. Table 2.2 lists all of the details of this API.

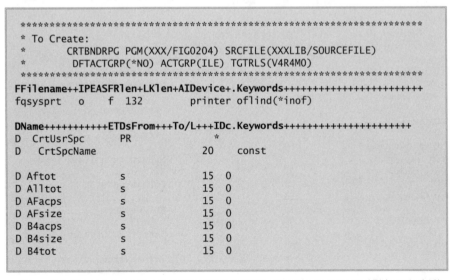

```
*****************************************************************
* To Create:
*        CRTBNDRPG PGM(XXX/FIG0204) SRCFILE(XXXLIB/SOURCEFILE)
*        DFTACTGRP(*NO) ACTGRP(ILE) TGTRLS(V4R4M0)
*****************************************************************
FFilename++IPEASFRlen+LKlen+AIDevice+.Keywords++++++++++++++++++++++++
fqsysprt   o    f  132           printer oflind(*inof)


DName+++++++++++ETDsFrom+++To/L+++IDc.Keywords+++++++++++++++++++++++
D CrtUsrSpc       PR              *
D   CrtSpcName                   20     const

D Aftot          s               15  0
D Alltot         s               15  0
D AFacps         s               15  0
D AFsize         s               15  0
D B4acps         s               15  0
D B4size         s               15  0
D B4tot          s               15  0
```

Figure 2.4: List and reorganize files with deleted records using the QUSPTRUS API (part 1 of 10).

```
D Diftot          s              15  0
D EstTitle        c                      'Files Needing to be Reorganized'
D FileLib         s              20
D FormatName      S               8
D InLib           S              10
D InPerc          s               2
D ListFormat      S               8
D MemberName      S              10
D ObjNamLIb       S              20      inz('*ALL      *LIBL    ')
D ObjType         S              10
D OvrPrc          s               1
D Perc            s               2  0
D PercHold        s              15  0
D Pronly          s               1
D PrtEstimat      s               9
D RcvLen          S              10i 0
D Reorg           s               1
D ReoTitle        c                      'Files Reorganized'
D Reslt           s               7  2
D SpacePtr        S               *
D Title           s              31
D Totfil          s               7  0
D Totout          s               5  1
D Totrec          s               9  0
D Totreo          s               7  0
D Tottyp          s               2
D Tstprc          s               2  0
D UserSpace       S              20      inz('MONRGZSPC QTEMP')


 * General Header Data structure as copied from QUSGEN in
 * source file QRPGLESRC in library QSYSINC

DQUSH0300         DS                      Based(GenDsPoint)
D*                                        Qus Generic Header 0300
D QUSUA00                 1      64
D*                                        User Area
D QUSSGH00               65      68B 0
D*                                        Size Generic Header
D QUSSRL00               69      72
D*                                        Structure Release Level
D QUSFN00                73      80
D*                                        Format Name
D QUSAU00                81      90
D*                                        Api Used
D QUSDTC00               91     103
D*                                        Date Time Created
D QUSIS00               104     104
D*                                        Information Status
```

Figure 2.4: List and reorganize files with deleted records using the QUSPTRUS API (part 2 of 10).

```
D QUSSUS00               105    108B 0
D*                                            Size User Space
D QUSOIP00               109    112B 0
D*                                            Offset Input Parameter
D QUSSIP00               113    116B 0
D*                                            Size Input Parameter
D QUSOHS00               117    120B 0
D*                                            Offset Header Section
D QUSSHS00               121    124B 0
D*                                            Size Header Section
D QUSOLD00               125    128B 0
D*                                            Offset List Data
D QUSSLD00               129    132B 0
D*                                            Size List Data
D QUSNBRLE00             133    136B 0
D*                                            Number List Entries
D QUSSEE00               137    140B 0
D*                                            Size Each Entry
D QUSSIDLE00             141    144B 0
D*                                            CCSID List Ent
D QUSCID00               145    146
D*                                            Country ID
D QUSLID00               147    149
D*                                            Language ID
D QUSSLI00               150    150
D*                                            Subset List Indicator
D QUSRSV1                151    192
D*                                            Reserved 1
D QUSEPN                 193    448
D*                                            Entry Point Name
D QUSRSV2                449    576
D*                                            Reserved 2

 * Format OUSL020002 List Objects. Copied from
 * member QUSLOBJ, source file QRPGLESRC, in library QSYSINC

DQUSL020002      DS               Based(ListPoint)
D*                                            Qus OBJL0200
D QUSOBJNU00               1     10

D*                                            Object Name Used
D QUSOLNU00               11     20
D*                                            Object Lib Name Used
D QUSOBJTU00              21     30
D*                                            Object Type Used
D QUSIS01                 31     31
D*                                            Information Status
D QUSEOA                  32     41
D*                                            Extended Obj Attr
```

Figure 2.4: List and reorganize files with deleted records using the QUSPTRUS API (part 3 of 10).

```
D QUSTD06                     42    91
D*                                              Text Description
D QUSUDA                       92   101
D*                                              User Defined Attr
D QUSERVED22                  102   108
D*                                              Reserved

  * Format OBJL0200 for the Retrieve Member Description API. Copied from
  * member QUSRMBRD, source file QRPGLESRC, in library QSYSINC

DQUSM0200         DS                   based(ReceivePtr)
D*                                              Qdb Mbrd0200
D QUSBRTN03                     1    4B 0
D*                                              Bytes Returned
D QUSBAVL04                     5    8B 0
D*                                              Bytes Available
D QUSDFILN00                    9   18
D*                                              Db File Name
D QUSDFILL00                   19   28
D*                                              Db File Lib
D QUSMN03                      29   38
D*                                              Member Name
D QUSFILA01                    39   48
D*                                              File Attr
D QUSST01                      49   58
D*                                              Src Type
D QUSCD03                      59   71
D*                                              Crt Date
D QUSSCD                       72   84
D*                                              Src Change Date
D QUSTD04                      85  134
D*                                              Text Desc
D QUSSFIL01                   135  135
D*                                              Src File
D QUSEFIL                     136  136
D*                                              Ext File
D QUSLFIL                     137  137
D*                                              Log File
D QUSOS                       138  138
D*                                              Odp Share
D QUSERVED12                  139  140
D*                                              Reserved
D QUSNBRCR                    141  144B 0
D*                                              Num Cur Rec
D QUSNBRDR                    145  148B 0
D*                                              Num Dlt Rec
D QUSDSS                      149  152B 0
D*                                              Dat Spc Size
D QUSAPS                      153  156B 0
```

Figure 2.4: List and reorganize files with deleted records using the QUSPTRUS API (part 4 of 10).

```
D*                                              Acc Pth Size
D QUSNBRDM             157     160B 0
D*                                              Num Dat Mbr
D QUSCD04              161     173
D*                                              Change Date
D QUSSD                174     186
D*                                              Save Date
D QUSRD                187     199
D*                                              Rest Date
D QUSED                200     212
D*                                              Exp Date
D QUSNDU               213     216B 0
D*                                              Nbr Days Used
D QUSDLU               217     223
D*                                              Date Lst Used
D QUSURD               224     230
D*                                              Use Reset Date
D QUSRSV101            231     232
D*                                              Reserved1
D QUSDSSM              233     236B 0
D*                                              Data Spc Sz Mlt
D QUSAPSM              237     240B 0
D*                                              Acc Pth Sz Mlt
D QUSMTC               241     244B 0
D*                                              Member Text Ccsid
D QUSOAI               245     248B 0
D*                                                      @A1A
D QUSLAI               249     252B 0
D*                                                      @A1A
D QUSRSV203            253     266
D*                                                      @A1C

 * Standard Error Code data structure
DQUSEC          DS            116
D QUSBPRV              1       4B 0
D QUSBAVL              5       8B 0       inz(116)

D*******************************************************************
 * Receiver structure to determine correct size for variable
D*******************************************************************
D Receiver1      DS
D  BytesRtn1                  10i 0
D  BytesAvl1                  10i 0

CL0N01Factor1+++++++Opcode&ExtFactor2+++++++Result++++++++Len++D+HiLoEq
C     *entry        Plist
C                   Parm                    InLib
C                   parm                    InPerc
C                   parm                    Pronly
```

Figure 2.4: List and reorganize files with deleted records using the QUSPTRUS API (part 5 of 10).

```
C                       move        InLIb           ObjNamLib
C                       move        InPerc          Perc
*   Create user space for file list information
C                       Eval        SpacePtr = CrtUsrSpc(UserSpace)
*
*   List files to user space
C                       Call        'QUSLOBJ'
C                       Parm                        UserSpace
C                       Parm        'OBJL0200'      ListFormat
C                       Parm                        ObjNamLib
C                       Parm        '*FILE'         ObjType
C                       Parm                        QusEc

*   Load the general data structure
C                       Eval        GenDsPoint = SpacePtr

*   If the list API was complete or partially complete
C                       if          QuSIS00 = 'C' OR
C                                   QuSIS00 = 'P'
*   Load the list data structure
C                       Eval        ListPoint = GenDsPoint + QusOLD00

*   Print heading
C                       eval        Title = ReoTitle
C                       if          PrOnly = 'Y'
C                       eval        Title = EstTitle
C                       endif
C                       except      Headng

C                       Do          QusNbrLE00

*   Only want to process physical files not in library QSYS
C                       if          QusEOA = 'PF' AND
C                                   QusOLNu00 <> 'QSYS'
*   If the list entry has no problems, otherwise ignore it
C                       if          QuSIS01 = ' '

C                       eval        Totfil = Totfil + 1
C                       movel       QusObjNu00      FileLib
C                       move        QusOLNu00       FileLib

*   Get number current records, deleted records and size information
C                       exsr        Rtvmbr
*   If no errors retrieving file information
C                       if          QusBAvl = 0
*   Check if percentage deleted exceeded
C                       move        *off            Reorg
C                       exsr        Rgzchk
```

Figure 2.4: List and reorganize files with deleted records using the QUSPTRUS API (part 6 of 10).

```
C                    if        Reorg = *on
C         QusDss     Mult      QusDSSM         B4Size
C         QusAPS     Mult      QusAPSM         B4Acps
C                    if        Pronly <> 'Y'
C                    exsr      Rgzfil
C                    endif
C                    exsr      Print
C                    eval      Totreo = Totreo + 1
C                    endif
C                    endif
C                    endif
C                    endif

C                    Eval      ListPoint = ListPoint + QusSEE00

C                    EndDo
C                    Endif

C                    if        Alltot > 1000000
C         Alltot     div(h)    1000000         Totout
C                    move      'MB'            Tottyp
C                    else
C                    if        Alltot > 1024
C         Alltot     div(h)    1024            Totout
C                    move      'KB'            Tottyp
C                    endif
C                    endif
C                    except    Total
C                    eval      *inlr = *on
 *
 * call cl program to perform reorg of file
C         Rgzfil     begsr
C                    call      'REORGCL'
C                    parm                      QusOLNu00
C                    parm                      QusObjNu00
 * Retrieve member to get size information after reorganize
C                    exsr      RtvMbr
C                    endsr
 * see if reorg needs to be done
C         Rgzchk     begsr
C                    move      *off            Reorg
C                    if        QusNbrCR = 0
C                              and QusNbrDR <> 0
C                    move      *on             Reorg
C                    endif
C                    if        QusNbrCR <> 0
C                              and QusNbrDR <> 0
C                    eval      Totrec = QusNbrDR + QusNbrCR
C                    if        Totrec <> 0
```

Figure 2.4: List and reorganize files with deleted records using the QUSPTRUS API (part 7 of 10).

```
C        QusNbrDr      div      Totrec         Reslt
C        Reslt         mult     100            Tstprc
C                      if       Tstprc >= Perc
C                      move     *on            Reorg
C                      endif
C                      endif
C                      endif
C                      endsr
 * accumulate totals and print detail
C        Print         begsr
C                      eval     B4tot = B4size + B4acps
C        QusDss        Mult     QusDSSM        AfSize
C        QusAPS        Mult     QusAPSM        AfAcps
C                      eval     Aftot = AfSize + AfAcps

 * If printing only, no reorganization took place. So estimate total.
C                      clear                   PrtEstimat
C                      eval     Title = ReoTitle
C                      if       PrOnly = 'Y'
C        Aftot         Mult     Reslt          PercHold
C                      sub      PercHold       Aftot
C                      eval     PrtEstimat = 'Estimated'
C                      eval     Title = EstTitle
C                      endif

C        B4tot         sub      Aftot          Diftot
C                      eval     Alltot = Alltot + Diftot
C                      except   Detail
C                      endsr
 * retrieve member description
C        Rtvmbr        begsr
C                      call     'QUSRMBRD'
C                      parm                    Receiver1
C                      parm     8              Rcvlen
C                      parm     'MBRD0200'     FormatName
C                      parm                    FileLib
C                      parm     '*FIRST'       MemberName
C                      parm     '0'            Ovrprc
C                      parm                    QusEc

 * If no errors retrieving file information
C                      if       QusBAvl = 0
 * Allocate enough storage for receiver
C                      Alloc    BytesAvl1      ReceivePtr
 * Call the api to get the information you want
C                      call     'QUSRMBRD'
C                      parm                    QusM0200
C                      parm     BytesAvl1      Rcvlen
C                      parm     'MBRD0200'     FormatName
```

Figure 2.4: List and reorganize files with deleted records using the QUSPTRUS API (part 8 of 10).

```
C                     parm                 FileLib
C                     parm      '*FIRST'   MemberName
C                     parm      '0'        Ovrprc
C                     parm                 QusEc
C                     endif
C                     endsr

OFilename++DF..N01N02N03Excnam++++B++A++Sb+Sa+....................
OQsysprt   e          Headng         2 02
O          or    of
O                                        5 'DATE:'
O                     Udate        y    14
O                     Title             85
O                                      121 'PAGE:'
O                     Page         z   127
OQsysprt   e          Headng         1
O          or    of
O                                        9 'LIBRARY'
O                                       18 'FILE'
O                                       44 'BEFORE SIZE'
O                                       64 'AFTER SIZE'
O                                       84 'FILE SAVED'
O                                      104 'TOTAL SAVED'
OQsysprt   ef         Detail         1
O                     QusOLNu00         12
O                     QusObjNu00        24
O                     B4tot        1    44
O                     Aftot        1    64
O                     Diftot       1    84
O                     Alltot       1   104
O                     PrtEstimat       114
OQsysprt   ef         Total          2 2
O                                       24 'TOTAL BYTES SAVED.....'
O                     Totout       1    44
O                     Tottyp            47
OQsysprt   ef         Total          1
O                                       24 'PHYSICAL FILES PROCESSED'
O                     Totfil       z    44
OQsysprt   ef         Total          1
O                                       24 'FILES REORGANIZED.......'
O                     Totreo       z    44
 *  Procedure to create extendable user space, return pointer to it.
P  CrtUsrSpc     B                   export

DName++++++++++ETDsFrom+++To/L+++IDc.Keywords++++++++++++++++++++++
D  CrtUsrSpc     PI              *
D    CrtSpcName            20     const

*  Local Variables
```

Figure 2.4: List and reorganize files with deleted records using the QUSPTRUS API (part 9 of 10).

```
D PasSpcName      DS           20
D  SLib                 11      20
D ChgAttrDs       DS           13
D  NumberAttr                   9B 0 inz(1)
D  KeyAttr                      9B 0 inz(3)
D  DataSize                     9B 0 inz(1)
D  AttrData                     1     inz('1')
D ListPtr         S                 *
D SpaceAttr       S           10     inz
D SpaceAuth       S           10     INZ('*CHANGE')
D SpaceLen        S            9B 0 INZ(2048)
D SpaceReplc      S           10     INZ('*YES')
D SpaceText       S           50
D SpaceValue      S            1


CLON01Factor1+++++++Opcode&ExtFactor2+++++++Result++++++++Len++D+HiLoEq
 * Create the user space
C                   move      CrtSpcName    PasSpcName
C                   CALL      'QUSCRTUS'
C                   PARM                    PasSpcName
C                   PARM                    SpaceAttr
C                   PARM                    SpaceLen
C                   PARM                    SpaceValue
C                   PARM                    SpaceAuth
C                   PARM                    SpaceText
C                   PARM      '*YES'        SpaceReplc
C                   PARM                    QusEc
 * Get pointer to user space
C                   CALL      'QUSPTRUS'
C                   PARM                    PasSpcName
C                   PARM                    ListPtr
 * Change user space to be extendable
C                   CALL      'QUSCUSAT'
C                   PARM                    Slib
C                   PARM                    PasSpcName
C                   PARM                    ChgAttrDs
C                   PARM                    QusEc
C                   return    ListPtr
P  CrtUsrSpc       E
```

Figure 2.4: List and reorganize files with deleted records using the QUSPTRUS API (part 10 of 10).

Table 2.3 lists all of the parameters of the Retrieve Member Description (QUSRMBRD) API. This API gives you the number of records in the file in field QUSNBRCR. The number of deleted records is in field QUSNBRDR. You can calculate the percentage of deleted records and print or reorganize the file only if it is greater than the parameter passed. As shown in Figure 2.4, the code is designed to list and reorganize files with deleted records using the QUSPTRUS API.

Table 2.2: Parameter Description of the List Objects API (QUSLOBJ)

Parameter	Description	Type	Attribute	Size
1	The user space name/library. The first 10 bytes are the name, and the second 10 are the library. Library names *LIBL and *CURLIB are acceptable.	Input	Char	20
2	The list format name, as follows:	Input	Char	8

Format Name	Description
OBJL0100	Object name.
OBJL0200	Text and extended attribute.
OBJL0300	Basic object information.
OBJL0400	Creation information.
OBJL0500	Save and restore information.
OBJL0600	Usage Information.
OBJL0700	All object information.

Parameter	Description	Type	Attribute	Size
3	The object and library name of objects to list. The first 10 bytes are the object name, and the second 10 bytes are the library name. The object can be a name, a generic name, or one of the special values *ALL, *ALLUSR, and *IBM. The library can be a name or one of the special values *ALL, *ALLUSR, *CURLIB, *LIBL, or *USRLIBL.	Input	Char	20
4	The type of object to list. It accepts a valid type name or the special value *ALL.	Input	Char	10
Optional Group 1				
5	A standard error data structure.	In/Out	Char	Varies
Optional Group 2				
6	The authority control.	Input	Char	Varies
7	The selection control.	Input	Char	Varies

Table 2.3: Retrieve Member Description (QUSRMBRD)

Parameter	Description	Type	Attribute	Size
1	The return variable, a field that holds information returned by the API.	Output	Char	Varies
2	The length of the return variable in parameter 1.	Input	Binary	4
3	The format name, as follows:	Input	Char	8

Name	Description
MBRD0100	The member name and basic source information.
MBRD0200	The member name with expanded information.
MBRD0300	The member name with full information.

Parameter	Description	Type	Attribute	Size
4	The file and library name. The first 10 bytes are the name, and the second 10 are the library. Library names *LIBL and *CURLIB are acceptable.	Input	Char	20
5	The member name within the file. The special values *FIRST and *LAST are acceptable.	Input	Char	10
6	Override, which determines whether to process overrides to find the file to retrieve information from. Zero means no; one means yes.	Input	Char	1
Optional Group 1				
7	An error data structure.	In/Out	Char	Varies
Optional Group 2				
8	Find member processing, which specifies how to search for a member. The default, zero, means find the member in the file. One means find the member name directly. This is a faster method if the member name is known but the library is specified as *LIBL.	Input	Char	1

The user space is overlaid with the General Header data structure by moving **SpacePtr** to **GenDsPoint**. This gets the pointers to the other data structures. Then, use the offset to the list data field QUSOLD00 in the General Data structure to get to the first entry in the list. QUSNBRLE00 is used as the basis for the DO loop that processes each entry in the list. Now, you can overlay the list data structure over the correct position in the user space and extract the information requested from the list entry. Then, add the size of the list entry structure, which is contained in QUSSEE00, to the **ListPoint** pointer to get the next entry in the list.

Each entry in the list provides a name of a file in the library. However, you don't want to reorganize every file in the library; you only want to reorganize files that have a particular percentage of deleted records. While the list object API doesn't return this information, the Retrieve Member Description (QUSRMBRD) API does return both the number of deleted records and the number of current records.

Within each iteration of the DO loop, the RTVMBR subroutine is executed. This subroutine executes the Retrieve Member Description (QUSRMBRD) API to retrieve the number of records and the number of deleted records in the member. If you look closely, you will notice that this subroutine calls the QUSRMBRD API twice. It uses the technique of calling the API to get the proper length of the receiver variable, allocates that length to the receiver variable, and then calls the API again to actually retrieve the information. (See chapter 1 for more information on this technique.) If there are some deleted records, consider reorganizing the file. If not, ignore this file and get another one.

Comparing Methods to Access the List Information

Now take a look at the same program, but this time use the Retrieve User Space (QUSRTVUS) API to retrieve the list information. Figure 2.5 shows the differences between the two techniques. Several changes were made to the program to use QUSRTVUS.

First, look at the definition for QUSH0300, the General Header data structure at the location labeled A in Figure 2.5. As shown in Figure 2.4, this data structure is defined based on the pointer field **GenDSPoint**. Because the user space isn't accessed via a pointer, the BASED keyword has been removed. This is also true for the List Entry Data Structure (QUSL0200).

Another change to note is the call to the **CrtUsrSpc** procedure located at reference point B in Figure 2.5. Because getting a pointer to the user space doesn't matter, this call has been changed from an EVAL statement to a CALLP.

The next change is the biggest. After the call to the List Objects (QUSLOBJ) API comes the code to access the user space. As shown in Figure 2.4, the use of pointers is accomplished with the statement **EVAL GenDSPoint = SpacePtr** to overlay the General Header data structure over the beginning of the user space. In Figure 2.5, this has been replaced with a call to the Retrieve User Space (QUSRTVUS) API with the General Header data structure name (QUSH0300) as the parameter in which to return data.

Now that the General Header data structure is loaded, you can use the list-offset field to get to the List Entry data structure. As shown in Figure 2.4, the pointer method simply adds the offset to the pointer field, like this:

```
Eval       ListPoint = GenDsPoint + QusOLD00.
```

The code in Figure 2.5 is a bit more cumbersome. You must again use the Retrieve User Space (QUSRTVUS) API to get at the data. You can use the offset field QUSOLD00 as the starting position parameter for this API, but you must add one to the offset value before using it. As previously mentioned, this is true for all offset fields. Their value is stored using zero as the first position. You cannot use zero as a starting position to retrieve data. The Retrieve User Space (QUSRTVUS) API recognizes the number 1 as the first position of data. So you must remember to add one to any offset field before using it (if you are not using pointers to access the data).

The Retrieve User Space (QUSTRVUS) API is located within the DO loop shown at reference point C in Figure 2.5, and is executed once each time through the loop. The starting position is incremented at the end of each loop by adding the size of the list entry field (QUSSEE00) to the last starting position. With the pointer method, the pointer field **ListPoint** is incremented by adding the QUSSEE00 field to it each time through.

It should be readily apparent that using pointers to access list information is actually easier than the Retrieve User Space (QUSTRVUS) API. It's also much faster because you don't have to repeatedly call the API. We highly recommend using the pointer method whenever you can. Refer to chapter 1 for a discussion on the reasons and limitations for using each method. Keep in mind that you cannot use the pointer method prior to V4R2 because pointer math wasn't available before then.

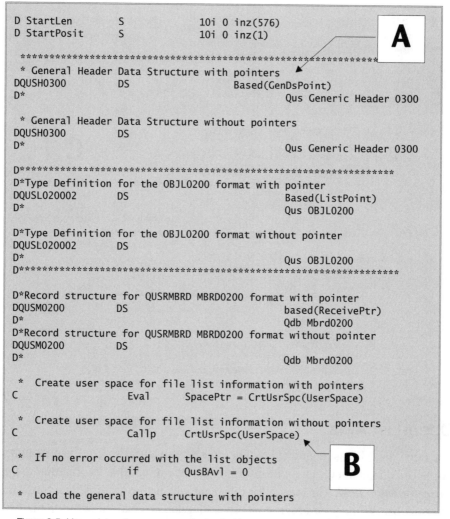

```
D StartLen          S                10i 0 inz(576)
D StartPosit        S                10i 0 inz(1)                                    A

     ************************************************************
     * General Header Data Structure with pointers
DQUSH0300           DS                         Based(GenDsPoint)
D*                                             Qus Generic Header 0300

     * General Header Data Structure without pointers
DQUSH0300           DS
D*                                             Qus Generic Header 0300

D***********************************************************************
D*Type Definition for the OBJL0200 format with pointer
DQUSL020002         DS                         Based(ListPoint)
D*                                             Qus OBJL0200

D*Type Definition for the OBJL0200 format without pointer
DQUSL020002         DS
D*                                             Qus OBJL0200
D***********************************************************************

D*Record structure for QUSRMBRD MBRD0200 format with pointer
DQUSM0200           DS                         based(ReceivePtr)
D*                                             Qdb Mbrd0200
D*Record structure for QUSRMBRD MBRD0200 format without pointer
DQUSM0200           DS
D*                                             Qdb Mbrd0200

 * Create user space for file list information with pointers
C                   Eval      SpacePtr = CrtUsrSpc(UserSpace)

 * Create user space for file list information without pointers
C                   Callp     CrtUsrSpc(UserSpace)                          B

 * If no error occurred with the list objects
C                   if        QusBAvl = 0

 * Load the general data structure with pointers
```

Figure 2.5: Use pointers to user spaces instead of just user spaces (part 1 of 2).

```
C                    Eval      GenDsPoint = SpacePtr
 *  Load the general data structure without pointers
C                    CALL      'QUSRTVUS'
C                    PARM                 UserSpace
C                    PARM                 StartPosit
C                    PARM                 StartLen
C                    PARM                 QUSH0300

 *  If the list API was complete or partially complete
C                    if        QuSISOO = 'C' OR
C                              QuSISOO = 'P'

 *  Load the list data structure with pointers
C                    Eval      ListPoint = GenDsPoint + QusOLD00

 *  Set initial starting point for retrieving list entry (no pointers)
C                    eval      StartPosit = QusOLD00 + 1
C                    eval      StartLen = QusSEE00

C                    Do        QusNbrLE00

 *  Load the list data structure without pointers
C                    CALL      'QUSRTVUS'
C                    PARM                 UserSpace
C                    PARM                 StartPosit
C                    PARM                 StartLen
C                    PARM                 QusL020002
 *  Only want to process physical files not in library QSYS

 * Set to next list entry with pointers
C                    Eval      ListPoint = ListPoint + QusSEE00
 * Set to next list entry with pointers
C                    Eval      StartPosit = StartPosit + QusSEE00

C                    EndDo
C                    Endif
C                    Endif
```

C

Figure 2.5: Use pointers to user spaces instead of just user spaces (part 2 of 2).

Open-List APIs

The open-list API, as mentioned earlier, doesn't use a user space. Even though open-list APIs can return a lot of information, they return this information into a *variable-length field*. The reason for this technique is that these APIs return a "partial" list. While your program is processing the original information the API returned, the API goes out to get more information for you to process. This sequence is referred to as *asynchronous processing*. This concept isn't a new one if you have been trained in the fine art of programming in an object-oriented environment.

Open-list APIs were created with one thought in mind: speed. An open-list API will return as many records as you request as soon as it can. While your program is acting on this partial list, the API will continue to finish the list. Because the program operator doesn't have to wait while the complete list is being created, this is especially helpful in interactive programming. Because both your program and the API are working on different parts of the same task, response time is improved. It's a variation of the old adage that "two heads are better than one."

Using open-list APIs requires that you have the Host Servers option of OS/400 installed. Because open-list APIs process asynchronously, they are only available if you have installed the Host Servers option. To install Host Servers, use option 1 from the LICPGM menu to access the Work with Licensed Programs display. From there, select the Host Servers option.

Another thing to be aware of when dealing with open-list APIs is that they reside in library QGY. You will have to take some action to ensure that your application program can find this library. Do this either by adding it to your library list, by hard-coding the call (an option we would never recommend), or by some other method.

Unfortunately, as of V4R4, only a handful of list APIs use this technique. We suspect that more will be in the works. Table 2.4 provides a list of the open-list APIs.

Each of these APIs returns only the number of records requested into a receiver variable, along with a request

Table 2.4: Open-List APIs	
API	**Description**
QGYOLJBL	Open list of job log messages.
QGYOLMSG	Open list of messages.
QGYOLOBJ	Open list of objects.
QEZOLBKL	Open list of objects to be backed up.
QGYRPRTL	Open list of printers.
QGYOLSPL	Open list of spooled files.

handle that can be used by another API to get the next set of records into the variable. The Get List Entry (QGYGTLE) API uses the request handle to fill the variable whenever it is called. Therefore, you call the open-list API once and the Get List Entry (QGYGTLE) API as many times as needed to get the rest of the records—one block of records at a time.

Most of these APIs return a control data structure that contains information about the list. The structure contains information such as how many records were returned and the length of each record returned, as well as a code to indicate if you have finished processing the list. This information allows you to process the list in the return variable. Figure 2.6 shows the data structure for the Open List of Spooled Files (QGYOLSPL) API.

Once again, this code was taken from the member QGYOLSPL, source file QRPGLESRC, found in library QSYSINC. Each of the open-list APIs appears to have its own data structure, with its own unique named fields, but the format is actually the same. Table 2.5 lists each of the fields in the data structure. The field names vary from API to API; field names from the Open List of Spooled Files API are used for this table.

```
DName++++++++++ETDsFrom+++To/L+++IDc.Keywords++++++++++++++++++++++++++
D*******************************************************************
D*Type Definition for the List Information Format
D*******************************************************************
DQGYOLIO2        DS
D QGYTR03                      1       4B 0
D QGYRR02                      5       8B 0
D QGYRH03                      9      12
D QGYRL03                     13      16B 0
D QGYIC03                     17      17
D QGYDT07                     18      30
D QGYLS02                     31      31
D QGYRSV108                   32      32
D QGYIL02                     33      36B 0
D QGYFR02                     37      40B 0
D QGYRSV207                   41      80
```

Figure 2.6: This code shows the open-list control data structure format.

Table 2.5: Fields in the Open-List Control Field Data Structure

Field	Description
QGYTR03	The total number of records in the list.
QGYRR02	The number of records returned to the variable field on this pass.
QGYRH03	The field to be used to access subsequent blocks of records into the variable field, used with QGYGTLE. It is valid until the Close List (QGYCLST) API is called.
QGYRL03	The length of each record returned. If the record is of variable length, this value is zero, and the actual length of each record is contained within each record.
QGYIC03	A code that indicates if the request for data has been fulfilled, as follows:
	Code / **Description**
	C — Complete and accurate. All done.
	I — Incomplete. Something went wrong; bad data.
	P — Partial. The variable is full, but more records exist.
QGYDT07	The date and time when the list was created, in CYYMMDDHHMMSS format.
QGYLS02	A code indicating the status of building the list, as follows:
	Code / **Description**
	0 — The building of the list is pending.
	1 — The list is being built.
	2 — The building of the list is completed.
	3 — An error occurred during the build. The next call to QGYGTLE will signal an error.
	4 — The list is primed and ready, but hasn't started building yet.
QGYRSV108	A field reserved for alignment purposes.
QGYIL02	The number of bytes returned to the variable field.
QGYFR02	The number of the first record returned in the receiver variable.
QGYRSV207	A field reserved for alignment purposes.

The Program to Display
Two Users' Spooled Files at Once

Figure 2.7 shows a program that will create a subfile of all spooled files belonging to User1 and User2. These are parameters passed to the program. The purpose of the program is to illustrate the use of the Open List of Spooled Files (QGYOLSPL) API and to show how to process open lists in general. Figure 2.8 shows the display file used by Figure 2.7, and Figure 2.9 shows an output screen presented when the program is run.

```
********************************************************************
* To Create:
*        CRTBNDRPG PGM(XXX/FIG0207) SRCFILE(XXXLIB/SOURCEFILE)
*        DFTACTGRP(*NO) ACTGRP(ILE) TGTRLS(V4R4M0)
*
*  Note: Add library QGY to your library list prior to running
*  this program
*
********************************************************************
FFilename++IPEASF.....L.....A.Device+.Keywords+++++++++++++++++++++++++
fFig0208    cf   e               workstn
f                                       sfile(sflrcd:rrn)
f                                       infds(info)


DName++++++++++++ETDsFrom+++To/L+++IDc.Keywords++++++++++++++++++++++++++
d F03            c                      const(x'33')
d Pageup         c                      const(x'F4')
d Pagedn         c                      const(x'F5')

d Info           ds
d  key                     369     369

d FmtName        s               8
d FormType       s              10      inz('*ALL')
d GetNbrRcds     s              10i 0 inz(10)
d JobName        s              26
d ListInfo       s              80
d Rrn            s               4  0
d StartRcd       s              10i 0 inz(1)
d Users          s              12      dim(2)
d User1          s              10
d User2          s              10
d UsrSpcData     s              10      inz('*ALL')
d Variable       s            1920
d VarLength      s              10i 0 inz(%len(Variable))
d VarStart       s               5  0
```

Figure 2.7: An RPG IV program can employ spooled files for multiple-user, open-list APIs (part 1 of 6).

```
d X                 S              4  0 Inz(1)
d Y                 S              4  0

 * Filter/select information data structure
dFilterInfo         DS            1000
d NbrUsrName              1        4b 0 inz(1)
d FilterInf               5     1000

 * OutQueue Selection array
dOutQueDs           DS            24
d NbrOutQs                1        4b 0 inz(1)
d OutqFilt                5       24      inz('*ALL')

 * Status selection array
dStatusDs           DS            16
d NbrStats                1        4b 0 inz(1)
d StatusFilt              5       16      inz('*ALL')

 * Device selection array
dDeviceDs           DS            16
d NbrDevices              1        4b 0 inz(1)
d DeviceFilt              5       16      inz('*ALL')

 * Sort information data structure
dSortInfo           DS            16
d NbrKeySort              1        4B 0 Inz(0)
d KeySortStr              5        8B 0 Inz(0)
d SortKeyLen              9       12B 0 inz(0)
d KeyDataTyp             13       14B 0 inz(x'0000')
d SortOrder              15       15      inz(x'00')
d Reserved               16       16      inz(x'00')

 * Standard Error Code data structure
dQUSEC              DS            116
d QUSBPRV                 1        4B 0           inz(116)

 * Format OGYV020000 Open List of Spooled Files. Copied from
 * member QGYOLSPL, source file QRPGLESRC, in library QSYSINC

dQGYV020000         DS            192
D*                                           Qgy Olsp RecVar 0200
D*QGYV010001                     160
D*                                           RecVar 0100
D  QGYSFILN04             1       10
D*                                           Spooled File Name
D  QGYJN02               11       20
D*                                           Job Name
D  QGYUN02               21       30
D*                                           User Name
D  QGYJN03               31       36
D*                                           Job No
```

Figure 2.7: An RPG IV program can employ spooled files for multiple-user, open-list APIs (part 2 of 6).

```
D   QGYSFILN05              37      40B 0
D*                                          Spooled File No
D   QGYTP00                 41      44B 0
D*                                          Total Pages
D   QGYCP05                 45      48B 0
D*                                          Current Page
D   QGYCTP00                49      52B 0
D*                                          Copies To Print
D   QGYOQN03                53      62
D*                                          Out Q Name
D   QGYOQLN01               63      72
D*                                          Out Q Lib Name
D   QGYUSD00                73      82
D*                                          User Spec Data
D   QGYTATUS01              83      92
D*                                          Status
D   QGYFT01                 93     102
D*                                          Form Type
D   QGYORITY00             103     104
D*                                          Priority
D   QGYIJID00              105     120
D*                                          Int Job ID
D   QGYISFID00             121     136
D*                                          Int SF ID
D   QGYDT06                137     146
D*                                          Device Type
D   QGYERVED36             147     160
D*                                          Reserved
D QGYDO                    161     167
D*                                          Date Opened
D QGYTO                    168     173
D*                                          Time Opened
D QGYPA                    174     174
D*                                          Printer Assigned
D QGYPN                    175     184
D*                                          Printer Name
D QGYERVED37               185     192
D*                                          Reserved

 * Format OGYOLIO2 Open List of Spooled Files. Copied from
 * member QGYOLSPL, source file QRPGLESRC, in library QSYSINC

DQGYOLI02          DS              80
D*                                          Qgy Olspl ListInfo
D QGYTR03                   1       4B 0
D*                                          Total Records
D QGYRR02                   5       8B 0
D*                                          Records Retd
D QGYRH03                   9      12
D*                                          Request Handle
D QGYRL03                  13      16B 0
```

Figure 2.7: An RPG IV program can employ spooled files for multiple-user, open-list APIs (part 3 of 6).

```
D*                                          Record Length
D QGYIC03                17      17
D*                                          Info Complete
D QGYDT07                18      30
D*                                          Date Time
D QGYLS02                31      31
D*                                          List Status
D QGYRSV108              32      32
D*                                          Reserved1
D QGYIL02                33      36B 0
D*                                          Info Length
D QGYFR02                37      40B 0
D*                                          First Record
D QGYRSV207              41      80
D*                                          Reserved2

CLON01Factor1+++++++Opcode&ExtFactor2+++++++Result++++++++Len++D+HiLoEq
c     *entry      plist
c                 parm                      User1
c                 parm                      User2
 *
c                 movel    '*ALL'           Users(1)
c                 movel    '*ALL'           User1o
c                 if       %parms >= 1
c                 movel    User1            Users(1)
c                 movel    User1            User1o
c                 endif
c                 if       %parms = 2
c                 add      1                NbrUsrName
c                 movel    User2            Users(2)
c                 movel    User2            User2o
c                 eval     *in05 = *on
c                 endif

 *   Create FilterInfo field
c                 exsr     CrtFiltInf

 *   List spooled files to variable
C                 Call     'QGYOLSPL'
C                 Parm                      Variable
C                 Parm                      VarLength
C                 Parm                      QgyOLI02
C                 Parm                      GetNbrRcds
C                 Parm                      SortInfo
C                 Parm                      FilterInfo
C                 Parm                      JobName
C                 Parm     'OSPL0200'       FmtName
C                 Parm                      QusEc

c                 Dou      Key <> PageDn
 * Process the variable field into subfile records
```

Figure 2.7: An RPG IV program can employ spooled files for multiple-user, open-list APIs (part 4 of 6).

```
C                    Exsr      ProcessVar

* If processed all the records, shut off page down
C                    If        QgyIC03 = 'C' AND
C                              QgyTR03 = RRN
C                    eval      *in24 = *on
C                    endif

C                    eval      *in22 = *on
C                    Exfmt     SflCtl
C                    eval      *in06 = *off

* If there were more records than what were returned
C                    if        Key = PageDn
C                    Exsr      GetMorRecs
C                    Endif
C                    Enddo

*  Close the list
C                    Call      'QGYCLST'
C                    Parm                  QgyRH03
C                    Parm                  QusEc

C                    eval      *inlr = *on

 **********************************************************************
 **
 ** Get more records from the open list via QGYGTLE
 **
 **********************************************************************
C     GetMorRecs     Begsr
C                    Eval      StartRcd = StartRcd + QgyRR02
*  Get more entries from the list
C                    Call      'QGYGTLE'
C                    Parm                  Variable
C                    Parm                  VarLength
C                    Parm                  QgyRH03
C                    Parm                  QgyOLI02
C                    Parm                  GetNbrRcds
C                    Parm                  StartRcd
C                    Parm                  QusEc
C                    Endsr
 **********************************************************************
 **
 ** Process variable returned from open-list API
 **
 **********************************************************************
C     ProcessVar     Begsr
C                    Eval      VarStart = 1
C                    Do        QgyRR02
C                    Eval      QgyV020000 = %subst(Variable:VarStart:
```

Figure 2.7: An RPG IV program can employ spooled files for multiple-user, open-list APIs (part 5 of 6).

```
C                                  QgyRL03)

* Process the information in data structure QgyV020000
*  Write to a subfile record, print it, whatever
*
C                    move      QgySFilN04     spname
C                    move      QgyJN02        jobnam
C                    move      QgyUN02        UserNam
C                    move      QgyJN03        Jobnum
C                    move      QgyTP00        Pages
C                    move      QgyOQN03       Outq
C                    move      QgyOQLN01      OutqLib

C                    eval      *in21 = *on
C                    eval      Rrn = Rrn + 1
C                    write     Sflrcd

* don't allow pageup key if writing first page of subfile
C                    if        Rrn = 1
C                    eval      *in06 = *on
C                    endif

C                    Eval      VarStart = VarStart + QgyRL03
C                    Enddo
C                    Endsr

     **********************************************************************
     **
     ** Create filter info field using parameters passed to program
     **
     **********************************************************************
C     CrtFiltInf     Begsr
C                    do        NbrUsrName     Y
C                    eval      FilterInf = %replace(Users(Y):FilterInf :x)
C                    eval      x = x + 12
C                    enddo
C                    eval      FilterInf = %replace(OutqueDs:FilterInf:x)
C                    eval      x = x + 24
C                    eval      FilterInf = %replace(FormType:FilterInf:x)
C                    eval      x = x + 10
C                    eval      FilterInf = %replace(UsrSpcData:
C                               FilterInf:x)
C                    eval      x = x + 10
C                    eval      FilterInf = %replace(StatusDs:FilterInf:x)
C                    eval      x = x + 16
C                    eval      FilterInf = %replace(DeviceDs:FilterInf:x)
C                    eval      x = x + 16
C                    Endsr
```

Figure 2.7: An RPG IV program can employ spooled files for multiple-user, open-list APIs (part 6 of 6).

```
A                              DSPSIZ(24 80 *DS3)
A                              PRINT
A                              CA03
A        R SFLRCD              SFL
A          SPNAME     10A  O  8  3
A          JOBNAM     10A  O  8 16
A          USERNAM    10A  O  8 28
A          JOBNUM      6A  O  8 40
A          PAGES       6Y 0O  8 48EDTCDE(Z)
A          OUTQ       10A  O  8 56
A          OUTQLIB    10A  O  8 68
A        R SFLCTL              SFLCTL(SFLRCD)
A                              SFLSIZ(0020)
A                              SFLPAG(0010)
A N24                          PAGEDOWN
A N06                          PAGEUP
A                              OVERLAY
A  21                          SFLDSP
A  22                          SFLDSPCTL
A  25                          SFLCLR
A  24                          SFLEND(*MORE)
A          RRN         4S 0H   SFLRCDNBR
A                            1 28'SPOOLED FILES'
A                              DSPATR(HI)
A                            3 27'For:'
A          USER10     10A  O  3 33
A  05                        4 27'And:'
A  05      USER20     10A  O  4 33
A                            7  3'Spool Name'
A                              DSPATR(HI)
A                            7 16'Job Name'
A                              DSPATR(HI)
A                            7 28'User'
A                              DSPATR(HI)
A                            7 40'Job#'
A                              DSPATR(HI)
A                            7 49'Pages'
A                              DSPATR(HI)
A                            7 56'Outqueue'
A                              DSPATR(HI)
A                            7 68'Library'
A                              DSPATR(HI)
A        R FORMAT1
A                              TEXT('Command keys')
A                           22  4'F3=Exit'
A                              COLOR(BLU)
```

Figure 2.8: The display file used by Figure 2.7 contains code displays of spooled files for multiple-user, open-list APIs.

```
                        SPOOLED FILES

                   For:   DOUG
                   And:   RON


    Spool Name    Job Name     User      Job#     Pages   Outqueue    Library
    WEBSPOOL      WEBSPOOL     DOUG      458377     12    NOPRINT     QUSRSYS
    WEBSIGNON     WEBSIGNON    DOUG      458493     11    NOPRINT     QUSRSYS
    WEBSIGNON     WEBSIGNON    DOUG      458496     11    NOPRINT     QUSRSYS
    WEBSIGNON     WEBSIGNON    DOUG      458501     11    NOPRINT     QUSRSYS
    SPLLIST       SPLLIST      RON       458787      8    NOPRINT     QUSRSYS
    WEBVALID8     WEBVALID8    DOUG      458789     13    NOPRINT     QUSRSYS
    SPLLIST       SPLLIST      RON       458790      9    NOPRINT     QUSRSYS
    WEBVALID8     WEBVALID8    DOUG      458792     13    NOPRINT     QUSRSYS
    SPLLIST       SPLLIST      RON       458796      9    NOPRINT     QUSRSYS
    WEBVALID8     WEBVALID8    DOUG      458816     13    NOPRINT     QUSRSYS
                                                              More...
```

Figure 2.9: The code for the program shown in Figure 2.7 produces this output.

As usual, most of the data structures were taken from QRPGLESRC in library QSYSINC. The exceptions to this are the **FilterInfo** and **SortInfo** parameters. We made up the names for the fields in these structures, as QSYSINC is not very helpful in these instances.

One of the first things the program does is to take the parameters passed into the program and convert them to the format that **FilterInfo** requires. This action takes place in the **CrtFiltInf** subroutine. The **FilterInfo** parameter is where the API is told exactly which spooled files to include in the list.

After **FilterInfo** is built, the Open List Spooled Files (QGYOLSPL) API is called. The details of the parameters to this API are listed in Table 2.6.

Table 2.6: Open List of Spooled files (QGYOLSPL) (part 1 of 2)

Parameter	Description	Type	Attribute	Size
1	A variable receiver field that will hold information returned by the API.	Output	Char	Varies
2	The length of the variable receiver in parameter 1.	Input	Binary	4
3	An open-list control data structure. See Table 2.5 for details.	Output	Char	80
4	The number of records to retrieve into the variable field after filtering and sorting. Valid values are as follows:	Input	Binary	4

Value	Description
-1	The list is built synchronously. The program will wait until the entire list is built before continuing.
0	The entire list is built asynchronously. The program will continue while the list is built by the server job.
Any number	The number of records specified will be created synchronously and returned to the variable. The rest of the list will be created asynchronously.

Parameter	Description	Type	Attribute	Size
5	The order in which to sequence the returning records. The format of the structure follows. If the last three fields in the structure are not used, they must be set to hexadecimal zeros.	Input	Char	Varies

Description	Attribute	Size
The number of keys to sort on. The following fields will repeat this many times.	Binary	4
The sort key field's starting position within the record.	Binary	4

Parameter	Description			Type	Attribute	Size
Table 2.6: Open List of Spooled files (QGYOLSPL) (part 2 of 2)						
Parameter	Description			Type	Attribute	Size
5 cont.	**Description**	**Attribute**	**Size**			
	The sort key field's length.	Binary	4			
	The sort key field's data type.	Binary	2			
	The sort order (ascending or descending).	Char	1			
	Reserved.	Char	1			
6	The filter list information. This information is used to determine which spooled filed should be included in the list. The file information is described in Table 2.7.			Input	Char	Varies
7	The qualified job name. Leave this blank to include all jobs.			Input	Char	26
8	The format name. Choose one of the following:			Input	Char	8
	Name	**Description**				
	OSPL0100	Basic information only.				
	OSPL0200	Basic plus additional.				
Optional Group 1						
9	An error data structure.			In/Out	Char	Varies

Make special note of parameter 6, which is the filter information. You can filter on user, output queues, form type, user data, status code, or device name. You can mix and match these filters to get very specific entries in the list, or you can ignore them entirely and get all spooled files.

This parameter is complex enough to merit its own description, in Table 2.7.

Table 2.7: Filter Information for the Open List of Spooled files API (QGYOLSPL)		
Description	**Attribute**	**Size**
The number of user names that are to be included in the list.	Binary	4
The user names to include in the list. Special values for the user name field are *ALL (spooled files for all users) and *CURRENT (spooled files for current user).	Char	12
The number of output queue names to include in the following list.	Binary	4
The output queue name and library. Only spooled files in these queues are included in the list. Special values for the output queue name are as follows: *ALL—Files on all queues. The library name must be blank. *CURLIB—Use the job's current library. *LIBL—Use the library list.	Char	20
The form type to be included in list. Special values for the form type are *ALL (files with any form type) and *STD (standard form type only).	Char	10
Only spooled files with this user-specified data would be included in the list. The only special value for this field is *ALL, for files with any user-specified data.	Char	10
The number of spooled file status codes that will be in the following list.	Binary	4
Only spooled files with this status code would be included in the list. The only special value for this field is *ALL, for files with any spooled status.	Char	12
The number of device names that will be in the following list.	Binary	4
Only spooled files with the following device names would be included in the list. The only special value for this field is *ALL, for files with any device name.	Char	12

The flexibility created by the Filter List Information (parameter 6) poses somewhat of a challenge when formatting the parameter. The parameter is basically a series of arrays. A binary number indicates how many entries are going to be in the array that follows. Because each array is variable in length, there are no set positions within the parameter. You have to build the parameter as you go, appending each new array to the end of the previous one. None of the arrays may be omitted.

If you don't want to use one of the filter capabilities, you must use the special value *ALL for the name and still indicate that there is one entry in the array. If you look at the **CrtFiltInf** subroutine, you will see that the %REPLACE built-in function is used to accomplish this. Because this example just provides the capability of filtering on specified users, we only had to load values into one array. If you want to make this program more robust, this subroutine can get complicated as you fill the other arrays. The technique would remain the same, however.

After calling the API, the variable receiver will contain 10 records. While you are processing these 10 records into a subfile, the API is continuing to create the list that you requested by employing asynchronous processing. The API will store the list in a hidden user space and return a handle you can use to access the rest of the list via the Get List Entries (QGYGTLE) API. The parameters for the Get List Entries API are found in Table 2.8. The parameters for the Close List API are shown in Table 2.9.

Table 2.8: Get List Entries (QGYGTLE) (part 1 of 2)				
Parameter	**Description**	**Type**	**Attribute**	**Size**
1	A variable receiver field that holds the information returned by the API.	Output	Char	Varies
2	The length of the variable receiver in parameter 1.	Input	Binary	4
3	The request handle retrieved from the call to the open-list API. It is used to access the list created by that call.	Input	Char	4
4	The open-list control data structure. (See Table 2.5 for details.)	Output	Char	80
5	The number of records to retrieve into the variable field, starting with the record indicated in parameter 6 (the starting-record parameter). This parameter must be zero or greater. If it is zero, only the open-list control data structure is returned.	Input	Binary	4

Table 2.8: Get List Entries (QGYGTLE) (part 2 of 2)

Parameter	Description	Type	Attribute	Size
6	The starting record; the number of the first record that will be put in the receiver variable. There are two special values: 	Value	Description
---	---
0	Only the open-list control data structure is returned. The number of records to return must also be zero.
-1	The whole list should be built before the list information is returned to the caller.		Input	Binary	4
7	A standard error data structure.	I/O	Char	Varies

Table 2.9: Close List (QGYCLST)

Parameter	Description	Type	Attribute	Size
1	The request handle to the list that is to be closed. The handle was generated by one of the open-list APIs.	Input	Char	4
2	A standard error data structure.	I/O	Char	Varies

The program has been coded as a loop to present a subfile of qualified spooled files for the operator. First, the loop processes the records found in the return variable into a subfile. Then, the subfile records are displayed. If the user presses the Page Down key, the subroutine **GetMoreRecs** executes and, appropriately enough, gets more records.

The GETMORERECS subroutine calls the Get List Entry (QGYGTLE) API. This API is used to retrieve another batch of records from the list already opened using the Open List of Spooled Files (QGYOLSPL) API. The same return variable field is used in both APIs to make it easier to process the information. Take a look at the parameters for the Get List Entry API in Table 2.8. Pay particular attention to parameters 3 and 6. Parameter 3 is the request handle. This field was retrieved from the open-list control data structure (parameter number 3 on QGYOLSPL). It tells the API which "hidden" user space contains the list.

Parameter 6 of the Get List Entry API is the starting record number that you want to retrieve from the list. This number is bumped by the number of records retrieved the last time. Basically, it is a counter for the number of records you have retrieved (plus one).

Summary

The list APIs are powerful tools. They return a lot of information relatively quickly, by way of user spaces. While each list API is unique, they all follow the same set of standards. Now that you know the standards, you should be able to process any of the list APIs.

The open-list APIs are even faster than the standard list APIs. They process asynchronously, so that you can get some of the records returned to process while the rest of the list is being built.

3

FILE APIs

The AS/400 is blessed with its own built-in database, DB2/400. One of the best decisions IBM ever made was to anoint the AS/400 with the fully integrated database originally developed on the System/38. Gone are the days of having to describe the file buffer layouts in every program you write. Externally described files are used to externalize and standardize database definition. This eliminates work and errors. Each file now contains a complete, definitive description of the data within it. Above and beyond the field definitions you use when writing your high-level-language programs, the description of the file can be accessed, too, using the file APIs.

The discussion of file APIs in this chapter opens with coverage of one of the most informative APIs, the Retrieve File Description (QDBRTVFD) API. This API returns everything you could ever want to know about a file, and then some. QDBRTVFD returns all of the same information that IBM's Display File Description (DSPFD) command does. From our perspective, though, IBM's Display File Description (DSPFD) command returns too much data! You'll see how to use QDBRTVFD to create your own pared-down, user-friendlier version of the Display File Description command.

Since we're in the mood for retrieving information about files, let's not forget about display files. The Retrieve Display Fil (QDFRTVFD)e API may be used to gather information about display files. This API tells you everything you want to know about a display file. In particular, you'll learn how to get the field names used in a format. The exercise demonstrating QDFRTVFD will take you on a wild ride, containing a lot of twists and turns. Hunker down and hang on to your hat, while you explore the mysterious world of file APIs!

Retrieve File Description

Have you ever run IBM's Display File Description (DSPFD) command? What kind of question is that? We might as well ask if you have been programming for longer than a week. You probably use this command all the time. What programmer doesn't? We *used* to use it all the time, too.

After all, IBM's Display File Description (DSPFD) command tells you everything there is to know about a file. Want to know the number of members, triggers, and constraints? It's in there. Want to know the type and size of the access path? It's in there. Is the file journaled? How about the name of the journal, the type of images being recorded, and the last date and time journaling was started? All of this, and much more, is in that single command.

There are pages and pages of information displayed whenever you run that command. Of course, you can filter the information by selecting different options for the TYPE parameter, but there doesn't seem to be one single view that gives us exactly what we're looking for 90% of the time. We have to page through panel after panel of extraneous information just to get what we are looking for.

Admittedly, the problem is really our own. We want to see a combination of record information, object information, and file information all on one single screen. Since we generally do not use multiple member files, we saw no reason why we could not accomplish this goal. However, since DSPFD cannot assume that the user doesn't have multiple member files, it has to be much more complex in order to provide flexibility.

If we ever want to see a list of members in a file, we'll use the Display File Description command. For that other 99.99% of the time, though, we're looking for some basic information. How many records are in the file, or how many fields? When was the file last created or saved? Who created the file? We want to easily get to the basic information about a file. Okay, we admit it: We're lazy. We don't want to have to scroll through page after page to get this information; we want it all on one screen!

Rather than just whine about it (which is generally our most common course of action), we decided to do something. Of course, we turned to APIs for the solution, and soon found the Retrieve File Description (QDBRTVFD) API. With this API in our arsenal, we could write a program that would display the information that we felt was most pertinent on a single screen.

In Figure 3.1, you can see the result of our efforts. This display combines the most pertinent object information (object owner, creator, and creation date) with the most important file information, all on a single panel.

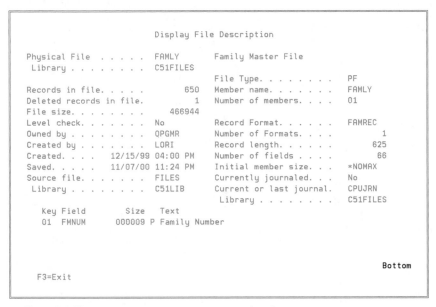

```
                      Display File Description

Physical File  . . . . .  FAMLY      Family Master File
  Library . . . . . . . .  C51FILES
                                     File Type. . . . . . . .  PF
Records in file. . . . .       650   Member name. . . . . . .  FAMLY
Deleted records in file.         1   Number of members. . . .  01
File size. . . . . . . .    466944
Level check. . . . . . .  No         Record Format. . . . . .  FAMREC
Owned by . . . . . . . .  QPGMR      Number of Formats. . . .         1
Created by . . . . . . .  LORI       Record length. . . . . .       625
Created. . . .  12/15/99 04:00 PM    Number of fields . . . .        66
Saved. . . . .  11/07/00 11:24 PM    Initial member size. . .  *NOMAX
Source file. . . . . . .  FILES      Currently journaled. . .  No
  Library . . . . . . . .  C51LIB     Current or last journal.  CPUJRN
                                       Library . . . . . . . .  C51FILES
    Key Field      Size   Text
    01  FMNUM    000009 P Family Number


                                                          Bottom

  F3=Exit
```

Figure 3.1: Use QDBRTVFD to create your own version of DSPFD.

In Figure 3.2, you can see the DDS to create the display file. As you can see from the figures, this program uses a simple, straightforward subfile. We made the program a subfile since we also wanted to show the key fields in the file. A description of every field in the file is contained within the file description.

```
AANO1NO2NO3T.Name++++++RLen++TDpBLinPosFunctions+++++++++++++++++++++++
A                                       DSPSIZ(24 80 *DS3)
A                                       CF03
A         R SFLRCD                      SFL
A           SFFLD       10A  0 18  9
A           SFTEXT      38A  0 18 29
A           SFKEY        2A  0 18  5
A           SFFSIZ       6  00 18 20
A           SFTYPE       1   0 18 27
A         R SFLCTL                      SFLCTL(SFLRCD)
A                                       SFLSIZ(0012)
A                                       SFLPAG(0004)
A                                       SFLDSPCTL
A                                       OVERLAY
A   21                                  SFLDSP
A   25                                  SFLCLR
A   27                                  SFLEND(*MORE)
A                                   1 28'Display File Description'
A                                   3  2'Physical File  . . . . .'
A           OUTFILENAM  10A  0  3 28
A           OUTLIBNAME  10A  0  4 28
A                                   5 40'File Type. . . . . . . .'
A           OUTTYPE      5A  0  5 67
A                                   6 40'Member name. . . . . . .'
A           OUTMEMBER   10A  0  6 67
A           OUTRECLEN    6Y 00 11 69EDTCDE(Z)
A                                   9 40'Record Format. . . . . .'
A           OUTFORMAT   10A  0  9 67
A                                  12 40'Number of fields . . . . '
A           NBRFLDS      4Y 00 12 71EDTCDE(Z)
A                                  17  5'Key'
A                                  17  9'Field'
A                                  17 29'Text'
A           FILDSC      40A  0  3 40
A                                   7 40'Number of members. . . . '
A           NBRMBR       2S 00  7 67
A                                  13 40'Initial member size. . . '
A           MBRSIZ       8A  0 13 67
A                                   9  2'Level check. . . . . . . '
A           LVLCHK       3A  0  9 28
A                                   6  2'Records in file. . . . . '
```

Figure 3.2: The DDS shows coding for the Display File Description (part 1 of 2).

```
A              NBRRCD         9Y 00  6 28EDTCDE(Z)
A                                    7  2'Deleted records in file.'
A              NBRDLT         9Y 00  7 28EDTCDE(Z)
A              LSTSVD         8A  O 13 19
A              CRTTIM         8A  O 12 28
A              SVDTIM         8A  O 13 28
A                                   11 40'Record length. . . . . .'
A                                   14 40'Currently journaled. . .'
A              JRNLD          3A  O 14 67
A                                   15 40'Current or last journal.'
A              JRNNAM        10A  O 15 67
A                                   16 40' Library . . . . . . . .'
A              JRNLIB        10A  O 16 67
A              CRTDAT         8A  O 12 19
A                                   12  2'Created. . . .'
A                                   11  2'Created by . . . . . . .'
A              CRTBY         10A  O 11 28
A                                   10  2'Owned by . . . . . . . .'
A              OWNER         10A  O 10 28
A                                   13  2'Saved. . . . .'
A                                   14  2'Source file. . . . . . .'
A              SRCFIL        10A  O 14 28
A                                   15  3'Library . . . . . . . .'
A              SRCLIB        10A  O 15 28
A                                    4  2' Library . . . . . . . .'
A                                   17 22'Size'
A                                    8  2'File size. . . . . . . .'
A              FILSIZ         9Y 00  8 28EDTCDE(Z)
A                                   10 40'Number of Formats. . . .'
A              NBROFFMTS      2Y 00 10 73EDTCDE(Z)
A            R FMT1
A                                   23  4'F3=Exit'  COLOR(BLU)
```

Figure 3.2: The DDS shows coding for the Display File Description (part 2 of 2).

The focus of this book, of course, is APIs. Take a look at the RPG program in Figure 3.3. It uses three different APIs to gather the information we elected to put on one screen.

```
FFig0302   CF   E              WORKSTN
F                                       SFILE(SFLRCD:RelRecNbr)

D DateField      S              d
D EntryFmt       S             10
D FileFormat     S              8
```

Figure 3.3: Use QDBRTVFD as a better display file description (part 1 of 11).

79

```
D FileLib         S             20
D FormatType      S             10
D I               S              7 0
D IQusDss         S              9 0
D IQusDssM        S              9 0
D IQusAps         S              9 0
D IQusApsM        S              9 0
D MemberName      S             10
D MessageTyp      S             10
D MessageQue      S             10
D MsgF            S             20    inz('QCPFMSG    QSYS        ')
D NameOSet        S              9 0
D ObjectType      S             10
D OverRide        S              1
D ReceiveVr2      S            300
D RelRecNbr       S              4 0
D S               S              7 0
D System          S             10
D TimeFld         S              t
D Time6           S              6 0
D WorkBin         S              9b 0
D X               S              9 0
D                 DS
D  SpaceLen              1       4B 0
D  ReceiveLen            5       8B 0
D  MessageKey            9      12B 0
D  MsgDtaLen            13      16B 0
D  MsgQueNbr            17      20B 0
D Receiver        DS         32000    based(ReceivePtr)
D ReceiverK       DS         32000    based(ReceiveKPt)
D FndSizeVar      DS             8
D  SizRtnd               1       4B 0
D  SizAvl                5       8B 0
D*****************************************************************
D*Record key information
D*****************************************************************
DQDBQ62           DS            32
D QDBRN                  1      10
D QDBNBROK              13      14B 0
D QDBKIO               29      32B 0
D*****************************************************************
D*Field information
D*****************************************************************
DQDBQ65           DS            64
D QDBEFN                11      20
D QDBDT01               21      22B 0
D QDBFL                 23      24B 0
D QDBNBROD              25      26B 0
D*****************************************************************
```

Figure 3.3: Use QDBRTVFD as a better display file description (part 2 of 11).

```
D*Type Definition for the OBJD0300 format.
D***************************************************************
DQUSD0300          DS           460
D QUSBRTN08                  1     4B 0
D QUSBAVL09                  5     8B 0
D QUSOBJN02                  9    18
D QUSOBJLN01                19    28
D QUSOBJT02                 29    38
D QUSOBJO06                 53    62
D QUSCDT14                  65    77
D   CrtDate                 66    71 0
D   CrtTimE                 72    77
D QUSCDT15                  78    90
D QUSEOA06                  91   100
D QUSSFILN07               151   160
D QUSSFLN07                161   170
D QUSSFMN04                171   180
D QUSOSDT02                194   206
D   SvdDate                195   200 0
D   SvdTimE                201   206
D QUSCUP03                 220   229
D QUSRD01                  238   244
D***************************************************************
D* Error Code data structure
D***************************************************************
DQUSEC             DS           116
D QUSBPRV                    1     4B 0           inz(116)
D QUSBAVL                    5     8B 0
D QUSEI                      9    15
D QUSERVED                  16    16
D QUSED01                   17   116
D***************************************************************
D*Record structure for QUSRMBRD MBRD0200 format
D***************************************************************
DQUSM0200          DS           266
D QUSBRTN03                  1     4B 0
D QUSBAVL04                  5     8B 0
D QUSDFILN00                 9    18
D QUSDFILL00                19    28
D QUSMN03                   29    38
D QUSFILA01                 39    48
D QUSNBRCR                 141   144B 0
D QUSNBRDR                 145   148B 0
D QUSDSS                   149   152B 0
D QUSAPS                   153   156B 0
D QUSDSSM                  233   236B 0
D QUSAPSM                  237   240B 0
D***************************************************************
D* Record structure for journaling information
```

Figure 3.3: Use QDBRTVFD as a better display file description (part 3 of 11).

```
D*****************************************************************
D JournalInf        DS           22    inz
D  Jrnnam                 2       11
D  JrnLib                12       21
D  JrnYesNo              22       22
D*****************************************************************
D*File Definition Template (FDT) Header
D*****************************************************************
DQDBQ25            DS          400
D QDBFYRET                 1      4B 0
D QDBFYAVL                 5      8B 0
D  FileType                9      9
D  Attribs                10     10
D QDBHMNUM                48     49B 0
D QDBMTNUM                62     63B 0
D QDBFHTXT00              85    134
D  FilDsc                 85    124
D QDBFOS                 317    320B 0
D QDBFPACT               337    338
D QDBPFOF                365    368B 0
D QDBFJORN               379    382B 0
D*****************************************************************
D*Header information
D*****************************************************************
DQDBQ41            DS          256
D QDBFRLEN                67     70B 0
D QDBFNAME                71     80
D QDBFTEXT                94    143
D QDBLDNUM               144    145B 0
D*****************************************************************
D*         FIELD HEADER
D*****************************************************************
DQDBQ42            DS
D QDBFDEFL                 1      4B 0
D QDBFFLDE                35     64
D QDBFTXTD               209    212B 0
D*****************************************************************
D* Physical file attributes
D*****************************************************************
DQDBQ26            DS           48
D QDBPRNUM                12     15B 0

C      *Entry       Plist
C                   Parm                      FileLib
C                   Parm                      MemberName
C                   Parm                      EntryFmt

 * Retrieve object description (verify exists, get object owner)
C                   Call       'QUSROBJD'
```

Figure 3.3: Use QDBRTVFD as a better display file description (part 4 of 11).

```
C                       Parm                    QusD0300
C                       Parm      460           ReceiveLen
C                       Parm      'OBJD0300'     FileFormat
C                       Parm                     FileLib
C                       Parm      '*FILE'        ObjectType
C                       Parm                     QusEc
 *   If file doesn't exist, send message and get out
C                       If        QusBAvl <> *zeros
C                       Exsr      SndMsg
C                       Else

 *   load object information to screen
c                       Eval      Owner = QusObj006
c                       Eval      CrtBy = QusCUp03
c                       Eval      SrcFil = QusSFilN07
c                       Eval      SrcLib = QusSFlN07
c                       Eval      Outtype = QusEOA06

c                       If        QusCDT14 <> *blanks
c        *ymd           Move      CrtDate       DateField
c        *mdy           Move      DateField     CrtDat
c                       Move      CrtTime       Time6
c        *HMS           Move      Time6         Timefld
c        *USA           Move      Timefld       CrtTim
c                       Endif
c                       If        QusOSDT02 <> *blanks
c        *ymd           Move      SvdDate       DateField
c        *mdy           Move      DateField     LstSvd
c                       Move      SvdTime       Time6
c        *HMS           Move      Time6         Timefld
c        *USA           Move      Timefld       SvdTim
c                       Endif

 *   Retrieve file description information and write subfile
 *     of key fields
C                       Exsr      RtvFd

 *   If not a physical or logical, get out
C                       If        QusEI <> *blanks
C                       Exsr      SndMsg
C                       Else
 *   Retrieve member description information
C                       Exsr      RtvMbr

c                       Move      QdbMtNum      NbrOfFmts
c                       Move      QdbFName      OutFormat
c                       Movel     FileLib       OutFileNam
c                       Move      FileLib       OutLibName
c                       Move      QusMn03       OutMember
```

Figure 3.3: Use QDBRTVFD as a better display file description (part 5 of 11).

```
C                    Move       QusNbrCR        NbrRcd
C                    Move       QusNbrDR        NbrDlt
C                    Move       QdbFRLen        OutRecLen
C                    Move       QdbLDNum        Nbrflds

C                    Write      Fmt1
C                    Exfmt      SflCtl
C                    Endif
C                    Endif
C                    Eval       *InLR = *ON

    *****************************************************************
    ** RTVFD - retreive file description subroutine              **
    *****************************************************************
C       RtvFd        Begsr
    *  Get correct size of receiver variable
C                    Call       'QDBRTVFD'
C                    Parm                       FndSizeVar
C                    Parm       8               ReceiveLen
C                    Parm                       FileLib
C                    Parm       'FILD0100'      FileFormat
C                    Parm                       FileLib
C                    Parm                       EntryFmt
C                    Parm       '0'             OverRide
C                    Parm       '*LCL'          System
C                    Parm       '*EXT'          FormatType
C                    Parm                       QusEc
    *  Allocate enough storage for receiver
C                    Alloc      SizAvl          ReceivePtr
    *  Get file information into ReceiveVar
C                    Call       'QDBRTVFD'
C                    Parm                       Receiver
C                    Parm       SizAvl          ReceiveLen
C                    Parm                       FileLib
C                    Parm       'FILD0100'      FileFormat
C                    Parm                       FileLib
C                    Parm                       EntryFmt
C                    Parm       '0'             OverRide
C                    Parm       '*LCL'          System
C                    Parm       '*EXT'          FormatType
C                    Parm                       QusEc

    *  If no errors with QDBRTVFD
C                    If         QusEI = *blanks
C                    Movel      Receiver        qdbq25
C                    TestB      '0'             Attribs             90
C                    If         *in90
C                    Move       'Yes'           LvlChk
C                    Else
```

Figure 3.3: Use QDBRTVFD as a better display file description (part 6 of 11).

```
C                   Move      'No '            LvlChk
C                   Endif
C                   Move      QDbHMNum         NbrMbr
 * If physical file type
C                   TestB     '2'              FileType              9
C                   If        *in90 = *off
C                   Eval      I = QdbPfOf
C                   Eval      QdbQ26 = %subst(Receiver:I:%len(qdbq26))

C                   If        QdbPrNum = 0
C                   Movel     '*NOMAX'         MbrSiz
C                   Else
C                   Move      QdbPrNum         MbrSiz
C                   Endif
C                   Endif
 * check journaling information
C                   Movel     'No'             Jrnld
C                   If        QdbFJorn <> *zeros
C                   Eval      I = QdbFJorn
C                   Eval      JournalInf = %subst(Receiver:I:
C                               %len(JournalInf))
C                   If        JrnYesNo = '1'
C                   Movel     'Yes'            Jrnld
C                   Endif
C                   Endif
 *  Get correct size of receiver variable
C                   Call      'QDBRTVFD'
C                   Parm                       FndSizeVar
C                   Parm      8                ReceiveLen
C                   Parm                       FileLib
C                   Parm      'FILD0200'       FileFormat
C                   Parm                       FileLib
C                   Parm                       EntryFmt
C                   Parm      '0'              OverRide
C                   Parm      '*LCL'           System
C                   Parm      '*EXT'           FormatType
C                   Parm                       QusEc
 * Allocate enough storage for receiver
C                   Alloc     SizAvl           ReceivePtr
 * Get member information into ReceiveVar
C                   Call      'QDBRTVFD'
C                   Parm                       Receiver
C                   Parm      SizAvl           ReceiveLen
C                   Parm                       FileLib
C                   Parm      'FILD0200'       FileFormat
C                   Parm                       FileLib
C                   Parm                       EntryFmt
C                   Parm      '0'              OverRide
C                   Parm      '*LCL'           System
```

Figure 3.3: Use QDBRTVFD as a better display file description (part 7 of 11).

```
C                    Parm      '*EXT'        FormatType
C                    Parm                    QusEc
 * If no errors with QDBRTVFD
C                    If        QusEI = *blanks
C                    Movel     Receiver      qdbq41
c                    Eval      NameOSet = 257
c                    Eval      QdbQ42 = %subst(Receiver:NameOSet:
c                               %len(QdbQ42))
c                    endif
 * If keyed file
c                    If        QdbFPACT = 'KC' OR
c                              QdbFPACT = 'KF' OR
c                              QdbFPACT = 'KL' OR
c                              QdbFPACT = 'KN' OR
c                              QdbFPACT = 'KU'

C                    Eval      I = QdbFOS
 *   Get correct size of receiver variable
C                    Call      'QDBRTVFD'
C                    Parm                    FndSizeVar
C                    Parm      8             ReceiveLen
C                    Parm                    FileLib
C                    Parm      'FILD0300'    FileFormat
C                    Parm                    FileLib
C                    Parm                    EntryFmt
C                    Parm      '0'           OverRide
C                    Parm      '*LCL'        System
C                    Parm      '*EXT'        FormatType
C                    Parm                    QusEc
 * Allocate enough storage for receiver
c                    Alloc     SizAvl        ReceiveKPt
 *   Get key information into ReceiverK variable
C                    Call      'QDBRTVFD'
C                    Parm                    ReceiverK
C                    Parm      SizAvl        ReceiveLen
C                    Parm                    FileLib
C                    Parm      'FILD0300'    FileFormat
C                    Parm                    FileLib
C                    Parm                    EntryFmt
C                    Parm      '0'           OverRide
C                    Parm      '*LCL'        System
C                    Parm      '*EXT'        FormatType
C                    Parm                    QusEc
 * If no errors with QDBRTVFD
C                    If        QusEI = *blanks
c                    z-add     25            I
 * do for each format in the file
C                    DOU       QdbRn = EntryFmt OR
C                              EntryFmt = '*FIRST'
```

Figure 3.3: Use QDBRTVFD as a better display file description (part 8 of 11).

```
C                   Eval        Qdbq62 = %subst(ReceiverK:I:
C                               %len(Qdbq62))
C                   If          QdbRN <> EntryFmt
C                   Eval        I = I + 32
C                   Endif
C                   EndDo

c                   z-add       QdbKIO          X
c                   add         1               X
 * do for number of keys in the format
c                   Do          QdbNbrOK
C                   Eval        Qdbq65 = %subst(ReceiverK:X:
C                               %len(Qdbq65))
c                   move        QdbEFN          SfFld
c                   move        QdbNbrOD        SfFSiz
c                   clear                       Sftype
 * If packed data
c                   if          QdbDt01 = x'0003'
c                   move        'P'             Sftype
c                   endif
 * If character use field length for size
c                   if          QdbDt01 = x'0004'
c                   move        QdbFL           SfFSiz
c                   endif
 * If date use field length for size
c                   if          QdbDt01 = x'000B'
c                   move        QdbFL           SfFSiz
c                   move        'L'             Sftype
c                   endif
c                   eval        RelRecNbr = RelRecNbr + 1
c                   move        RelRecNbr       SfKey
 * control more/bottom indicator
c                   if          RelRecNbr = QdbNbrOK
c                   eval        *in27 = *on
c                   endif
 * Get text description of key field
c                   exsr        GetFldText
c                   eval        SfText = %subst(Receiver:
c                               (QdbFtxtd + NameOSet): 50)
c                   write       SflRcd
c                   eval        *in21 = *on
 * 64 bytes is the size of the key field attribute data structure
 *  there is no field that gives the size of this structure so
 *  you have to hard code it. Bummer.
C                   EVAL        X = (X + 64)
c                   enddo

C                   Endif
c                   endif
```

Figure 3.3: Use QDBRTVFD as a better display file description (part 9 of 11).

```
c                      endif
C                      EndSR

      **************************************************************
      ** RtvMbr - Retrieve member description subroutine          **
      **************************************************************
C       RtvMbr         BegSR
C                      Call      'QUSRMBRD'
C                      Parm                    QusM0200
C                      Parm      240           ReceiveLen
C                      Parm      'MBRD0200'    FileFormat
C                      Parm                    FileLib
C                      Parm                    MemberName
C                      Parm      '0'           OverRide
c                      z-add     QusDss        IQusDss
c                      z-add     QusDssM       IQusDssM
c                      z-add     QusAps        IQusAps
c                      z-add     QusApsM       IQusApsM
c                      Eval      WorkBin = (IQusDss * IQusDSSM) +
c                                           (IQusAps * IQusApsM)
c                      z-add     WorkBin       FilSiz
C                      EndSR


      **************************************************************
      ** SndMsg - Send error messages subroutine                  **
      **************************************************************
C       SndMsg         BegSR
*   Send error message
C                      Call      'QMHSNDPM'
C                      Parm                    QusEi
C                      Parm                    MSGF
C                      Parm                    FileLib
C                      Parm      20            MsgDtaLen
C                      Parm      '*DIAG'       MessageTyp
C                      Parm      '*'           MessageQue
C                      Parm      2             MsgQueNbr
C                      Parm                    MessageKey
C                      Parm                    QusEc
C                      EndSR


      **************************************************************
      ** GetFldText - Get key field text descriptions subroutine  **
      **************************************************************
C       GetFldText     BegSR
c                      Eval      NameOSet = 257
c                      Eval      QdbQ42 = %subst(Receiver:NameOSet:
c                                        %len(QdbQ42))
c                      Do        QdbLDNum
c                      If        Qdbfflde = SfFld
```

Figure 3.3: Use QDBRTVFD as a better display file description (part 10 of 11).

```
C                        leave
C                        Else
C                        Add       QdbFdEF1        NameOSet
C                        Eval      QdbQ42 = %subst(Receiver:NameOSet:
C                                      %len(QdbQ42))
C                        Endif
C                        EndDo
C                        EndSR
```

Figure 3.3: Use QDBRTVFD as a better display file description (part 11 of 11).

The first API the program uses is the Retrieve Object Description (QUSROBJD) API. This API is actually pulling double duty. If the API returns an error (such as file not found), then it passes the error back to the caller and terminates the program. This is similar to the EXISTS procedure described in chapter 8. If an error is found, it evokes the **SndMsg** subroutine, which uses the Send Program Message (QMHSNDMSG) API. (This API is covered in detail in chapter 6.)

If calling QUSROBJD did not result in an error, then the API has returned the requested object information into a receiver variable, where it can be processed and pushed out to the screen.

The Retrieve Object Description (QUSROBJD) API is relatively easy to use. It is typical of the retrieve APIs, in that the first parameter is the receiver variable to hold the returned information, and the second parameter is the length of the receiver variable field. The third parameter contains the record format description. For our purposes, we chose the OBJD0300 format because we want some information contained in that format. If the Retrieve Object Description (QUSROBJD) API wasn't doing double duty, and we were only interested in checking for the existence of an object, we would have used OBJD0100. (The less the information, the less time required to retrieve it.) The next two parameters are the object name (with library) and object type. The last parameter is the standard error-handling data structure. (See Table 3.1.)

The execution of the next API, the Retrieve File Description (QDBRTVFD) API, is accomplished when the RTVFD subroutine is executed. If you look closely, you will notice that the routine calls QDBRTVFD twice, once to get the proper size of the variable, and then a second time (using the proper size) to get the file information. (This technique is covered in detail in chapter 1.)

Take a look at QDBRTVFD's parameters in Table 3.2. QDBRTVFD is typical of most retrieve APIs, but it has a few deviations. The API is typical in that the first two parameters are the receiver variable and the length of the variable. The third parameter returns the file name (with library) that the API actually retrieved information about. If overrides were used to access the file, this parameter might be different from the file name specified in parameter 5. The fourth parameter is the format name. It is here that the API begins to deviate from the norm.

Usually, format names are consecutively larger in respect to the amount of information that they contain. For example, Format 0001 contains the least information, while Format 0002 contains everything Format 0001 contained, and then some. Format 0003 contains everything from both Formats 0001 and 0002, and yet more. That's not the case with the Retrieve File Description API, though.

Each format for this API contains totally different information about the file. Consequently, if you want information that's contained in more than one format, you have to call the API multiple times. And that's exactly what we have done here.

The program calls QDBRTVFD three times: once for file information using FILD0100 format, once for format information using FILD0200, and once again using FILD0300 for key field information. Actually, the API is called a total of six times, using the aforementioned double-call technique for each different format. It's a testament both to the speed of APIs and to the speed of the AS/400 that this tool still responds with sub-second performance.

The fifth parameter is the name and library of the file you want information about. Parameter 6 is the record format name in the file. You use parameter 7 to specify if you want the API to honor any existing overrides. If this parameter is zero, the API will use the name and library in parameter 5 and ignore any other overridden parameters. If you specify a one, and the file is overridden, the API will apply the override and then return the information including any overridden parameters.

Parameter 8 allows you to indicate whether you want to access information from a local or remote file. Parameter 9 deals with returning internal or external field information from logical files. The last parameter is the standard error-handling data structure.

So, the RTVFD subroutine calls the API and uses the %SUBST built-in function to load the returned information into various data structures. The record format information is repeated for every format in the file. The key field information is also repeated for each format. The code "walks" through these structures until it finds the ones that define the format we requested. Then, for each key field in the format, it writes a subfile record.

Oops! We seem to have hit a slight problem. The key-field information data structure (QDBQ65) does not contain the text description of the key field. So, before the program can write the subfile record, it executes subroutine **GetFldText** to take care of this.

Subroutine **GetFldText** walks through the names of all the fields in the file until it finds the name of the key field that is about to be written to the subfile. It then gets the text description for that field, and the subfile record can be written.

The only thing left for the program to do is to get the member information. To do that, the Retrieve Member Description (QUSRMBRD) API is used. This is a typical retrieve API that gets the file and access path size. The only parameter that is any different from the other retrieve APIs is the override parameter (number 6). Since this serves the same function as the override parameter on the Retrieve File Description (QDBRTVFD) API, we don't need to go over it again.

Table 3.1: Retrieve Object Description (QUSROBJD)

Parameter	Description	Type	Attribute	Size
1	The variable receiver field that will hold information returned by the API.	Output	Char	Varies
2	The length of the variable receiver in parameter 1.	Input	Binary	4
3	The format name, as follows: **Format Name** | **Description** OBJL0100 | Basic information. OBJL0200 | The same information as PDM. OBJL0300 | Service information. OBJL0400 | Full information.	Input	Char	8
4	The object name and library name of the objects to list. The first 10 bytes are the object name, and the second 10 bytes are the library name. The object can be a name, a generic name, or one of the special values *ALL, *ALLUSR, and *IBM. The library can be a name or one of the special values *ALL, *ALLUSR, *CURLIB, *LIBL, or *USRLIBL.	Input	Char	20
5	The type of object to list. It accepts a valid type name or the special value *ALL.	Input	Char	10
Optional Group 1				
6	A standard error data structure.	In/Out	Char	Varies

Table 3.2: Retrieve File Description (QDBRTVFD) (part 1 of 2)

Parameter	Description	Type	Attribute	Size
1	The variable receiver field that will hold information returned by the API.	Output	Char	Varies
2	The length of the variable receiver in parameter 1.	Input	Binary	4
3	The qualified return file name, which is the actual file name and library from which information was retrieved.	Input	Char	20

Parameter	Description	Type	Attribute	Size
4	The format name, as follows:	Output	Char	8
	Name / **Description** FILD0100 — The file definition. FILD0200 — The format definition. FILD 0300 — The key field information.			
5	The qualified file name, which is the file name and library name to retrieve information about. The first 10 bytes are the file name, and the second 10 bytes are the library name. The library can be a name or one of the special values *CURLIB or *LIBL.	Input	Char	20
6	The name of the record format in the file specified in parameter 5. The special value *FIRST indicates the use of the first format in the file.	Input	Char	10
7	Override processing, which indicates if existing overrides are to be honored when extracting data. Zero means no; one means yes.	Input	Char	1
8	The system parameter, which indicates whether the database file is located on local (*LCL), remote (*RMT), or both local and remote (*FILETYPE) machines.	Input	Char	10
9	The format type, used only with format FILD0200. It indicates, for logical files, if the returned data is based on the physical file fields. A value of *EXT indicates that the data comes from logical field definitions, while *INT indicates physical field definitions. If it is a physical file, *EXT and *INT are the same.	Input	Char	10
Optional Group 1				
10	A standard error data structure.	In/Out	Char	Varies

Table 3.2: Retrieve File Description (QDBRTVFD) (part 2 of 2)

Retrieve Display File Information

There is another type of file on the AS/400 that you are probably familiar with. It's the good ol' green-screen interface, more commonly known as the *display file*. While both the database file and the display file are files that contain fields, that's about all that they have in common. A display file is concerned with screen sizes, display attributes, fonts, and a lot of other stuff that a database file would have no use for. That is precisely why the display file has its own Retrieve Display File (QDFRTVFD) API, to extrapolate this very unique information.

The Display File API is like most other retrieve APIs, in that it uses a receiver variable into which the API puts various data structures that contain pointers to other structures. Unlike most other retrieve APIs, however, the QDFRTVFD pointers are not offsets based from the beginning of the receiver variable. With this API, the offsets are usually based from the beginning of whatever base data structure you are processing. This "quirk" makes this API a little more difficult to use, so you have to pay more attention to detail when walking through the various structures.

Because of the vast amount of information that this API generates, the information has been organized into seven sections. Table 3.3 lists the different categories that the data has been sectioned into. We have included the data structure format names and information about how to get to the first structure in each section.

Table 3.3: Structures Returned by Retrieve Display File API (QDFRTVFD) (part 1 of 3)		
Section		**Description**
Base File Formats:		The first structure returned, located at offset 0 of the receiver variable.
Format Name	**Description**	
QDFFBASE	The base file section.	
QDFFSCRA	The screen size table.	
QDFFSEQ	The sort sequence table.	

Table 3.3: Structures Returned by Retrieve Display File API (QDFRTVFD) (part 2 of 3)	
Section	**Description**
File formats:	The first file structure (QDFFINFO) accessed from field QDFFINFO in structure QDFFBASE.

Format Name	Description
QDFFINFO	The file header section.
QDFFDPDD	The file-level device-dependent section.
QDFARFTE	The record format table.
QDFFSEQT	The sequence number table.

Record formats:

The first format structure (QDFFRINFO) accessed from field QDFARFOF in structure QDFARFTE. The offset is from the beginning of QDFFINFO.

Format Name	Description
QDFFRINF	The record header section.
QDFFRDPD	The record-level device-dependent section.
QDFFXRDP	The record-level device-dependent extension.
QDFFSRCR	The subfile control record.
QDFFSRCREXT	The subfile control record extension.
QDFFRCTB	The row-column table.
QDFFRCTE	The row-column table entry.
QDFFNTB	The field name table.
QDFFOT	The field order table.
QDFFFITB	The field indexing table.

Field formats:

The first format structure (QDFFFINF) accessed from field QDFFFOFS in structure QDFFFITB. The offset is from the beginning of QDFFRINF.

Format Name	Description
QDFFFINF	The field header section.
QDFFFCON	The constant field header table.
QDFFFNAM	The named field header table.

Table 3.3: Structures Returned by Retrieve Display File API (QDFRTVFD) (part 3 of 3)

Section	Description
Field Formats (continued)	

Format Name	Description
QDFFFDPD	The field-level device-dependent section.
QDFFFDIC	The input-capable field-level device-dependent section.
QDFFXFDP	The field-dependent extension.
QDFFSELT	The selection table.
QDFFSTBL	The selection table entry.
QDFFCOSA	The keyword-category displacement string.
QDFFCCOA	The keyword-category displacement-string entry.

Keyword Formats:	The first format structure (QDFKFILK) accessed from field QDFFCAOF in structure QDFFCCOA. The offset is from the beginning of the appropriate section (file, record, or field). There are too many keyword formats to list. See manual for details.

Where-used Formats:	The first format structure (QDFWFLEI) accessed from field QDFFWUOF in structure QDFFINFO. The offset is from the beginning of QDFFINFO.

Format Name	Description	
QDFWFLEI	The where-used file information structure.	
QDFWRCDI	The where-used record information structure.	Tables in this section map to the row-column table (QDFFRCTB) to determine the correct entry in the keyword table.
QDFWFLDI	The where-used field information structure.	
QDFWITBE	The indicator-table entry structure.	Tables in this section map to the row-column table (QDFFRCTB) to determine the correct entry in the keyword table.
QDFWKWDA	The keyword area structure.	
QDFWATTR	The keyword entry structure.	
QDFWATYP	The variable length structure.	
QDFWBTYP	The multiple variable length structure.	
QDFWRSTR	The reference information structure.	
QDFWNTBL	The name table structure.	

As you can see, the Retrieve Display File (QDFRTVFD) API returns quite a lot of structures. This many structures can be a chore to navigate through. Further complicating the process is the fact that all offset positions are not based on the same starting position. The best way to explore this API is by example.

Retrieving Display File Fields

One useful bit of information you might want to retrieve from a compiled display file is the name of the fields in a particular record format. Armed with this information, you could write a single program to call from any report program that would print legends at the bottom of the report. As shown in Figure 3.4, the program lists all of the fields in a given record format within a given display file. Because this book is mainly concerned with APIs, the rest of the code for the generic print-legends program isn't included here. You can use this program as the basis to write your own.

```
fqsysprt   o   f  132          printer oflind(*inof)

 * Prototype for procedure to create user space
d  CrtUsrSpc      PR               *
d   CrtSpcName                     20     const

D InFormat        S               10
D InLibrary       S               10
D InFile          S               10
d Length          S                5   0 inz
d Name            S               10
d NbrFlds         S                4   0
d SfLength        S                5   0
D X               S                4   0
D XX              S                4   0

D FileFmt         S                8
D FldName         S               10
D FmtCounter      S                4   0
D ICounter        S                4   0
D RcvSpace        S               20     inz('RTVFDSPC  QTEMP')
D ReceiveLen      S                9B  0
D RecordFmt       S               10
D SFileLib        S               20     inz('RPTDRIVEDS*LIBL   ')
D TotCtr          S                5   0
D Y               S                4   0
```

Figure 3.4: To create a program to retrieve display file fields, list fields in a display file using QDFRTVFD (part 1 of 6).

```
D Z               S           4 0

D* Base File Section
DQDFFBASE        DS                    Based(SpacePtr)
D QDFFINOF                 9    10B 0
D QDFFFRCS                11    12B 0

D* File Header Section
DQDFFINFO        DS                    based(QdffInfoPt)
D QDFFDFLO                 1     4B 0
D QDFFWUOF                 5     8B 0

D* Record Format Table
DQDFARFTE        DS                    Based(QDFARFTEPT)
D QDFARFNM                 1    10
D QDFARFOF                13    16B 0

D* Record Header Section
DQDFFRINF        DS                    based(qdffrinfpt)
D QDFFRDDO                 1     4B 0
D QDFFOFIT                 5     8B 0
D QDFFFFLD                17    18B 0
D QDFFRAOF                29    30B 0

D* Field name table
DQDFFNTB         DS                    Based(Qdffntbpt)
D QDFFFNAMA              10    dim(1000)

D* Field indexing table
DQDFFFITB        DS                    based(qdfffitbpt)
D QDFFFOFS                 1     4B 0
D QDFFDLEN                 7     8B 0

D* Field header section
DQDFFFINF        DS                    based(qdfffinfpt)
D QDFFFLEN                 1     2B 0
D QDFFFIOA                 3     3
D QDFFFTBE                 7    18

D* Named field header table
DQDFFFNAMO       DS
D QDFFOUTO                 3     4B 0
D QDFFPLEN                 5     6B 0
D QDFFFDEC                 7     7

D* Where used file level information structure
DQDFWFLEI        DS                    based(QdfwFleiPt)
D QDFWXLEN                 1     2B 0
D QDFWWULN                 5     8B 0
D QDFWNTBO                 9    12B 0
```

Figure 3.4: To create a program to retrieve display file fields, list fields in a display file using QDFRTVFD (part 2 of 6).

```
D* Name table structure
DQDFFNTBL       DS                       based(qdffntblPt)
D QDFFFNMS                  1     4B 0
D QDFFNMES                       10     DIM(00100)

D* Where used record information structure
DQDFWRCDI       DS                       based(QdfwRcdiPt)
D QDFWRLEN                  1     2B 0
D QDFWNXTR                  5     8B 0

D* Where used field information structure
DQDFWFLDI       DS                       based(qdfwfldipt)
D QDFWFLDL                  1     2B 0
D QDFWFOKW                  3     4B 0
D QDFWRRDX                  5     6B 0
D QDFWNMEI                  7    10B 0

D* Keyword area structure
DQDFWKWDA       DS                       based(qdfwkwdapt)
D QDFWKWDC                  1     2B 0
D QDFWKWDS                  3    102

DQUSEC          DS               116
D QUSBPRV                   1     4B 0              inz(116)
D QUSBAVL                   5     8B 0
D QUSEI                     9    15
D QUSERVED                 16    16
D QUSED01                  17   116

C       *ENTRY      PLIST
C                   PARM                      InFormat
C                   PARM                      InLibrary
C                   PARM                      InFile

c                   if        %parms > 1
c                   move      InLibrary       SFileLIb
c                   endif
c                   if        %parms > 2
c                   movel     InFile          SFileLIb
c                   endif
c                   Except    Heding
 * Create user space for retrieve file description
c                   Eval      SpacePtr = CrtUsrSpc(RcvSpace)

 * Get the display information into the user space
c                   EXSR      GETFIL
 * If not errors with retrieving display file information
c                   If        QusBAvl = 0
```

Figure 3.4: To create a program to retrieve display file fields, list fields in a display file using QDFRTVFD (part 3 of 6).

```
 * Get file information structure
 c                Eval      QDffInFoPt = SpacePtr + QdFFInOf
 * Get pointer to structure containing format name
 c                Eval      QdFarFtePt = QdffInFoPt + QDFFDFLO
 * Look at name of each record format....
 c                DO        QdffFrCs        FmtCounter
 * Until a match is made with the requested format
 c                If        QdFarFnm = InFormat OR
 c                          InFormat = '*FIRST'
 c                Eval      QdFFRinfPt = QdFfInfoPt + QDfarfof
 * Get where used structure (to point to file field names table)
 c                Eval      QDfWFlEIPt = QdffInfoPt + QdFFWuOf
 c                Eval      QDffNtblPt = QdfWflEiPt + QdfWntbo
 * Get pointer to first where-used record information structure
 c                Eval      QdfWRcdIPt = QdfWFlEiPt + QdfwXLen
 * Get to structure that corresponds to record format table entry
 c                eval      ICounter = 1
 c                dow       ICounter < FmtCounter
 c                Eval      QdfWrcdIpt = QdfWrcdIpt + QdfWNxtr
 c                eval      Icounter = Icounter + 1
 c                enddo
 * Get pointer to where used field information structure
 c                eval      QdfWFldiPt = QdfWrcdIPt + Qdfwrlen
 c                clear                     x
 * Get and print field information
 c                exsr      GetFlds
 c                Leave
 c                else
 * Add increment to look at next record format structure
 c                Eval      QdFarFtePt = QdFarFtePt + 16
 c                endif

 c                Enddo
 c                Endif
 c                eval      *inlr = *on
 *
 C    GETFLDS     BEGSR
 * Pointer to field indexing table
 c                Eval      QdfffitbPt = QdffrinfPt + Qdffofit
 * Pointer to field header section
 c                Eval      Qdfffinfpt = Qdffrinfpt + Qdfffofs

 c                do        Qdfffld        X

 c                z-add     Qdfwnmei       z
 c                if        Z <> 0
 c                movel     QDffnmes(Z)    Name
 c                z-add     QDffdlen       Length
 c                except    PrtDetail
 c                eval      TotCtr = TotCtr + 1
```

Figure 3.4: To create a program to retrieve display file fields, list fields in a display file using QDFRTVFD (part 4 of 6).

```
C                 else
* constant
C                 eval      QdfWkWdapt = Qdfwfldipt + qdfwfokw
C                 endif

C                 if        x <> Qdffffld
* Get pointer to next where used field
C                 eval      QdfWFldiPt = QdfWFldIPt + Qdfwfldl
C                 Eval      QdfffitbPt = QdffrinfPt + Qdffofit +
C                             ((QdfwRrdx * 8) - 8)
* Add increment to get next field size from table of fields
C                 Eval      Qdfffinfpt = Qdfffinfpt + Qdffflen
C                 endif
C                 enddo
C                 Except    LastTot
C                 Endsr
*
C     GETFIL      BEGSR
*   Retrieve display information into user space (looking for
*   format and field names)
C                 CALL      'QDFRTVFD'
C                 PARM                  QDFFBASE
C                 PARM      16776704    ReceiveLen
C                 PARM      'DSPF0100'  FileFmt
C                 PARM                  SFileLib
C                 PARM                  QusEc
C                 ENDSR

oqsysprt   e            Heding        1 02
o          or    of
o                                          5 'DATE:'
o                       Udate         y   14
o                                         53 'Fields in display file
o                       Infile            63
o                                         71 'Format:'
o                       Informat          81
o                                        125 'Page:'
o                       Page          z  130
o          e            Heding        1   1
o          or    of
o                                         39 'NAME'
o                                         56 'LENGTH'
o          ef           PrtDetail     1
o                       Name              45
o                       Length        z   55
o          ef           Lasttot       2 1
o                                         50 'Number of fields:'
o                       TotCtr        z   55
*
*   Procedure to create extendable user space, return pointer to it.
```

Figure 3.4: To create a program to retrieve display file fields, list fields in a display file using QDFRTVFD (part 5 of 6).

```
      *
P CrtUsrSpc        B                    export
d CrtUsrSpc        PI             *
d   CrtSpcName                    20     const

    * Local Variables
D PasSpcName       DS             20
D  SName                   1      10
D  SLib                   11      20
D ChgAttrDs        DS
D  NumberAttr                      9B 0 inz(1)
D  KeyAttr                         9B 0 inz(3)
D  DataSize                        9B 0 inz(1)
D  AttrData                        1    inz('1')
D ListPtr          S              *
D SpaceAttr        S              10    inz
D SpaceAuth        S              10    INZ('*CHANGE')
D SpaceLen         S               9B 0 INZ(2048)
D SpaceReplc       S              10    INZ('*YES')
D SpaceText        S              50
D SpaceValue       S               1

    * Create the user space
C                  move    CrtSpcName    PasSpcName
C                  CALL    'QUSCRTUS'
C                  PARM                  PasSpcName
C                  PARM                  SpaceAttr
C                  PARM                  SpaceLen
C                  PARM                  SpaceValue
C                  PARM                  SpaceAuth
C                  PARM                  SpaceText
C                  PARM    '*YES'        SpaceReplc
C                  PARM                  QusEc
    * Get pointer to user space
C                  CALL    'QUSPTRUS'
C                  PARM                  PasSpcName
C                  PARM                  ListPtr
    * Change user space to be extendable
C                  CALL    'QUSCUSAT'
C                  PARM                  Slib
C                  PARM                  PasSpcName
C                  PARM                  ChgAttrDs
C                  PARM                  QusEc

C                  return  ListPtr
P CrtUsrSpc        E
```

Figure 3.4: To create a program to retrieve display file fields, list fields in a display file using QDFRTVFD (part 6 of 6).

The program in Figure 3.4 accepts three input parameters: the record format name, library name, and display file. The program then creates a user space by calling the **CrtUsrSpc** procedure. (**CrtUsrSpc** is covered in detail in chapter 2. This procedure is used throughout this book when a user space is needed, so if you do not already have a grasp of the concept of user spaces, take a few minutes to review chapter 2.)

The next step executes the **GetFil** subroutine to...well, get the display file information. All this subroutine does is execute the Retrieve Display File (QDFRTVFD) API. As you can see, calling the API is a very simple task. It accepts five parameters, the details of which are shown in Table 3.3. The challenge in using this API lies not in calling it, but rather in the complexity of the structures that it returns.

The first parameter is the receiver variable that is to contain the information returned by the API. QDFRTVFD normally returns data into a receiver variable, but because of the potential for large amounts of data to be returned, the output is directed into a user space. So, you pass the name of a variable field based on the same pointer that points to the user space you created. This causes the output of the API to be directed into the user space. (This concept is covered in chapter 1.)

Parameter 2 is the length of parameter 1. You are passing a value of 16 MB! This is an enormous number, far larger than the 32 KB that is the maximum size of a variable field in a program. However, since parameter 1 is actually a user space, 16 MB is not actually allocated. The user space will automatically extend to the size it needs, to hold the data returned. Theoretically, this value could be up to a maximum of 16 MB.

Parameter 3 is the format name that describes the data being returned. Currently, the only valid format is DSPF0100. Parameter 4 is the qualified name of the display file that you want the API to retrieve information about. The fifth parameter is the standard error data structure.

That's all there is to calling the Retrieve Display File API. If the call was successful, it starts walking through the various data structures shown in Table 3.3. The base file structure is the first structure in the user space. It contains a pointer

(QDFFINOF) to the file header structure, and a pointer (QDFFFRCS) to the where-used structure. The file header structure contains a pointer (QDFFDFLO) to the record format table.

The record format table contains the name of every record format in the display file, and a corresponding pointer that points to the record header for each format. So, a loop is set up based on the total number of record formats in the file looking for the record format name that was passed into the program. (This value is found in the base file header structure, QDFFFRCS.) Once there is a match, you use the corresponding pointer (QDFARFOF) to get to the record header structure.

The record header structure contains a pointer to the field-indexing table. The field-indexing table contains a pointer (QDFFOFS) to the field header file. It also contains the length of the field (QDFFDLEN). But this doesn't have the field names. To get the names of the fields used in the record format, you have to back up a little and follow another path.

The where-used formats contain a structure called the name table structure. This table contains the names of all the fields used in the file. Since display files can contain more than one record format, the challenge is to pick out only the fields that are in the record format you want.

The pointer to the file-level-where-used structure comes from the file header section. It is a field called QDFFWUOF. The first field in the file-level-where-used structure is a pointer (QDFWXLEN) to the where-used record information structure. This structure, in turn, contains a pointer (QDFWRLEN) to the where-used field level information structure. The where-used field information structure contains an index (QDFWNMEI) into the table of names. This, finally, gives the name of the field in the format. The only trouble with this is that you are looking at the fields in the first record format in the file. This might not be the record format you want.

Through trial and error, we discovered that the where-used record format structures are contiguous, as are the record format structures. Furthermore, both structures are in the same sequence. The first record format structure corresponds to the first where-used record format structure, the second record format structure

104

corresponds to the second where-used record format structure, and so on. Since the record format structure contains the format name, you simply need to keep track of how deep into the stack of record format structures you went to match up the record format names earlier. In other words, were you on the first record format in the file, or the second, or the third, etc.? Knowing this, you simply set up a loop and walk through the where-used record formats the same number of times to get to the structure that corresponds to the correct record format.

That's it! You now have the name and length of the first field in the record format you are interested in. The where-used field structure also contains a pointer (QDFWFLDL) to the next field in the format. So, you just set up a loop and read each field name in the record format, printing as you go.

We should point out that each of the structures used in this program contains far more information than we actually used. As we have mentioned before, you can find the definitions of these structures in QSYSINC/QRPGLESRC under the member name that corresponds to the API you are using (QDFRTVFD). We have limited the definitions in our program because it does not make sense to print a 1,000-line program in a book. However, you should copy the definitions into your program and leave them alone when you use APIs. IBM has done a good job here, and the definitions are pretty well documented.

Summary

This chapter just skims the surface of file APIs. By whetting your appetite, we hope to encourage you to look into some of the other file-level APIs. There are a lot of other tools you can write using these types of APIs.

Just as we have shown how to write a better DSPFD command, you can use other file APIs to improve on other IBM commands. We have used APIs to write a better Display File Field (DSPFFD) command, limiting the information shown about each field to one single subfile record. We have also improved on IBM's Display Database Relations command by using the List Database Relations (QDBLDBR) API to display *all* the logical files over a given physical, showing the key fields for each logical file.

4

COMMAND-PROCESSING APIs

This chapter covers some of the APIs used to process commands from within your RPG and CL programs. It includes three very useful examples to show you how to use the QCMDEXC API to run commands from within your RPG programs. It also covers the QCMDCHK API, which allows you to check a command string for validity from within your program. Last but certainly not least, it covers the QCAPCMD API, which allows you to edit a command string for validity, allows for prompting, and returns command parameters to your RPG program. As you will see, the command-processing APIs enhance the usability and flexibility of your existing RPG programs, and give you many more options when writing new ones.

Defining the QCMDEXC API

QCMDEXC, the Execute Command API, just might be the most common and well-known API of them all. It has been around since the beginning and has become a longstanding friend to RPG programmers everywhere. The beauty of QCMDEXC is its simplicity and power. It was designed with a single purpose: to let you process AS/400 commands from within your RPG programs (and other high-level-language programs, including CL). QCMDEXC is a powerful tool that you should become intimately familiar with. Almost anything you would ever want to do with a single command can be done using QCMDEXC, without ever leaving your program. For instance, you can submit jobs, manipulate library lists, override printer parameters, perform Open Query File on your database files, or execute any of a myriad of other functions, all from within your RPG program.

This chapter provides examples of several ways to use QCMDEXC to get flexibility from within your RPG programs:

- Run a simple command like Work with Spooled Files (WRKSPLF) from within your RPG program.

- Run the Open Query File (OPNQRYF) command from within a print program to sequence a file into the order you want, before listing it.

- Override printer parameters within an RPG program to send the printed output to a specific printer and change the number of copies.

- Submit a job from within an RPG program.

As mentioned earlier, QCMDEXC is both versatile and easy to use. All you need to do is call QCMDEXC and pass it two parameters: the command you want to run and the length of the command. Table 4.1 lists the definitions of these parameters.

You can even "fudge" a little on the length of your command; the system does not seem to mind if you pad the end with blanks. It is important, however, that the length of the second parameter, which specifies the command length, be defined as a 15-digit field with five decimal positions.

Table 4.1: Required Input Parameters for the Execute Command API (QCMDEXC)

Parameter	Description	Type	Attribute	Size
1	The source command string that is to be run from within your program.	Input/Output	Char	Varies
2	The length of the command string being processed.	Input	Packed	15/5

The example in Figure 4.1 shows how to embed the Work with Spool Files (WRKSPLF) command into an RPG program. You can see how simple it is.

```
DName++++++++++ETDsFrom+++To/L+++IDc.Keywords+++++++++++++++++++++++++++++
D Command         S              7
D CmdLength       S             15  5 INZ(7)

CLON01Factor1+++++++Opcode&ExtFactor2+++++++Result++++++++Len++D+HiLoEq+
C                   CALL      'QCMDEXC'
C                   PARM      'WRKSPLF'      Command
C                   PARM                     CmdLength
```

Figure 4.1: Use QCMDEXC to run WRKSPLF from within an RPG program.

Using QCMDEXC to Run OPNQRYF from within an RPG Program

Most report programs have a variety of sequence and sort options provided to the end user. If you could sequence and select your data dynamically, you could add a great deal of flexibility to your programs, thus reducing the amount of maintenance performed.

The sample program in Figure 4.2 allows you to do just that. This RPG program is a simple list program that prints the customer file in customer-name or customer-number order. It does so by executing the Open Query File (OPNQRF) command from within an RPG program. When the program is called, a parameter is passed that determines the sequence in which the records are printed. If a one is passed to the program, the list will be printed in customer-name sequence. Otherwise, the list prints in customer-number order.

Take a look at the code in Figure 4.2. In particular, note the USROPN (User Controlled Open) keyword specified on the File Description Specification for the CUST file. This tells the system that the open and close of the CUST database file is user-controlled; in other words, it is controlled from within the program.

The program must not be allowed to open the file during program initialization because you could not perform file overrides or create an alternate path for the data. The override for OPNQRYF is not allowed once the file has been opened. Therefore, before opening the file, you must perform the overrides on it. The Override Database File (OVRDBF) command tells the system that you want this RPG program and the OPNQRYF command to share the same data path as the CUST database file.

```
************************************************************************
*   TO COMPILE:
*       CRTBNDRPG PGM(XXXLIB/FIG0402)
************************************************************************

FFilename++IPEASF.....L.....A.Device+.Keywords++++++++++++++++++++++++
FCustomer  IF   E            Disk    UsrOpn
FQsysPrt   O    F   132       Printer OFLIND(*InOF)

DName++++++++++++ETDsFrom+++To/L+++IDc.Keywords++++++++++++++++++++++++
D CmdAry          S                 80    DIM(5) CTDATA PERRCD(1)
D Sequence#       S                  1
D Command         S                 80
D CmdLength       S                 15  5 INZ(80)

CL0N01Factor1+++++++Opcode&ExtFactor2+++++++Result+++++++Len++D+HiLoEq
C     *Entry      Plist
C                 Parm                    Sequence#
 * Over-ride the Open Data Path of the CUSTOMER file
C                 Eval       Command = CmdAry(1)
C                 Call       'QCMDEXC'
C                 Parm                    Command
C                 Parm                    CmdLength
C                 If         Sequence# = '1'
 * Perform OPNQRYF to sequence records into customer name order
C                 Eval       Command = %TRIMR(CmdAry(2))
C                              + ' ' + CmdAry(3)
C                 Else
 * Perform OPNQRYF to sequence records into customer number order
C                 Eval       Command = %TRIMR(CmdAry(2))
C                              + ' ' + CmdAry(4)
C                 EndIf
C                 Call       'QCMDEXC'
C                 Parm                    Command
C                 Parm                    CmdLength
 * Now that OPNQRYF has been performed, the file may be opened
C                 Open       Customer
C                 Except     Heading
 * Read and print records
C                 DoU        %Eof(Customer)
```

Figure 4.2: This program uses QCMDEXC to run OPNQRYF from within an RPG program (part 1 of 2).

```
C                    Read      CusRec
C                    If        not %Eof(Customer)
C                    Except    Detail
C                    EndIf
C                    EndDo
 * Close the CUSTOMER file
C                    Eval      Command = CmdAry(5)
C                    Call      'QCMDEXC'
C                    Parm                Command
C                    Parm                CmdLength
C                    Eval      *InLr = *ON

OFilename++DF..N01N02N03Excnam++++B++A++Sb+Sa+.....................
OQSYSPRT   E              Heading        2 02
O          OR    OF
O                                         72 'CUSTOMER LIST'
O          E              Heading        1
O          OR    OF
O                                         15 'CUSTOMER NUMBER'
O                                         45 'CUSTOMER NAME'
O          EF             Detail         1
O                         Customer#           15
O                         Custname            65

** CmdAry compile time array
OVRDBF FILE(CUSTOMER) SHARE(*YES)
OPNQRYF FILE((CUSTOMER)) ALWCPYDTA(*OPTIMIZE)
KEYFLD((CUSTNAME))
KEYFLD((CUSTOMER#))
CLOF CUSTOMER
```

Figure 4.2: This program uses QCMDEXC to run OPNQRYF from within an RPG program (part 2 of 2).

The program uses QCMDEXC to perform the Override Data Base File command for the CUST database file, and then again to perform the Open Query File operation to sequence the data. An EVAL expression concatenates the primary element of OPNQRYF to the appropriate KEYFLD parameter. The KEYFLD parameter chosen depends on the parameter value passed to the program. Once the OPNQRYF command has been performed, the CUST file can be opened for use within the RPG program.

The QCMDEXC API is called three times in the example in Figure 4.2. First, it is used to run the OVRDBF command so that the system knows to share the open data path between the OPNQRYF command and the RPG program. Second, QCMDEXC is used to perform the OPNQRYF command, where the data is sequenced. Third, QCMDEXC is used to close the CUST file once the program is finished with the list. Failure to close the file could cause some interesting and unintended results in subsequent programs that used the CUST database file, if the program was being called interactively.

In the sample program in Figure 4.2, the data can be dynamic, eliminating the need to code and maintain additional programs with similar output. It can also process the data in the CUST file in arrival sequence, rather than the less-efficient method of reading the file by key.

Using QCMDEXC to Override Printer Parameters from within an RPG Program

Directing report output to desired printers and output queues is standard fare for an RPG programmer. If you have not used QCMDEXC for the task, however, you'll want to check out the example in Figure 4.3.

Figure 4.3 uses the QCMDEXC API to change printers and the number of copies printed from within the RPG print program. Parameter 1 is the number of copies to print, and parameter 2 is the printer device to which to direct the output.

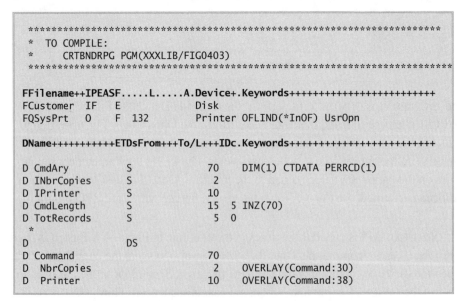

```
**************************************************************************
*   TO COMPILE:
*      CRTBNDRPG PGM(XXXLIB/FIG0403)
**************************************************************************

FFilename++IPEASF.....L.....A.Device+.Keywords+++++++++++++++++++++++++++
FCustomer  IF   E              Disk
FQSysPrt   O    F   132        Printer OFLIND(*InOF) UsrOpn

DName+++++++++++ETDsFrom+++To/L+++IDc.Keywords+++++++++++++++++++++++++++

D CmdAry            S              70     DIM(1) CTDATA PERRCD(1)
D INbrCopies        S               2
D IPrinter          S              10
D CmdLength         S              15 5   INZ(70)
D TotRecords        S               5 0
 *
D                   DS
D Command                          70
D  NbrCopies                        2     OVERLAY(Command:30)
D  Printer                         10     OVERLAY(Command:38)
```

Figure 4.3: This program uses QCMDEXC to override printer attributes (part 1 of 2).

```
CLON01Factor1+++++++Opcode&ExtFactor2++++++Result++++++++Len++D+HiLoEq
C     *Entry      Plist
C                 Parm                    INbrCopies
C                 Parm                    IPrinter
 * Perform the printer over-rides
C                 If        %Parms > 0
C                 Movea     CmdAry(1)     Command
C                 Eval      NbrCopies = INbrCopies
C                 Eval      Printer = IPrinter
C                 Call      'QCMDEXC'
C                 Parm                    Command
C                 Parm                    CmdLength
C                 EndIf
 * Open printer file and begin output operations
C                 Open      QsysPrt
C                 Except    Heading
 * Read and print customer file records
C                 DoU       %Eof(Customer)
C                 Read      Customer
C                 If        not %Eof(Customer)
C                 Eval      TotRecords = TotRecords + 1
C                 Except    Detail
C                 EndIf
C                 EndDo
C                 Except    Totals
C                 Close     QsysPrt
C                 Eval      *InLr = *ON


OFilename++DF..N01N02N03Excnam++++B++A++Sb+Sa+......................
OQsysPrt   E          Heading      3 02
O          OR    OF
O                                     5 'DATE:'
O                      Udate       Y  14
O                                    70 'CUSTOMER LIST'
O                                   121 'PAGE:'
O                      Page        Z 127
O          E          Heading      1
O          OR    OF
O                                    20 'CUSTOMER NUMBER'
O                                    46 'CUSTOMER NAME'
O          EF         Detail       1
O                      Customer#      20
O                      CustName       66
O          E          Totals     2 1
O                      TotRecords 1   14
O                                    35 'TOTAL RECORDS LISTED'
** Cmdary compile time array
OVRPRTF FILE(QSYSPRT) COPIES( ) DEV(            ) OUTQ(*DEV)
```

Figure 4.3: This program uses QCMDEXC to override printer attributes (part 2 of 2).

As in the previous example, the file being overridden must remain closed while the file overrides are performed. Notice the USROPN keyword specified on the File Description Specification of the printer file (QSYSPRT). It tells the system this file is user-controlled. You code the open and close of QSYSPRT yourself, once you have performed the desired file overrides.

The %PARMS built-in function tells the program whether or not parameters are passed to it. (We could have also used the PARMS keyword in the Program Status Information data structure.) If the customer-file-list program is called with parameters 1 and 2 specified (the %PARMS value is greater than zero), printer file overrides are performed, specifying the desired printer and number of copies. If no parameters are passed to the program, the override is not performed.

The single element of the CMDARY compile-time array (defined in the Definition Specification in Figure 4.3) holds the shell of the Override Printer File (OVRPRTF) command. (We chose to use a data structure as a tool to load the parameters of the OVRPRTF command because it is generally easier to follow than concatenating the various components together.) The program loads the CMDARY compile-time array element into the data structure and then overlays it with the values passed into the program as parameters 1 and 2. The result is a complete OVRPRTF command that is ready to be executed. The OVRPRTF command is executed by calling the QCMDEXC API. Once the override to the printer file has been performed, the printer file is opened, and the rest of the simple list program is completed.

Prototyping QCMDEXC to Submit a Job to the Job Queue from within an RPG Program

Have you ever wondered why there is no Submit Job (SMBJOB) opcode that allows you to submit jobs from within your RPG program? We have too. Fortunately, you can use QCMDEXC to do the job.

This example uses a little RPG prompt program, which prompts for a printer ID and the number of copies, validates the values entered, and then submits a program to the job queue. The program being submitted is the customer list program, written in the previous example (Figure 4.3). The display file coded in Figure 4.4 presents the prompt screen shown in Figure 4.5.

```
A*********************************************************************
A*  TO COMPILE:
A*      CRTDSPF FILE(XXXLIB/FIG0404)
A*********************************************************************
AAN01N02N03T.Name++++++RLen++TDpBLinPosFunctions+++++++++++++++++++++++
A              R FORMAT1
A                                        CHGINPDFT
A                                        CF03
A                                   1 26'List Customer File'
A                                        DSPATR(HI)
A                                   8  7'Printer to send report to.........-
A                                     ................'
A              PRINTER       10A  B  8 58DSPATR(HI)
A                                        DSPATR(UL)
A   41                                   ERRMSG('Invalid Printer Id Entered')
A   43                                   ERRMSG('Your list was submitted...')
A                                  10  7'Number of copies to print.........-
A                                     ................'
A              NBRCOPIES     2D 0B 10 58DSPATR(HI)
A                                        CHECK(RZ)
A   42                                   ERRMSG('Invalid Number of Copies')
A                                  23  4'F3=Exit'
A                                        COLOR(BLU)
```

Figure 4.4: This DDS produces the Customer-List Prompt Screen display file.

In the RPG program in Figure 4.6, we chose to prototype the call to the QCMDEXC command. Prototyping offers an advantage in that the syntax for the QCMDEXC API will be validated when the program is compiled, instead of at program runtime.

Take a look at the code in Figure 4.6. It first establishes the default values for the number-of-copies field, and then presents a prompt screen. The program has been coded to continue presenting the prompt screen until F3 is pressed.

If the entries keyed pass the edits, the values are passed to the **PassCmd** data structure, which in turn is passed to the **SbmJob** prototype of the Submit Job

(SBMJOB) command. The CALLP operand is then executed to submit the job to the job queue, and a confirmation message is sent to the screen.

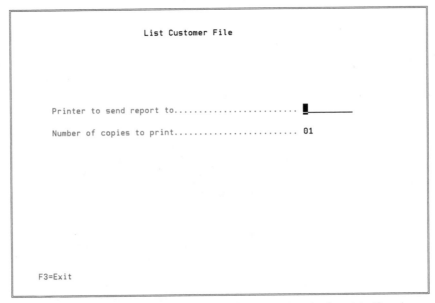

```
                        List Customer File




        Printer to send report to........................ ▮_____

        Number of copies to print........................ 01







        F3=Exit
```

Figure 4.5: The Customer-List Prompt Screen allows users to enter the printer ID and number of copies.

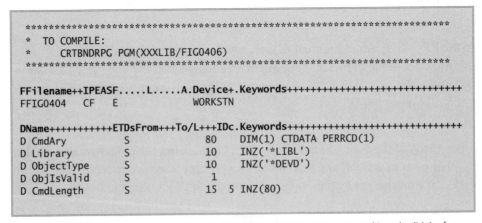

```
 ********************************************************************
 *   TO COMPILE:
 *      CRTBNDRPG PGM(XXXLIB/FIG0406)
 ********************************************************************

FFilename++IPEASF.....L.....A.Device+.Keywords+++++++++++++++++++++++++++++++
FFIG0404   CF   E           WORKSTN

DName++++++++++ETDsFrom+++To/L+++IDc.Keywords+++++++++++++++++++++++++++++++++
D CmdAry          S              80     DIM(1) CTDATA PERRCD(1)
D Library         S              10     INZ('*LIBL')
D ObjectType      S              10     INZ('*DEVD')
D ObjIsValid      S               1
D CmdLength       S              15  5 INZ(80)
```

Figure 4.6: This program is an example of prototyping the QCMDEXC command to submit jobs from within an RPG program (part 1 of 2).

```
     *
     D               DS                    INZ
     D PassCmd                    80
     D  PassCopies                 2        OVERLAY(PassCmd:36)
     D  PassPrintr                10        OVERLAY(PassCmd:41)
     *


     D SbmJob         PR                    ExtPgm('QCMDEXC')
     D  Command                 32727       Options(*VARSIZE) Const
     D  Length                     15  5 Const
     CL0N01Factor1+++++++Opcode&ExtFactor2+++++++Result++++++++Len++D+HiLoEq
     *   Establish defaults
     C                 MOVEA      Cmdary(1)      Command
     C                 Eval       NbrCopies = 1
     *   Do until an EOJ request is encountered
     C                 DoU        *InKC = *ON
     C                 Exfmt      Format1
     C                 MoveA      '000'          *IN(41)
     *   End of job request
     C                 If         *InKC = *On
     C                 Leave
     C                 EndIf
     *   Must specify printer
     C                 If         Printer = *blanks
     C                 Eval       *In41 = *ON
     C                 Iter
     C                 EndIf
     *   Must specify the number of copies
     C                 If         NbrCopies = *Zeros
     C                 Eval       *In42 = *ON
     C                 Iter
     C                 EndIf
     *   Submit Customer List
     C                 Eval       *In43 = *ON
     C                 Move       NbrCopies      PassCopies
     C                 Eval       PassPrintr = Printer
     C                 Callp      SbmJob(PassCmd:80)
     C                 EndDo
     **
     C                 Eval       *InLr = *ON

     ** Cmdary compile time array
     SBMJOB CMD(CALL PGM(FIG0403) PARM('99' 'Printer ID')) JOB(LISTCUST)
```

Figure 4.6: This program is an example of prototyping the QCMDEXC command to submit jobs from within an RPG program (part 2 of 2).

Using the System Function
Instead of Calling QCMDEXC

One of the primary driving forces behind the Integrated Language Environment, or ILE, was to create a certain level of homogenization, where different languages could be combined to create a "best of breed" atmosphere. By having the ability to use many different languages in the same operating environment, AS/400 developers would have the ability to pick exactly the right tool for each job. The *system function* is a fine example of this idea.

The system function exploits RPG IV's ability to execute system-provided C functions. In this case, the function is called "system." The system function provides the same capability as the QCMDEXC API, but you don't have to pass the size of the command. Just pass the command you want executed (as a parameter), and the function will figure out the length of the command.

Figure 4.7 shows an example of the code necessary to execute the system function. The call to the system function is prototyped and accessed using the EXTPROC keyword. It accepts one parameter, the command to be executed. As noted, the length of the command does not have to be passed to this function. Both keywords VALUE and **Options(*STRING)** must be used on the command parameter. C functions expect strings to be null-terminated; the **Options(*STRING)** keyword handles this requirement for you.

When working with C functions, remember that the case of the characters is important. The system function must be entered in lowercase. Also, notice the definition of the CPFMSGID field. Defining the field with import('_EXCP_MSGID') causes the field to be loaded with the contents of the global variable EXCP-MSGID. This will be the CPF message number of any error encountered while executing the command. This is a big advantage over QCMDEXC.

The logic of the program is very simple, as it is only intended to demonstrate how to code using the system function. The program accepts a command as a parameter and passes that command to the system function. If any errors are encountered, it will display the CPF message number. If not, the command is executed.

There are two important issues to note when working with the system function. The first is that you must compile the program using the QC2LE binding directory. This is the case with any of the system-provided C functions. Second, and perhaps more important, is that using the system function will not leave any kind of audit trail in your job log. If your job fails, the system function will return the CPF message where the failure occurred, but there will be no trail left to help you further determine the nature of the error.

```
DName+++++++++++ETDsFrom+++To/L+++IDc.Keywords+++++++++++++++++++++++++++
d System            PR             10i 0 extproc('system')
d Cmd                                 *   value options(*string)
d CpfMsgId          s               7   import('_EXCP_MSGID')
d RunCmdIn          s              50


CLON01Factor1++++++Opcode&ExtFactor2++++++Result++++++++Len++D+HiLoEq
c      *entry       Plist
c                   Parm                         RunCmdIn

 * execute the command passed to the program
c                   If         System(RunCmdIn) <> 0

 * If procedure returned not zero, display the error msgid
c      CpfMsgId     dsply
c                   endif

c                   eval       *inlr = *On
```

Figure 4.7: This program example uses the system function to execute commands.

The QCMDCHK API

The Check Command Syntax (QCMDCHK) API lets you edit and prompt a command from within your program. This API is reasonably simple; it only requires that you pass the command you want to run and the length of the command string. The only downside to this API is that it does not actually run the command. It edits the command, and when prompted, returns the prompted values back to your program.

As you can see in Table 4.2, the QCMDCHK parameters are virtually the same as those for QCMDEXC.

Table 4.2: Required Input Parameters for the Check Command Syntax API (QCMDCHK)				
Parameter	**Description**	**Type**	**Attribute**	**Size**
1	The source command string that is to be processed (either prompted for or run).	Input/Output	Char	Varies
2	The length of the command string being processed.	Input	Packed	15/5

The Ultimate Command-Processing API

By now, you probably feel that you have a pretty good understanding of the QCMDEXC and the QCMDCHK APIs. You know that QCMDEXC can be used to execute almost any command from within your program, and that QCMDCHK can be used to prompt for and edit a command from within your program.

But what if you simply wanted the operator to press a function key to get a window where a command could be entered? You would probably want to edit the command for validity, rather than presenting one of those nasty CPF errors if an invalid command happened to be entered. You might also want to trap the information that the user entered in response to that prompt.

One way to accomplish these goals would be to combine the QCMDCHK and QCMDEXC APIs, but a better way would be to use the Process Commands (QCAPCMD) API. QCAPCMD lets you edit a command string for validity, allow prompting, and return the command parameters to your program. It can either process the entered command or simply verify that the command is valid, and let you pass the changed command on to QCMDEXC to be run.

Table 4.3 documents the parameters for QCAPCMD. They might seem complicated at first, but a practical example is provided in Figure 4.8 to help you see that this API is really worthwhile.

120

Table 4.3: Required Input Parameters for the Command Processing API (QCAPCMD)

Parameter	Description	Type	Attributes	Size
1	The source command string that is to be processed (either prompted for or run).	Input	Character	Varies
2	The length of the source command string. Valid values are between one and 6,000. Trailing blanks in the command string can count in the length.	Input	Binary	4
3	The option control block. Currently, only one format is allowed. This format is described in Table 4.4.	Input	Char	Varies
4	The length of the option control block parameter. It must be a minimum of 20 bytes.	Input	Binary	4
5	The name of the data structure defining the data in the control block. Currently, the only valid entry is CPOP0100.	Input	Char	8
6	The updated command string. This may be considerably longer than the source command string, as it contains the keywords. No padding is performed on this field; you must use the length of changed command string field to determine the number of characters returned. This field will not be changed if an error occurred during the execution of QCAPCMD.	Output	Char	Varies
7	The total number of bytes QCAPCMD has to return in the changed command string. If the string is larger than this number, the returned command string will be truncated to fit.	Input	Binary	4
8	The total number of bytes QCAPCMD is going to return.	Input	Binary	4
9	The standard error-code data structure.	Both	Character	Varies

Table 4.4: Format of the Option Control Block (CPOP0100) in QCAPCMD

Offset	Attribute	Size	Description
0	Binary	4	The type of command processing. Valid values and their meaning are as follows: • 0—Command running. Processes the same as QCMDEXC. • 1—Command syntax check. Processes the same as QCMDCHK. • 2—Command line running. Processes the same as QCMDEXC except limited user-checking and prompting for missing required parameters is performed. • 3—Command-line syntax checking. The complement of type 2. • 4—CL program statement. Checked according to the same rules as SEU for CL. Variable names are allowed. • 5—CL input stream. Checked according to the same rules as the input batch stream. • 6—Command definition statements. • 7—Binder definition statements. Checked according to the same rules as SEU for BND. • 8—A user-defined option that allows the user to create commands similar to those used in PDM. • 9—ILE CL programs source. Checked according to the rules of SEU for ILE CL.
4	Char	1	DBCS handling, which indicates whether the command analyzer should handle the SO/SI characters as DBCS. If zero, ignore DBCS; if one, handle DBCS.
5	Char	1	The prompter action, which indicates whether the prompter should be called for the command string. Valid values are as follows: • 0—Never call the prompter, even if prompting characters (?, *?, etc.) are embedded in the command string. • 1—Always call the prompter, even if there are no prompting characters embedded in the string. • 2—Prompt only if prompting characters are present. Error code CPF3CF1 is issued if this code is used with command-processing types 4 through 8. • 3—Provide a help display for the command.
6	Char	1	The command string syntax, which specifies whether the command is in the AS400 syntax (library/object) or the System 38 syntax (object.library). It will be truncated to fit.
7	Char	4	The message-retrieve key of the request message that contains the source command statements to process.
11	Char	9	Reserved

An example of QCAPCMD in action will help to bring everything together. Remember the simple list program, where QCMDEXC is used to override the printer attributes (Figure 4.3)? The sample program in Figure 4.8 submits that job to the job queue. Granted, that is really no big deal in itself, but the program prompts for the Submit Job command, allowing the operator to change whatever job-queue parameters he or she wants. The command will then not only be submitted to the job queue, but the completed command (including whatever parameters were added during the prompting process) will be returned to the program.

```
**************************************************************************
*   TO COMPILE:
*       CRTBNDRPG PGM(XXXLIB/FIG0408)
**************************************************************************

DName++++++++++ETDsFrom+++To/L+++IDc.Keywords++++++++++++++++++++++++++++
* Program Information Data Structure
D                   SDS
D JobName           244    253
D JobUser           254    263
D JobNumber         264    269  0

 * QCAPCMD format CPOP0100 as copies from library QSYSINC
DQCAP0100           DS
D*                                              Format CPOP0100
D QCACMDPT           1      4B 0                 inz(0)
D*                                              Command Process Type
D QCABCSDH           5      5                    inz('0')
D*                                              DBCS Data Handling
D QCAPA              6      6                    inz('1')
D*                                              Prompter Action
D QCACMDSS           7      7                    inz('0')
D*                                              Command String Syntax
D QCAMK              8     11
D*                                              Message Key
D QCAERVED          12     20     inz(x'000000000000000000')
D*                                              Reserved

 * QUSRJOBI format JOBI0300 as copied from library QSYSINC
DQUSI030000         DS
D*                                              Qwc JOBI0300
D QUSBR02            1      4B 0
D*                                              Bytes Return
D QUSBA02            5      8B 0
D*                                              Bytes Avail
```

Figure 4.8: This example uses QCAPCMD to prompt commands from within an ILE RPG program (part 1 of 4).

```
D QUSJN04                     9    18
D*                                            Job Name
D QUSUN04                    19    28
D*                                            User Name
D QUSJNBR04                  29    34
D*                                            Job Number
D QUSIJID02                  35    50
D*                                            Int Job ID
D QUSJS07                    51    60
D*                                            Job Status
D QUSJT05                    61    61
D*                                            Job Type
D QUSJS08                    62    62
D*                                            Job Subtype
D QUSJN05                    63    72
D*                                            Jobq Name
D QUSJL                      73    82
D*                                            Jobq Lib
D QUSJP                      83    84
D*                                            Jobq Priority
D QUSON                      85    94
D*                                            Outq Name
D QUSOL                      95   104
D*                                            Outq Lib
D QUSOP                     105   106
D*                                            Outq Priority
D QUSPDN                    107   116
D*                                            Prt Dev Name
D QUSSJN                    117   126
D*                                            Subm Job Name
D QUSSUN                    127   136
D*                                            Subm User Name
D QUSSJNBR                  137   142
D*                                            Subm Job Num
D QUSSMN                    143   152
D*                                            Subm Msgq Name
D QUSSML                    153   162
D*                                            Subm Msgq Lib
D QUSSOJ                    163   172
D*                                            Sts On Jobq
D QUSDPOJ                   173   180
D*                                            Date Put On Jobq
D QUSJD                     181   187
D*                                            Job Date

 * Data Structure for standard Error Data Structure
DQUSEC          DS
D QUSBPRV                     1     4B 0      inz(116)
```

Figure 4.8: This example uses QCAPCMD to prompt commands from within an ILE RPG program (part 2 of 4).

```
D QUSBAVL                      5      8B 0
D QUSEI                        9     15
D QUSED01                     17    116

D CapCommand        S               256     INZ
D CapLength         S                9B 0   INZ(256)
D CapRetrnd         S               256     INZ
D CapRtnLen         S                9B 0   INZ(256)
D CapARtnLen        S                9B 0   INZ(256)
D CapBlkLen         S                9B 0   INZ(20)
D CapBlkFmt         S                 8     INZ('CPOP0100')
D Library           S                10     INZ('*LIBL')
D NbrCopies         S                 4     INZ('''01''')
D ObjectType        S                10     INZ('*DEVD')
D ObjIsValid        S                 1
D Quote             S                 1     INZ('''')
D UsrFormat         S                 8     INZ('JOBI0300')
D UsrJobName        S                26     INZ
D UsrJobID          S                16     inz
D UsrLength         S                 9B 0  INZ(187)

CLON01Factor1+++++++Opcode&ExtFactor2+++++++Result++++++++Len++D+HiLoEq...
 *  Build qualified job name
C                   Eval      UsrJobName = JobName + JobUser +
C                             %Char(JobNumber)

 *  Retrieve Job Attributes
C                   Call      'QUSRJOBI'
C                   Parm                    QUSI030000
C                   Parm                    UsrLength
C                   Parm                    UsrFormat
C                   Parm                    UsrJobName
C                   Parm                    UsrJobID

 *  Build the Submit Job Command to be executed
C                   Eval      CapCommand =
C                             'SBMJOB CMD(CALL PGM(FIG0403) PARM(' +
C                             NbrCopies + ' ' +
C                             Quote + QUSPDN + Quote + '))' +
C                             ' JOB(LISTCUST)'

 *  Perform prompted Submit Job Command
C                   Call      'QCAPCMD'
C                   Parm                    CapCommand
C                   Parm                    CapLength
C                   Parm                    QCap0100
C                   Parm                    CapBlkLen
C                   Parm                    CapBlkFmt
```

Figure 4.8: This example uses QCAPCMD to prompt commands from within an ILE RPG program (part 3 of 4).

```
C                      Parm                    CapRetrnd
C                      Parm                    CapRtnLen
C                      Parm                    CapARtnLen
C                      Parm                    QusEc
   **
C                      Eval        *InLr = *ON
```

Figure 4.8: This example uses QCAPCMD to prompt commands from within an ILE RPG program (part 4 of 4).

Before performing the prompt for the Submit Job command, another API needs to be run to establish the default values for the operator of the program. The Retrieve Job Information (QUSRJOBI) API retrieves job attributes and returns them to your program. For the purposes of this program, the user's default printer ID is retrieved. That value is used as a default when the list program is submitted to the job queue. The parameters for QUSRJOBI are described in Table 4.5.

Parameter	Description		Type	Attributes	Size
Table 4.5: Required Input Parameters **for the Retrieve Job Information API (QUSRJOBI) (part 1 of 2)**					
1	The receiver variable, which receives the requested job information.		Output	Character	Varies
2	The length of the receiver variable (must be at least 8 bytes).		Input	Binary	4
3	The name of the format whose information you are requesting. Possible values are as follows:		Input	Char	8
	Name	**Description**			
	JOBI0100	Basic performance information.			
	JOBI0150	Additional performance information.			
	JOBI0200	WRKACTJOB information.			

Parameter	Description		Type	Attributes	Size
Table 4.5: Required Input Parameters **for the Retrieve Job Information API (QUSRJOBI) (part 2 of 2)**					
3 cont.	**Name**	**Description**			
	JOBI0300	Job queue and output queue information.			
	JOBI0400	Job attribute information.			
	JOBI0500	Message logging information.			
	JOBI0600	Active job information.			
	JOBI0700	Library list information.			
	JOBI0800	Active-job signal information.			
	JOBI0900	Active-job SQL cursor information.			
4	The qualified job name, which is either a name or one of two special values. These values are * (asterisk), which represents the current job, or *INT, which represents the internal job identifier assigned by the system. The qualified job name consists of these three parts:		Input	Char	26
	Description	**Attr**	**Size**		
	Job Name	Char	10		
	Job User	Char	10		
	Job Number	Char	6		
5	An internal ID that the system generates to define a job. This is the quickest way for the system to find a job.		Input	Char	16

127

The QUSRJOBI API is actually very simple to use and returns a veritable plethora of useful job information to your program. As you can see from the format list in Table 4.5, you can extract a lot of job information using this API. If you take a look at the QUSRJOBI source member in source file QRPGLESRC (library QSYSINC), you will see a detailed list of what each of these formats actually provides. From library list to performance data, you can extract all kinds of information about a job.

The Qualified Name Parameter

Most APIs that ask for the Qualified Name parameter will accept an asterisk (*), which tells the API to use the job that is currently running. QUSRJOBI is no exception. The program in Figure 4.8, however, specifies the qualified name by extracting the required information from the Program Information data structure. As you can see, the first step in the calculation specifications concatenates three fields (job name, job user, and job number) to create the qualified job name. The qualified job name is then passed to QUSRJOBI to extract information about the job. This exercise was mainly for educational purposes, since you could have just used the asterisk to tell the API to gather information about the current job. We just wanted to show that the information is all there. All you need is to know where to go to get it.

We specified the JOBI0300 format when calling the QUSRJOBI API because we were interested in information about the job and output queues. Within the information returned, we used the default printer ID (QUSPDN) in putting together the Submit Job command. If you look at the definition specifications for format JOBI0300, however, you'll see that there is a lot of other information at your disposal.

The next step in putting together the Submit Job command involves concatenating the various components. The Submit Job command will be the first parameter used when calling QCAPCMD. You will notice that we defaulted several of the QCAPCMD parameters during the definition process because it saved steps later in the process.

When the program is run, you will see a screen similar to the one in Figure 4.9. Operators can use the prompting features as desired to modify the Submit Job commands, but all of the default information has been provided for them up front. Once the prompting is complete, the job will be submitted (unless it is terminated by the operator).

The unique feature of this API is that the final command submitted to the job queue (after prompting) is actually returned to the program as the sixth parameter of the API (**CapRetrnd**, in the program). We elected not to do anything with it for this example, but this information could be written to a log file or printed on a submitted job report somewhere.

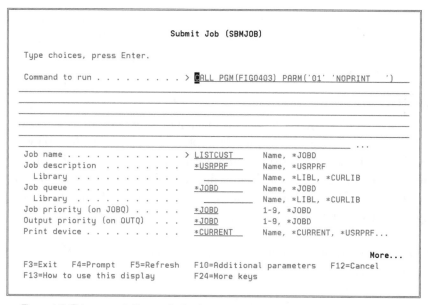

Figure 4.9: This screen is the result of using QCAPCMD to prompt commands from within an ILE RPG program.

The IBM Command-Line API

If all you want to do is provide the user a command line, you can use the Command Line (QUSCMDLN) API. This is probably the easiest of all APIs to use. It is even easier than using QCMDEXC. All you do is call it; there are no parameters to worry about.

Figure 4.10 shows the command entry screen that is presented when you run QUSCMDLN. Commands entered on the command line can be prompted via the F4 function key. Using the F9 function key retrieves previous commands. The API provides both of these capabilities. There is no coding necessary to provide these functions, other than calling the API!

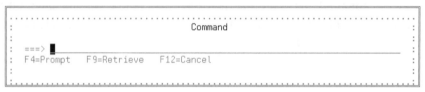

Figure 4.10: A command entry screen results from using the Command Line API (QUSCMDLN).

Summary

As you have seen, the QCAPCMD API is much more flexible, and more complex, than the QCMDEXC, QCMDCHK, and QUSCMDLN APIs. We think that you will agree, however, that QCAPCMD performs a very useful function. This unique API allows you to provide a command entry line in your programs where you can both validate and execute the requested user action. As an added bonus, you can "trap" what the user entered.

Take the time to learn how to use the command-processing APIs. You will find that your will is the system's command!

5

WORK-MANAGEMENT APIs

Since you're reading this book, you probably spend long hours of hard work programming. All of your hard work won't mean a thing, however, if your programs can't be properly managed. We are, and always will be, programmers at heart, so we find it somewhat difficult to tout the virtues of management. But there comes a time in every programmer's life when you have to stand up and look the truth straight in the eye.

Anybody who has ever seen a system "thrashing" for available resources can attest to the importance of work management. Thrashing is when a system is constantly swapping pages back and forth between disk and memory. A system that is thrashing is working very hard indeed, but because the work is not managed well, the system is not accomplishing much of anything.

Fortunately, the AS/400 has the best operating system on the planet. Since OS/400 is such a great operating system, it easily manages the work done on the AS/400. It also has some great built-in tools to allow you to see and control how well it performs this task.

Work System Status (WRKSYSSTS), Work Active Job (WRKACTJOB), Work Subsystem Job (WRKSBSJOB), and Work Job (WRKJOB) are all great commands that help you see exactly what's happening on the system, as well as what's happening with a particular job. As you might have already guessed, all of these commands have APIs that give you access to the work-management information programmatically. This chapter looks at some of these work-management APIs.

This chapter begins with a look at the Retrieve Data Area (QWCRDTAA) API. You are probably asking yourself "What does a data area API have to do with work management?" Well, to be perfectly honest, we're not sure, but since this API is covered in IBM's *API Work Management Manual*, we are including it in our work management chapter, to be consistent with IBM's documentation. We're not sure if we are perpetuating some illogical deviation in IBM's documentation (as if that ever happens), or if there actually is some valid reason for considering data areas to be part of work management. In any case, you'll see a nice example of how to use the Retrieve Data Area API in this chapter. You might have noticed that the Edit Data Area command that comes standard on the AS/400 is extremely limiting. When dealing with values in data areas, you can either display the data, or you can change the data. However, neither option shows you the current value in the data area while you are working with it. You might have found that the Edit Data Area (EDTDTAARA) command in library QUSRTOOL (a library of tools that used to ship free of charge with every AS/400) shows you the current data while changing it. However, the Edit Data Area Command in QUSRTOOL only shows data areas up to 450 characters long (at least on the version that we have), and it doesn't use APIs to accomplish the task. In this chapter, you'll learn how to create your own Edit Data Area command using APIs.

Following the diversion into data areas, you'll explore the basic unit of work on the AS/400, which is, of course, the job. All work on the AS/400 is done within a job. The Work With Active Jobs (WRKACTJOB) command does a great job of showing the state of all the jobs on the system, but it can't show all information for every job; there is just not enough real estate on the screen. If you want to list all the jobs on the system, but show information other than the default, you need the power of APIs. Specifically, you need the List Jobs (QUSLJOBS) API. You'll see this API in depth with a simple list-jobs program.

Once you have created a list of jobs, the next logical step is to take a complete look at an individual job. The Retrieve Job Information (QUSRJOBI) API does just that. It retrieves everything you could possibly want to know about any given job.

One potential problem with processing a list of jobs on the system is that jobs are not static. Between the time the list is created and the time you take some action on a particular job in the list, the status of the job could have changed. Therefore, you should check the status of the job after processing a job from the list. You could use the QUSRJOBI API to do that, but you need something that works really, really fast. The Retrieve Job Status (QWCRJBST) API was created just for checking the status of a job, and it is blazingly fast.

Batch jobs become active on a system by going through a job queue, of course. Occasionally, you need to know that there are no jobs waiting on a job queue before starting another job. You can accomplish this by putting the Retrieve Job Queue Information (QSPRJOBQ) API to work.

To round out this chapter, you'll learn about system values. Specifically, you'll see a program that will return any system value. Of course, the Work System Values command does everything you could want with system values, but it's sometimes handy to access that information from within a program.

The Edit Data Area Program

Imagine using an interactive tool like DFU to change data in a record, and not being able to view the data that you are changing. Absurd! Idiotic! Yet, that is exactly what you are asked to do if you want to change the information in a data area.

The IBM's Change Data Area (CHGDTAARA) command allows you to change the data in a data area (just like DFU for a file), but it does not show you the data that is currently in the data area. To display the data area, you have to use IBM's Display Data Area (DSPDTAARA) command. So, when you want to change a data area, you first need to run DSPDTAARA to see the data, and then use CHGDTAARA to change the data. To be sure you got the data and positions correct, you need to run DSPDTAARA once again. This process seems to leave a lot of room for error, doesn't it? It's not a very productive use of your time, either.

To replace all those steps, we have written a small program that uses the Retrieve Data Area (QWCRDTAA) API to get the information from any given data area and present it in an edit-capable subfile on the screen. From there, you can change the data as desired by typing over the existing data presented in the subfile. The program uses the Command Execute (QCMDEXC) API to execute the Change Data Area command, which effects the change. The code for the Edit Data Area program, shown in Figure 5.1, is followed by the code for the associated display file in Figure 5.2. To see what the program looks like, a sample of the screen is provided in Figure 5.3.

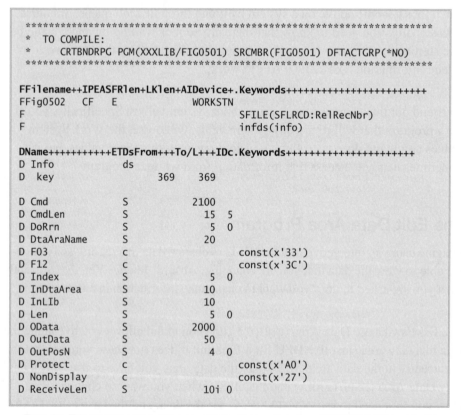

```
****************************************************************************
*   TO COMPILE:
*       CRTBNDRPG PGM(XXXLIB/FIG0501) SRCMBR(FIG0501) DFTACTGRP(*NO)
****************************************************************************

FFilename++IPEASFRlen+LKlen+AIDevice+.Keywords++++++++++++++++++++++++++++
FFig0502   CF  E                  WORKSTN
F                                            SFILE(SFLRCD:RelRecNbr)
F                                            infds(info)

DName+++++++++++ETDsFrom+++To/L+++IDc.Keywords++++++++++++++++++++++++
D Info           ds
D  key                  369     369

D Cmd            S              2100
D CmdLen         S                15 5
D DoRrn          S                 5 0
D DtaAraName     S                20
D F03            c                       const(x'33')
D F12            c                       const(x'3C')
D Index          S                 5 0
D InDtaArea      S                10
D InLIb          S                10
D Len            S                 5 0
D OData          S              2000
D OutData        S                50
D OutPosN        S                 4 0
D Protect        c                       const(x'A0')
D NonDisplay     c                       const(x'27')
D ReceiveLen     S               10i 0
```

Figure 5.1: This program edits a data area using the Retrieve Data Area (QWCRDTAA) API (part 1 of 6).

```
D RelRecNbr        S                  4 0
D Remainder        S                  5 0
D Result           S                  5 0
D RtvLength        S                 10i 0
D Size             S                  4 0
D StrPosit         S                 10i 0 inz(1)
D X                S                  5 0
D Y                S                  5 0
D ChgCon           c                       'CHGDTAARA DTAARA('

D Receiver         DS             32000    based(ReceiverPt)
D  BytesAvl                          10i 0
D  BytesAct                          10i 0
D  TypeReturn                        10
D  RecLib                            10
D  RtnLength                         10i 0
D  NbrDecimal                        10i 0
D  RcvData                         2000

D Receiver1        DS                       INZ
D  BytesPoss              1          4B 0
D  BytesRtrnd             5          8B 0

 *  API error data structure
D ErrorDs          DS                       INZ
D  BytesProvd             1          4B 0 inz(116)
D  BytesAvail             5          8B 0
D  MessageId              9         15
D  Err###                16         16

D PackedNums       DS
D  packed1                1          1p 0
D  packed2                1          2p 0
D  packed3                1          3p 0
D  packed4                1          4p 0
D  packed5                1          5p 0
D  packed6                1          6p 0
D  packed7                1          7p 0
D  packed8                1          8p 0
D  packed9                1          9p 0
D  packed10               1         10p 0
D  packed11               1         11p 0
D  packed12               1         12p 0
D  packed13               1         13p 0
D  packed14               1         14p 0
D  packed15               1         15p 0
```

Figure 5.1: This program edits a data area using the Retrieve Data Area (QWCRDTAA) API (part 2 of 6).

```
CLON01Factor1+++++++Opcode&ExtFactor2+++++++Result+++++++++Len++D+HiLoEq
C          *ENTRY       PLIST
C                       PARM                    InDtaArea
C                       PARM                    InLib

C                       movel     InDtaArea     DtaAraName
C                       move      InLib         DtaAraName
     *
C                       CALL      'QWCRDTAA'
C                       PARM                    Receiver1
C                       PARM      8             ReceiveLen
C                       PARM                    DtaAraName
C                       PARM      -1            StrPosit
C                       PARM      32000         RtvLength
C                       PARM                    ErrorDs

C                       alloc     BytesPoss     ReceiverPt

C                       CALL      'QWCRDTAA'
C                       PARM                    Receiver
C                       PARM      BytesPoss     ReceiveLen
C                       PARM                    DtaAraName
C                       PARM      -1            StrPosit
C                       PARM      BytesPoss     RtvLength
C                       PARM                    ErrorDs

C                       z-add     RtnLength     Size
C                       z-add     RtnLength     Len
C                       If        Len > 50
C                       eval      Len = 50
C                       Endif
C                       z-add     RtnLength     OutLen
C                       z-add     NbrDecimal    OutDec
C                       Eval      Outtyp = TypeReturn

C                       Eval      Index = 37
C                       Eval      OutPosN = 1

C                       Dou       (Index + Len) > BytesPoss

C                       If        (Index + Len) > BytesPoss
C                       Eval      Len = (BytesPoss - Index) + 1
C                       else
C                       Eval      Len = 50
C                       If        Len > Rtnlength
C                       Eval      Len = RtnLength
C                       Endif
C                       End
```

Figure 5.1: This program edits a data area using the Retrieve Data Area (QWCRDTAA) API (part 3 of 6).

136

```
C                    Eval        Data = %subst(Receiver:Index:Len)

C                    If          TypeReturn = '*DEC'
C                    movel       data              PackedNums
C                    select
C                    When        Len <= 1
C                    movel       Packed1           OutData
C                    When        Len <= 2
C                    movel       Packed2           OutData
C                    When        Len <= 3
C                    movel       Packed3           OutData
C                    When        Len <= 4
C                    movel       Packed4           OutData
C                    When        Len <= 5
C                    movel       Packed5           OutData
C                    When        Len <= 6
C                    movel       Packed6           OutData
C                    When        Len <= 7
C                    movel       Packed7           OutData
C                    When        Len <= 8
C                    movel       Packed8           OutData
C                    When        Len <= 9
C                    movel       Packed9           OutData
C                    When        Len <= 10
C                    movel       Packed10          OutData
C                    When        Len <= 11
C                    movel       Packed11          OutData
C                    When        Len <= 12
C                    movel       Packed12          OutData
C                    When        Len <= 13
C                    movel       Packed13          OutData
C                    When        Len <= 14
C                    movel       Packed14          OutData
C                    When        Len <= 15
C                    movel       Packed15          OutData
C                    endsl
C      RtnLength     Div         2                 Result
C                    Mvr                           Remainder
C                    if          Remainder <> 0
C                    movel(p)    OutData           Data
C                    else
C                    eval        Data = %subst(OutData:2:RtnLength)
C                    Endif
C                    Eval        %subst(Data:RtnLength + 2:1) = Protect
C                    Eval        %subst(Data:RtnLength + 1:1) = NonDisplay
C                    else
C                    If          Len < 50
```

Figure 5.1: This program edits a data area using the Retrieve Data Area (QWCRDTAA) API (part 4 of 6).

```
C                   Eval      %subst(Data:RtnLength + 2:1) = Protect
C                   Eval      %subst(Data:RtnLength + 1:1) = NonDisplay
C                   Endif
C                   Endif

C                   EVAL      RelRecNbr = RelRecNbr + 1
C                   move      OutPosN        OutPos
C                   WRITE     SFLRCD
C                   Eval      OutPosN = OutPosN + 50

C                   Eval      Index = Index + Len

C                   Enddo

C                   If        Index < BytesPoss
C                   eval      Len = (BytesPoss - Index) + 1
C                   Eval      Data = %subst(Receiver:Index:Len)
C                   If        len <> 50
C                   Eval      %subst(Data:Len + 2:1) = Protect
C                   Eval      %subst(Data:Len + 1:1) = NonDisplay
C                   Endif
C                   Eval      RelRecNbr = RelRecNbr + 1
C                   move      OutPosN        OutPos
C                   WRITE     SFLRCD
C                   Endif

C                   If        RelRecNbr > 0
C                   Eval      *In21 = *ON
C                   Endif
C                   WRITE     FORMAT1
C                   EXFMT     SFLCTL

C                   If        Key <> F03 AND
C                             Key <> F12
C                   Exsr      UpdateSR
C                   Endif
C                   Eval      *inlr = *on

C         UpdateSR  Begsr
C                   Eval      DoRRN = RelRecNbr
C                   Eval      Index = 1

C                   Do        DoRRN          x
C         x         chain     SflRcd
C                   eval      %subsT(OData:Index:50) = Data
C                   eval      index = Index + 50
C                   enddo
```

Figure 5.1: This program edits a data area using the Retrieve Data Area (QWCRDTAA) API (part 5 of 6).

```
C                   If         TypeReturn <> '*DEC'
C                   Eval       Cmd = ChgCon + %trim(Inlib) + '/' +
C                              %trim(InDtaArea) +
C                              ') VALUE(''' + %subst(OData:1:Size) +
C                              ''')'
C                   Else
C                   Eval       Cmd = ChgCon + %trim(Inlib) + '/' +
C                              %trim(InDtaArea) + ') VALUE(' +
C                              %subst(OData:1:Size) + ')'
C                   Endif
C
C      ' '          Checkr     Cmd               Len
C                   z-add      Len               CmdLen
C                   call       'QCMDEXC'
C                   parm                         Cmd
C                   parm                         CmdLen
C                   Endsr
```

Figure 5.1: This program edits a data area using the Retrieve Data Area (QWCRDTAA) API (part 6 of 6).

```
AANO1NO2NO3T.Name++++++RLen++TDpBLinPosFunctions+++++++++++++++++++++++
A                                        DSPSIZ(24 80 *DS3)
A                                        CF03
A                                        CF12
A           R SFLRCD                     SFL
A             DATA        50A  B  9 13
A             OUTPOS       4A  O  9  6DSPATR(HI)
A           R SFLCTL                     SFLCTL(SFLRCD)
A                                        SFLSIZ(0024)
A                                        SFLPAG(0012)
A                                        OVERLAY
A    21                                  SFLDSP
A                                        SFLDSPCTL
A                                      1 29'Edit data area information'
A                                      3  2'Data area name . . . . . . . .:
A             INDTAAREA   10A  O  3 34
A             INLIB       10A  O  4 35
A                                      8 13'....5...10...15...20...25...30.
A                                          5...40...45...50'
A                                        DSPATR(HI)
A                                      7 14'Value'
A                                      8  4'Offset'
A                                      3 48'Type:'
A                                      4 48'Length:'
A             OUTTYP      10A  O  3 56
A             OUTLEN       4S 00  4 56
```

Figure 5.2: The display file for the Edit Data Area program in Figure 5.1 produces the screen shown in Figure 5.3 (part 1 of 2).

```
A                                    4  3'Library . . . . . . . . . . .:'
A              OUTDEC         2Y 00  4 61EDTCDE(Z)
A          R FORMAT1
A                                   23  4'F3=Exit'    COLOR(BLU)
A                                   23 18'F12=Previous'  COLOR(BLU)
```

Figure 5.2: The display file for the Edit Data Area program in Figure 5.1 produces the screen shown in Figure 5.3 (part 2 of 2).

```
                        Edit data area information

       Data area name . . . . . . . .: RONTEST      Type:   *CHAR
         Library . . . . . . . . . . .:  RON        Length: 0130


                    Value
         Offset   ....5...10...15...20...25...30...35...40...45...50
           0001   DDDDSDFKSDFLKDJSFLKJDFS456789012345678901234567890
           0051   12345678901234567890123456789012345678901234567890
           0101   12345678901234567890123456789X




       F3=Exit      F12=Previous
```

Figure 5.3: This sample output from the Edit Data Area program allows the user to edit information in a data area.

The Edit Data Area program accepts two parameters: the name of the data area and the library where it resides. The program passes the two input parameters to QWCRDTAA. Table 5.1 describes the parameters for QWCRDTAA. This is an easy API to use, as it only needs five parameters, plus the obligatory standard error data structure.

The first parameter is the name of the receiver variable to hold the output from the API. Parameter 2 is the length of the receiver variable named in parameter 1. The third parameter is the qualified name of the data area. A qualified name is the name of an object, directly followed by the library name where the object resides. Parameter 4 is the starting position within the data area to begin retrieving data. Using -1 for this parameter tells the API to retrieve all the data in the data area, from the beginning. Last, but not least, parameter 5 is the length of the data to retrieve.

Parameter 5 can be used in conjunction with parameter 4 to substring out part of the data from the data area. The example specifies 32 KB, which is roughly the maximum size of a variable field. We did this because we are using the (previously covered) technique of double-calling the API to determine the true size of the variable. The API is called the first time using 32 KB as the number-of-bytes to return parameter, specifying 8 bytes as the length of the receiver. After the first call of the API, the first field in the receiver variable (BYTESPOSS) will contain the number of bytes that could have been returned by the API. Once the length is established, the ALLOC command is used to allocate storage for that amount and the API is called again, this time specifying the BYTESPOSS field as the size of the receiver variable.

The rest of the program parses through the returned receiver variable in 50-byte increments. There's nothing magical about the number 50, it just fits pretty good on the screen in a subfile record. So each 50-byte "chunk" of data area equals one subfile record. This is pretty easy code if you are dealing with character-type data areas.

If you started at the beginning of this book, you have already covered a large number of APIs. You are probably starting to get a pretty good feel for how most of them work. There is something missing in this one, however. Did you spot it? Did you notice that no parameter specifies a record format? Most "retrieve" APIs have a parameter that describes the data to be returned. In this case, the parameter is omitted because there is only one possible format.

The receiver variable definition in Table 5.1 shows the format of the returned data. The first two fields are the "standard bytes returned" and "total bytes possible" fields common to most retrieve APIs. The third field is the type of data area you are dealing with, while the fourth field is the length of the data area. The next field is the number of decimal positions, used when dealing with a decimal data area. If you total the lengths of all of these fields, you get 36. The actual data that resides in the data area begins in position 37. So, the beginning of the data is defined in 37 and runs for a length of 2,000 more bytes, which is the maximum length of a data area. We only substring-out the actual length, as given in the fourth field in the receiver variable.

Table 5.1: Retrieve Data Area API (QWCRDTAA) (part 1 of 2)

Parameter	Description						Type	Attribute	Size
1	The receiver variable, which takes the following format:						Output	Char	Varies
		From	To	Description	Attr	Size			
		1	4	Possible bytes to return	Binary	4			
		5	8	Actual number of bytes returned	Binary	4			
		9	18	Type of data area	Char	10			
		19	28	Library name	Char	10			
		29	32	Length of data area	Binary	4			
		33	36	Number of decimal positions	Binary	4			
		37	??	Information stored in data area	Char	Varies			
2	The length of the receiver variable specified in parameter 1.						Input	Binary	4

Table 5.1: Retrieve Data Area API (QWCRDTAA) (part 2 of 2)				
Parameter	Description	Type	Attribute	Size
3	The qualified data area name, where the first 10 bytes of data are the area name, and the second are the library name. There are three special name values: • *LDA—The local data area. • *GDA—The group data area. • *PDA—The program's initialization-parameter data area. There are two special library values: • *LIBL—The library list. • *CURLIB—The job's current library.	Input	Char	20
4	The starting position, with the data area to begin retrieving data. A negative means retrieve all data from the data area. There is a 2,000-byte maximum.	Input	Binary	4
5	The length of data to retrieve, which cannot be zero. This length, plus the starting position minus one cannot exceed the actual length of the data area.	Input	Binary	4
6	The standard error data structure.	I/O	Char	Varies

There is a slight problem with numeric data areas, though. The data returned in the receiver variable is packed data, in a character variable. The data must be unpacked to make it useable. Since the actual size of the data varies from data area to data area, however, you can't code a simple move to a proper sized packed field, even though that is what you need to do to unpack the data. We needed to get a little creative when unpacking the decimal data. We defined a data structure with 15 subfields. Each subfield is defined as packed and increases in size by 1 byte over the previous definition. All we have to do is move the packed data into the inclusive data structure, determine the actual size of the data, and then move the correctly sized packed field definition to the character output field.

In looking through the code, you might see something else that looks a little unusual. The subfile is defined so that each subfile record is 50 bytes long and underlined. The underlined field should not extend past the actual end of the data, but the length of every data area will not always be divisible by 50. For purely aesthetic reasons, therefore, the "protect" and "non-display" control characters are concatenated to the end of the last subfile record.

As you can see, this program is both simple and functional. It does not perform any edits on the data entered to ensure validity of data types. In other words, if you entered alphabetic characters into a numeric data area, the program would blow up. You should probably add your own edit routines.

List Jobs

As you are probably aware, the job is the basic unit of work on the AS/400. Everything on the AS/400 happens within a job. To get a clear picture of everything that is happening on your system, you need to look at the jobs that your system is processing. A lot of commands allow you to do this interactively. To analyze this data programmatically, however, you need an API. The API for this particular job, the List Jobs API (QUSLJOBS), provides information about every job on the system.

The List Jobs API is a little different from most of other "retrieve" APIs. It is relatively standard in the way it delivers record format structures into a user space, but if you want more information than the standard record format delivers, it deviates from the standard. You would normally just give an API a different record format name that contained more information. With this API, you do specify another record format name to indicate that you want more data, but this API really only has one record format. To get more information than the format contains, it shifts into using keys to indicate the information you want.

The reason this API uses keyed access is speed. There are usually a tremendous number of jobs running on any given system, and there are hundreds of pieces of information about each job that you might be interested in. To gather all information about every job on the system could potentially eat up a great deal of system resources. So, the API gives you the basic information in a record layout format, and then will retrieve any bit of information that you request, but you must supply the appropriate key. This gets a little tedious when you have to request each bit of information by specifying the key that has been assigned to represent that bit of information. On the other hand, this provides much more flexibility because you can pick and choose the information you want returned.

As we have said before, flexibility breeds complexity. If you want a lot of information, you have to specify a lot of keys.

The source code for the display jobs program is shown in Figure 5.4, and the display in Figure 5.5. A sample of the program is shown in Figure 5.6. Take a couple of minutes to look through the source code for the program.

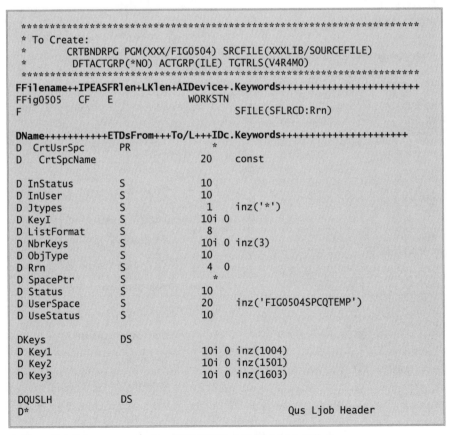

```
 ********************************************************************
 * To Create:
 *      CRTBNDRPG PGM(XXX/FIG0504) SRCFILE(XXXLIB/SOURCEFILE)
 *      DFTACTGRP(*NO) ACTGRP(ILE) TGTRLS(V4R4M0)
 ********************************************************************
FFilename++IPEASFRlen+LKlen+AIDevice+.Keywords+++++++++++++++++++++++
FFig0505   CF   E           WORKSTN
F                                     SFILE(SFLRCD:Rrn)

DName+++++++++++ETDsFrom+++To/L+++IDc.Keywords+++++++++++++++++++++++
D  CrtUsrSpc     PR                  *
D    CrtSpcName               20      const

D InStatus       S            10
D InUser         S            10
D Jtypes         S             1      inz('*')
D KeyI           S            10i 0
D ListFormat     S             8
D NbrKeys        S            10i 0 inz(3)
D ObjType        S            10
D Rrn            S             4 0
D SpacePtr       S                 *
D Status         S            10
D UserSpace      S            20      inz('FIG0504SPCQTEMP')
D UseStatus      S            10

DKeys            DS
D Key1                        10i 0 inz(1004)
D Key2                        10i 0 inz(1501)
D Key3                        10i 0 inz(1603)

DQUSLH           DS
D*                                     Qus Ljob Header
```

Figure 5.4: This program employs QUSLJOBS to list jobs (part 1 of 6).

145

```
D QUSJN00                         1     10        inz('*ALL')
D*                                                Job Name
D QUSUN00                        11     20        inz('*ALL')
D*                                                User Name
D QUSJNBR00                      21     26        inz('*ALL')
D*                                                Job Number
DQUSLKF           DS
D*                                                Qus Ljob Key Fields
D QUSLFIR                         1      4B 0
D*                                                Length Field Info Rtnd
D QUSKF                           5      8B 0
D*                                                Key Field
D QUSTOD                          9      9
D*                                                Type Of Data
D QUSERVED17                     10     12
D*                                                Reserved
D QUSLD00                        13     16B 0
D*                                                Length Data
D*QUSDATA06                      17     17
D*
D*                                      Varying length
D*QUSERVED17                     18     18
D*
D*                                      Varying length

DQUSL020001      DS                               based(ListPoint)
D*                                                Qus JOBL0200
D QUSJNU00                        1     10
D*                                                Job Name Used
D QUSUNU00                       11     20
D*                                                User Name Used
D QUSJNBRU00                     21     26
D*                                                Job Number Used
D QUSIJI00                       27     42
D*                                                Internal Job Id
D QUSTATUS01                     43     52
D*                                                Status
D QUSJT01                        53     53
D*                                                Job Type
D QUSJS00                        54     54
D*                                                Job Subtype
D QUSERVED18                     55     56
D*                                                Reserved
D QUSJIS                         57     57
D*                                                Job Info Status
D QUSRSV205                      58     60
D*                                                Reserved2
D QUSNBRFR                       61     64B 0
D*                                                Number Fields Rtnd
d KeyData                        65    180
```

Figure 5.4: This program employs QUSLJOBS to list jobs (part 2 of 6).

```
D QUSKFI          DS             16
D   QUSLFIR01                    9B 0 OVERLAY(QUSKFI:00001)
D   QUSKF00                      9B 0 OVERLAY(QUSKFI:00005)
D   QUSTOD01                     1    OVERLAY(QUSKFI:00009)
D   QUSERVED33                   3    OVERLAY(QUSKFI:00010)
D   QUSLD01                      9B 0 OVERLAY(QUSKFI:00013)
D*
D*                                    Varying length
DQUSH0300         DS                  Based(GenDsPoint)
D*                                    Qus Generic Header 0300
D QUSUA00                1    64
D*                                    User Area
D QUSSGH00              65    68B 0
D*                                    Size Generic Header
D QUSSRL00              69    72
D*                                    Structure Release Level
D QUSFN00               73    80
D*                                    Format Name
D QUSAU00               81    90
D*                                    API Used
D QUSDTC00              91   103
D*                                    Date Time Created
D QUSIS00              104   104
D*                                    Information Status
D QUSSUS00             105   108B 0
D*                                    Size User Space
D QUSOIP00             109   112B 0
D*                                    Offset Input Parameter
D QUSSIP00             113   116B 0
D*                                    Size Input Parameter
D QUSOHS00             117   120B 0
D*                                    Offset Header Section
D QUSSHS00             121   124B 0
D*                                    Size Header Section
D QUSOLD00             125   128B 0
D*                                    Offset List Data
D QUSSLD00             129   132B 0
D*                                    Size List Data
D QUSNBRLE00           133   136B 0
D*                                    Number List Entries
D QUSSEE00             137   140B 0
D*                                    Size Each Entry
D QUSSIDLE00           141   144B 0
D*                                    CCSID List Ent
D QUSCID00             145   146
D*                                    Country ID
D QUSLID00             147   149
D*                                    Language ID
D QUSSLI00             150   150
D*                                    Subset List Indicator
D QUSRSV1              151   192
```

Figure 5.4: This program employs QUSLJOBS to list jobs (part 3 of 6).

```
D*                                              Reserved 1
D QUSEPN             193     448
D*                                              Entry Point Name
D QUSRSV2            449     576
D*                                              Reserved 2

 * Standard Error Code data structure
DQUSEC            DS           116
D QUSBPRV               1      4B 0              inz(116)
D QUSBAVL               5      8B 0

CLON01Factor1+++++++Opcode&ExtFactor2+++++++Result++++++++Len++D+HiLoEq
C      *entry        Plist
C                    parm                       InUser
C                    parm                       InStatus

C                    eval       ScUser = '*ALL'
C                    eval       ScStat = '*ALL'

C                    If         %parms >= 1
C                    eval       QusUN00 = Inuser
C                    eval       ScUser = Inuser
C                    Endif

C                    If         %parms >= 2
C                    eval       UseStatus = InStatus
C                    eval       ScStat = InStatus
C                    Endif

 *  Create user space for file list information
C                    Eval       SpacePtr = CrtUsrSpc(UserSpace)
 *
 *  List jobs to user space
C                    Call       'QUSLJOB'
C                    Parm                       UserSpace
C                    Parm       'JOBL0200'      ListFormat
C                    Parm                       QusLH
C                    Parm       '*ALL'          Status
C                    Parm                       QusEc
C                    Parm                       Jtypes
C                    Parm                       NbrKeys
C                    Parm                       Keys

 *  Load the general data structure
C                    Eval       GenDsPoint = SpacePtr

 *  If the list API was complete or partially complete
C                    if         QuSIS00 = 'C' OR
C                               QuSIS00 = 'P'
 *  Load the list data structure
C                    Eval       ListPoint = GenDsPoint + QusOLD00
```

Figure 5.4: This program employs QUSLJOBS to list jobs (part 4 of 6).

```
C                       Do         QusNbrLE00

C                       If         UseStatus = *blanks OR
C                                  UseStatus = Qustatus01
C                       Move       QusJnU00      SfName
C                       Move       QusUnU00      SfUser
C                       Movel      Qustatus01    SfStatus

 * Process keys returned
C                       Eval       KeyI = 1
C                       Do         QusNbrFr
C                       Eval       QusKFI = %subst(KeyData:KeyI:16)

C                       Select
 * Jobq info
C                       When       QusKf00 = 1004
C                       Eval       SfJobq = %subst(KeyData:KeyI+16:QusLd01)
 * Qutput queue info
C                       When       QusKf00 = 1501
C                       Eval       SfOutq = %subst(KeyData:KeyI+16:QusLd01)
 * Printer device
C                       When       QusKf00 = 1603
C                       Eval       SfPrtD = %subst(KeyData:KeyI+16:QusLd01)
C                       Endsl

C                       Eval       KeyI = KeyI + QusLFir01
C                       Enddo

C                       Eval       Rrn = Rrn + 1
C                       Write      SflRcd
C                       EndIF

C                       Eval       ListPoint = ListPoint + QusSEE00
C                       EndDo
C                       EndIf

C                       If         Rrn > 0
C                       Eval       *in21 = *on
C                       Endif

C                       Eval       *in24 = *on
C                       Write      Format1
C                       Exfmt      SflCtl
C                       Eval       *inlr = *on

 *
 *  Procedure to create extendable user space, return pointer to it.
 *
PName+++++++++++..T.................Keywords+++++++++++++++++++++++++++
P  CrtUsrSpc      B                 export
```

Figure 5.4: This program employs QUSLJOBS to list jobs (part 5 of 6).

```
DName++++++++++++ETDsFrom+++To/L+++IDc.Keywords++++++++++++++++++++++++
D CrtUsrSpc       PI                  *
D   CrtSpcName                       20      const

 * Local Variables
D PasSpcName      DS                 20
D  SLib                       11     20
D ChgAttrDs       DS                 13
D  NumberAttr                         9B 0 inz(1)
D  KeyAttr                            9B 0 inz(3)
D  DataSize                           9B 0 inz(1)
D  AttrData                            1    inz('1')
D ListPtr         S                   *
D SpaceAttr       S                  10      inz
D SpaceAuth       S                  10      INZ('*CHANGE')
D SpaceLen        S                   9B 0 INZ(4096)
D SpaceReplc      S                  10      INZ('*YES')
D SpaceText       S                  50
D SpaceValue      S                   1

CL0N01Factor1+++++++Opcode&ExtFactor2+++++++Result++++++++Len++D+HiLoEq
 * Create the user space
C                    move      CrtSpcName    PasSpcName
C                    CALL      'QUSCRTUS'
C                    PARM                    PasSpcName
C                    PARM                    SpaceAttr
C                    PARM                    SpaceLen
C                    PARM                    SpaceValue
C                    PARM                    SpaceAuth
C                    PARM                    SpaceText
C                    PARM      '*YES'        SpaceReplc
C                    PARM                    QusEc
 * Get pointer to user space
C                    CALL      'QUSPTRUS'
C                    PARM                    PasSpcName
C                    PARM                    ListPtr
 * Change user space to be extendable
C                    CALL      'QUSCUSAT'
C                    PARM                    Slib
C                    PARM                    PasSpcName
C                    PARM                    ChgAttrDs
C                    PARM                    QusEc

C                    return    ListPtr

PName+++++++++++..T..................Keywords++++++++++++++++++++++++++
P CrtUsrSpc       E
```

Figure 5.4: This program employs QUSLJOBS to list jobs (part 6 of 6).

```
AAN01N02N03T.Name++++++RLen++TDpBLinPosFunctions++++++++++++++++++++++++
A                                       DSPSIZ(24 80 *DS3)
A                                       CF03 CF12
A         R SFLRCD                      SFL
A           SFNAME      10A  0  6  2
A           SFUSER      10A  0  6 13
A           SFSTATUS     4A  0  6 24
A           SFJOBQ      20   0  6 29
A           SFOUTQ      20   0  6 50
A           SFPRTD      10   0  6 71
A         R SFLCTL                      SFLCTL(SFLRCD)
A                                       SFLSIZ(0032) SFLPAG(0016)
A                                       OVERLAY
A  21                                   SFLDSP
A                                       SFLDSPCTL
A  24                                   SFLEND(*MORE)
A                                     1 26'List Jobs Information'
A                                       DSPATR(HI)
A                                     5  2'Job Name'
A                                       DSPATR(HI)
A                                     5 13'User'
A                                       DSPATR(HI)
A                                     5 24'Sts'
A                                       DSPATR(HI)
A                                     5 29'Job queue'
A                                       DSPATR(HI)
A                                     5 50'Output queue'
A                                       DSPATR(HI)
A                                     5 71'Printer'
A                                       DSPATR(HI)
A                                     1 62'Selection criteria:'
A                                     2 63'Status.'
A           SCSTAT      10   0  2 71
A                                     3 63'User.'
A           SCUSER      10   0  3 71
A         R FORMAT1
A                                    23  4'F3=Exit'    COLOR(BLU)
A                                    23 18'F12=Previous'  COLOR(BLU)
```

Figure 5.5: The DDS for listing jobs with the QUSLJOBS program produces the screen shown in Figure 5.6 .

The program in Figure 5.4 accepts two parameters: user and status. This lets you display jobs only for a given user, or jobs only at a certain status. If you wanted to view jobs for user *JOE*, for example, you would specify that name in parameter 1. If you wanted only jobs that were currently on a job queue, you would specify *JOBQ for the second parameter. The valid entries for this parameter are shown in Table 5.2 in the STATUS parameter.

```
                    List Jobs Information              Selection criteria:
                                                       Status.  *ALL
                                                       User.    *ALL

  Job Name    User      Sts  Job queue           Output queue        Printer
  QZSCSRVS    QUSER     *ACT                      *DEV                NOPRINT
  JWALKXXGO   JDOUG     *ACT                      *DEV                NOPRINT
  JWALKXXGO   JDOUG     *ACT                      *DEV                NOPRINT
  QPADEV0075  KITT      *ACT                      *DEV                NOPRINT
  SENDMBS     QPGMR     *OUT  QBATCH      QGPL    *DEV                NOPRINT
  SENDMED     QPGMR     *OUT  QBATCH      QGPL    *DEV                NOPRINT
  MCR0448     LEONARD   *OUT  QBATCH      QGPL    MC2P1      QGPL     USRPRF
  QZSCSRVS    QUSER     *ACT                      *DEV                USRPRF
  QNPSERVS    QUSER     *ACT                      *DEV                USRPRF
  MAINTENEW   JOHN      *OUT  QBATCH      QGPL    *DEV                NOPRINT
  SENDSSI     QPGMR     *OUT  QBATCH      QGPL    *DEV                NOPRINT
  C51PMTANAL  TOM       *OUT  QBATCH      QGPL    *DEV                NOPRINT
  COLLECTOR   KEN       *OUT  QBATCH2     QGPL    AWOUTQ     SEACOL   VPRTO1
  MCR0806     LEONARD   *OUT  QBATCH      QGPL    MC2P1      QGPL     USRPRF
  QDFTJOBD    TOM       *OUT  QINTER      QGPL    *DEV                NOPRINT
  QPWFSERVSO  QUSER     *ACT                      *DEV                NOPRINT
                                                                     More...

    F3=Exit         F12=Previous
```

Figure 5.6: Employing QUSLJOBS creates a list of jobs.

The first thing the program does is load these parameters into variables that will be passed as parameters to the API. It then executes the procedure to create a user space that the list API can use. (See Chapter 1 for more information about user spaces.)

Next, the program executes the List Jobs (QUSLJOBS) API. The program specifies eight parameters with this API. Parameter 1 is the name of the user space just created. Parameter 2 is the name of the API-supplied record format that describes the type of information you want. If you specify JOBL0100, for example, you will only get the general information. This example specifies JOBL0200, which means you want the general information and will supply keys for the additional information you want. This key information is supplied in the optional parameter group 2.

Table 5.2: List Jobs API (QUSLJOBS)				
Parameter	Description	Type	Attribute	Size
1	The name and library of the user space into which the API will return the list of jobs.	Input	Char	20
2	The record format name that describes the format of the data that will be returned. There are two possible values: JOBL0100—Basic information. JOBL0200—Basic information plus key fields.	Input	Char	8
3	The qualified job name or special value, as follows:<table><tr><td>Parameter</td><td>Value</td></tr><tr><td>Job name</td><td>*CURRENT or *ALL</td></tr><tr><td>Job user</td><td>*CURRENT or *ALL</td></tr><tr><td>Job number</td><td>ALL</td></tr></table>	Input	Char	26
4	The status filter. Only jobs that meet the filter criteria will be included in the list. There are four possible filter values: • *ALL—All jobs, regardless of status. • *ACTIVE—Only active jobs, including group jobs and disconnected jobs. • *JOBQ—Jobs currently on a job queue. • *OUTQ—Jobs that have finished, but still have output on an output queue.	Input	Char	10

Parameter 3 is the job name. This parameter lets you filter the information that will be returned by an individual job or user. This parameter is a three-field data structure consisting of the job name, user, and job number. All three subfields accept *ALL to indicate that you want all jobs. The user part of this parameter holds the second parameter passed to the program.

Parameter 4 is a filter that allows for filtering by job status. Parameter 5 is the optional standard error data structure. The next three parameters form the second optional parameter group. (See Chapter 1 if you are unfamiliar with the concept.)

Parameter 6 is another filter, by job type. Passing an asterisk (*) indicates that you want all job types. The next two parameters work together. Parameter 7 indicates the number of keys that are passed in parameter 8. Parameter 8 is a data structure that contains 4-byte binary fields that, in turn, contain the key value representing the data you want returned.

Table 5.3 shows a selection of interesting key values. There are many more keys than those listed here. Refer to IBM's *Work Management API* manual for a complete list.

Table 5.3: Selected Key Values for QUSLJOBS

Key	Description	Attribute	Size
101	The active job status.	Char	4
305	The current user profile.	Char	10
306	The completion status.	Char	1
401	The date and time when the job became active.	Char	13
402	The date and time when the job entered the system.	Char	13
403	The date and time when the job is scheduled to run.	Char	8
404	The date and time when the job was put on this job queue.	Char	8
411	The device name.	Char	10
502	The end status.	Char	1
601	The function name.	Char	10
602	The function type.	Char	1
701	The signed-on job.	Char	1
1001	The job's accounting code.	Char	15
1004	The job's queue name.	Char	10
1012	The job's user identity.	Char	10
1013	The job's user identity setting.	Char	1
1501	The output queue name.	Char	20
1603	The printer device name.	Char	10
1903	The status of the job on the job queue.	Char	10
1904	The submitter's job name.	Char	26
1906	The subsystem description name.	Char	20

After executing the API, the program walks through the user space, processing each list entry. (See chapter 2 for more information on this type of API.) This information is used in the General Header data structure to get each list entry.

Each list entry contains the basic information indicated in record type JOBL0200. Remember that the definitions for these record formats may be found in library QSYSINC, as discussed in chapter 1. The basic information found in record type JOBL0200 is followed by X number of key structures, where X represents the number of keys indicated in parameter 7 when the API was called. In other words, if you asked for three keys (as in this example), you should expect to find three key structures here. One large field, **KeyData**, is defined, which will be parsed into key structures.

Since each key can represent a different type of information, each of the structures could differ in length. However, to process each key structure, you must know its length. Therefore, the first field within the key structure happens to be the length of the structure. This field can be added to an index to get to the next key structure. The next field in each structure is another 4-byte binary field containing the key for the structure. Next, a 1-byte field represents the data type, followed by a 3-byte reserved field used to maintain the appearance of a 4-byte boundary. The next field is very important in processing the structure. It is the length of the key data that immediately follows.

Retrieve Job Information

You just learned how to generate a list of jobs on the system. However, what if you are interested in information about a particular job on the system? That is when you will need the Retrieve Job Information (QUSRJOBI) API. This API returns just about everything there is to know about a job. Ten different record formats describe the data that can be returned from this API! Table 5.4 lists all possible record formats that can be used with QUSRJOBI. Since each record format has different performance implications, the table includes notes about the relative speed of the formats.

Table 5.4: Record Format Names for QUSRJOBI

Format	Description
JOBI0100	Basic performance information. Since it returns a minimal amount of information, this is faster than the other formats that also return job performance information.
JOBI0150	Basic performance plus. This format is slower than JOBI0100 but faster than JOBI0200.
JOBI0200	Maximum performance information. This is the slowest of the three formats that return performance information. It is similar to the Work Active Job.
JOBI0300	Information about the job queue and the submitter's job.
JOBI0400	Job attribute types.
JOBI0500	Message logging information.
JOBI0600	Information about active jobs. It supplements JOBI0400, but is slower.
JOBI0700	Library list information about an active job.
JOBI0800	Signal information for an active job.
JOBI0900	SQL open cursor information for an active job

In spite of the enormous amount of information that the Retrieve Job Information API deals with, it is not very difficult to use. The sample program in Figure 5.7 runs the Retrieve Job Information API. Since this program was intended to demonstrate how to use the API to retrieve information about a job, it doesn't really do anything with the information except display it to the screen. You might find some interesting uses for this sample code—using it as a template—should the right application arise.

```
DName++++++++++ETDsFrom+++To/L+++IDc.Keywords+++++++++++++++++++++++
DQUSI020000        DS
D*                                              Qwc JOBI0200
D QUSBR01            1      4B 0
D*                                              Bytes Return
D QUSBA01            5      8B 0
D*                                              Bytes Avail
D QUSJN03            9     18
D*                                              Job Name
D QUSUN03           19     28
D*                                              User Name
```

Figure 5.7: This program uses the Retrieve Job Information (QUSRJOBI) API (part 1 of 3).

156

```
D QUSJNBR03                  29    34
D*                                          Job Number
D QUSIJID01                  35    50
D*                                          Int Job ID
D QUSJS05                    51    60
D*                                          Job Status
D QUSJT04                    61    61
D*                                          Job Type
D QUSJS06                    62    62
D*                                          Job Subtype
D QUSSN                      63    72
D*                                          Subsys Name
D QUSRP01                    73    76B 0
D*                                          Run Priority
D QUSSPID00                  77    80B 0
D*                                          System Pool ID
D QUSCPUU00                  81    84B 0
D*                                          CPU Used
D QUSAIOR                    85    88B 0
D*                                          Aux IO Request
D QUSIT                      89    92B 0
D*                                          Interact Trans
D QUSRT                      93    96B 0
D*                                          Response Time
D QUSFT                      97    97
D*                                          Function Type
D QUSFN15                    98   107
D*                                          Function Name
D QUSAJS                    108   111
D*                                          Active Job Stat
D QUSNDBLW                  112   115B 0
D*                                          Num DBase Lock Wts
D QUSNIMLW                  116   119B 0
D*                                          Num Internal Mch Lck Wts
D QUSNDBLW00                120   123B 0
D*                                          Num Non DBase Lock Wts
D QUSTDBLW                  124   127B 0
D*                                          Wait Time DBase Lock Wts
D QUSTIMLW                  128   131B 0
D*                                          Wait Time Internal Mch L
D QUSNDBLW01                132   135B 0
D*                                          Wait Time Non DBase Lock
D QUSERVED45                136   136
D*                                          Reserved
D QUSCSPID                  137   140B 0
D*                                          Current System Pool ID
D QUSTC01                   141   144B 0
D*                                          Thread Count
```

Figure 5.7: This program uses the Retrieve Job Information (QUSRJOBI) API (part 2 of 3).

```
DQUSEC              DS             116    inz
D QUSBPRV                   1        4B 0 inz(116)
D QUSBAVL                   5        8B 0 inz(0)
D QUSEI                     9       15
D QUSERVED                 16       16
D QUSED01                  17      116

D FormatName        S               8    Inz('JOBI0200')
D InJobName         S              26
D IntJobName        S              16
D JobName           S              26    Inz('*')
D Outcount          S               5 0
D ReceiveLen        S              10i 0 Inz(187)

CLON01Factor1+++++++Opcode&ExtFactor2+++++++Result++++++++Len++D+HiLoEq
C     *entry        Plist
C                   Parm                        InJobName
C                   If        %parms > 0
C                   Eval      JobName = InJobName
C                   Endif

 * Call the API to get the information you want
C                   Call      'QUSRJOBI'
C                   Parm                        QusI020000
C                   Parm                        ReceiveLen
C                   Parm                        FormatName
C                   Parm                        JobName
C                   Parm                        IntJobName
C                   Parm                        QusEc

 * Display the subsystem name
c     QusSN         dsply
 * Display the interactive transaction count
c                   z-add     QusIT           Outcount
c     Outcount      dsply

c                   Eval      *inlr = *on
```

Figure 5.7: This program uses the Retrieve Job Information (QUSRJOBI) API (part 3 of 3).

The program accepts a single parameter, and it's optional. If you want, you can pass in the qualified name of a job, and that job name will be passed along to the API. If you omit this optional parameter, the program defaults to the current job name. Initializing the field JOBNAME to an asterisk (*) tells the system to use the current job name, unless you tell the program otherwise (by passing the optional parameter). The program then calls the API using six parameters, listed in Table 5.5.

Parameter 1 is the name of the receiver variable. The second parameter defines the size of the first. (Is this starting to sound familiar? By now, it should.) Parameter 3 is the name of the record format that describes how the data will be returned, as defined in Table 5.4. The fourth parameter is the name of the job. Parameter 5 is another way to indicate the name of the job. This is called an *internal job name*, and when utilized, enables QUSRJOBI to run faster. The internal job name may be retrieved by using other APIs (such as QUSLJOB) and then passed on to QUSRJOBI. Parameter 6 is the standard error-handling data structure that has been described many times before.

Table 5.5: Parameters for QUSRJOBI				
Parameter	**Description**	**Type**	**Attribute**	**Size**
1	The receiver variable.	Output	Char	Varies
2	The receiver length.	Input	Binary	4
3	The format name, described in Table 5.4.	Input	Char	8
4	The job name, as follows: • Asterisk (*)—The current job. • *INT—Use the internal job name specified in parameter 5.	Input	Char	26
5	The internal job name, which must be blank if the job name parameter is not *INT. The API performs faster using the internal job name.	Input	Char	16
Optional Parameter Group 1				
6	The standard error data structure.	I/O	Char	Varies

Once the program calls the Retrieve Job Information API, the receiver variable will contain the requested data. This is verified using the DSPLY opcode to show a couple of the fields on the screen. The data structure formats (in this case, QUSIO20000) can be found in member QUSRJOBI, in file QRPGLESRC, in library QSYSINC. By taking advantage of the source found in library QSYSINC, we were able to put this program together in about 20 minutes!

Retrieve Job Status API

Sometimes, all you want to know about a job is where it went. Is the job still on the job queue, or is it running? Is it active, or is it waiting on a message? Did it finish? If so, what happened to the spooled output? These are all questions that could be answered if there were a way to easily retrieve the current status of the job. Surely, you know where we are going with this. APIs to the rescue once again!

The Retrieve Job Information (QUSRJOBI) API returns the status of the job, along with anything else you could possibly want to know about a job. Because of the vast amount of information it can return, though, it can be somewhat slow. Because the nature of a job status is to change, you need a lightning-quick API to retrieve its current status. The Retrieve Job Status (QWCRJBST) API is the perfect tool for the job (and yes, the pun was intended).

Imagine you were to use QUSRJOBI to bring a list of jobs to the screen and then allow the user to take some action based on the current status of the job. You would need to ensure that the current status of the job was still as it was when the list was created. QWCRJBST was created for just such a purpose. It's sole reason for existence is to retrieve a single bit of information about a job as fast as possible. It fulfills that mission admirably, indeed.

Figure 5.8 shows the sample code required to use QWCRJBST. It's a very small, simple program because that's the nature of this API. The program accepts one parameter: the internal job name of the job whose status you are inquiring about. This internal job name was returned from the List Job (QUSLJOBS)s API. The program then calls the Retrieve Job Status (QWCRJBST) API using five parameters. The details for the parameters are given in Table 5.6.

```
DName++++++++++++ETDsFrom+++To/L+++IDc.Keywords+++++++++++++++++++++++
DQwcrDs            DS
D BytesRtn                  1      4B 0
D*                                           Bytes Return
D BytesAvl                  5      8B 0
```

Figure 5.8: Using five parameters, this program calls the Retrieve Job Status (QWCRJBST) API (part 1 of 2).

```
D*                                        Bytes Avail
D JobStatus                9     18
D*                                        Job Status
D IntJobId                19     34
D*                                        Internal job id
D FullJobNam             35     60
D*                                        Full job name

DQUSEC           DS             116   inz
D QUSBPRV                 1      4B 0 inz(116)
D QUSBAVL                 5      8B 0 inz(0)
D QUSEI                   9     15
D QUSERVED               16     16
D QUSED01                17    116

D FormatName     S              8     Inz('JOBS0200')
D IntJobName     S             16
D ReceiveLen     S             10i 0 Inz(60)

CLON01Factor1+++++++Opcode&ExtFactor2+++++++Result+++++++Len++D+HiLoEq
C       *entry          Plist
C                       Parm                      IntJobName

 * Call the API to get the information you want
C                       Call      'QWCRJBST'
C                       Parm                      QwcrDs
C                       Parm                      ReceiveLen
C                       Parm                      IntJobName
C                       Parm                      FormatName
C                       Parm                      QusEc

 * Display the job status
C       JobStatus       dsply

C                       Eval      *inlr = *on
```

Figure 5.8: Using five parameters, this program calls the Retrieve Job Status (QWCRJBST) API (part 1 of 2).

As with all retrieve-type APIs, the first parameter is the receiver variable, and the second parameter is the length of the first parameter. Parameter 3 is the name of the job you are interested in, which was retrieved in the previous step.

Parameter 4 is the format name. Unlike other retrieve APIs, parameter 4 is not a record format name that describes the format of the data being returned. Remember, this API has only one function: to return the current status of the job. There is only one format needed for the data, so a record format code is not needed. Parameter 4 is actually a code that describes parameter 3, the job name parameter. JOBS0200 is used in the example, which means parameter 3 is the 16-byte internal name of the job. If you were to use JOBS0100, it would indicate that parameter 3 is the qualified 26-byte name of the job. The last parameter is the standard error-handling data structure.

After calling the API, the receiver variable (the data structure **QwcRDS** in the sample program) contains the status of the job in the field aptly named **JobStatus**. The program simply displays it on the screen using the DSPLY opcode. You, however, could do whatever you wanted with the information.

Table 5.6: Parameters for QWCRJBST				
Parameter	Description	Type	Attribute	Size
1	The receiver variable.	Output	Char	Varies
2	The receiver length.	Input	Binary	4
3	The job name, which is either the 26-byte qualified job name or the 16-byte internal job name.	Input	Char	Varies
4	The format name, which has two possible values: • JOBS0100—The qualified job name. • JOBS0200—The internal job name.	Input	Char	8
Optional Parameter Group 1				
6	The standard error data structure.	I/O	Char	Varies

Retrieve Job Queue Information

As the name implies, the Retrieve Job Queue Information (QSPRJOBQ) API returns information about a job queue. For the purposes of this example, the information we are most interested in retrieving is the number of jobs on the job queue.

When would this information be considered important? Well, some applications (our primary one, for instance) have certain job queues that are only used for certain kinds of jobs. You might use a *single-threaded job queue* to process transaction posting and also to print statements. Making this particular job queue single-threaded means only one job can be processed from the job queue at a time. This enables jobs in this queue to be processed sequentially, since it is important that these jobs not run at the same time. Going back to the example earlier in this chapter, we do not want statements to print at the same time a batch of transactions is being posted. On the other hand, there are other multi-threaded job queues, where more than one job should process at a time. These job queues are generally used for low-level batch jobs, like printing reports.

What if you need to know if there are any jobs that have not yet been processed on a particular job queue? Using the previously described example application, what if you were ready to perform a critical function like month-end processing, and you needed to know that there were not any transactions waiting to post? You would need to know if there were any jobs remaining on that specific single-threaded job queue. The Retrieve Job Queue Information (QSPRJOBQ) API will tell you exactly that. The code required to use QSPRJOBQ is shown in Figure 5.9. The parameters for the API are listed in Table 5.7.

```
DName+++++++++++ETDsFrom+++To/L+++IDc.Keywords+++++++++++++++++++++++
DQspQ010000      DS
D*                                        Qsp JOBQ0100
D QSPBRTN00       1      4B 0
D*                                        Bytes Returned
D QSPBAVL00       5      8B 0
D*                                        Bytes Available
D QSPJQN          9      18
D*                                        Job Queue Name
D QSPJQLN        19      28
D*                                        Job Queue Lib Name
D QSPOC01        29      38
D*                                        Operator Controlled
D QSPAC          39      48
D*                                        Authority Check
D QSPNBRJ        49      52B 0
D*                                        Number Jobs
D QSPJQS         53      62
D*                                        Job Queue Status
```

Figure 5.9: This example program uses the Retrieve Job Queue Information (QSPRJOBQ) API (part 1 of 2).

```
D QSPSN                    63      72
D*                                          Subsystem Name
D QSPTD                    73     122
D*                                          Text Description

DQUSEC          DS                116     inz
D QUSBPRV                   1       4B 0 inz(116)
D QUSBAVL                   5       8B 0 inz(0)
D QUSEI                     9      15
D QUSERVED                 16      16
D QUSED01                  17     116

D FormatName    S                   8     inz('JOBQ0100')
D Jobq          s                  10
D JobqLib       s                  20     Inz('            *LIBL      ')
D Library       s                  10
D ReceiveLen    S                  10i 0 Inz(122)
CLON01Factor1+++++++Opcode&ExtFactor2+++++++Result++++++++Len++D+HiLoEq
c     *entry        Plist
c                   Parm                       Jobq
c                   Parm                       Library
c                   movel    Jobq              JobqLib
c                   If       %parms > 1
c                   move     Library           JobqLib
c                   endif

 * Call the API to get the information you want
c                   Call     'QSPRJOBQ'
c                   Parm                       QspQ010000
c                   Parm                       ReceiveLen
c                   Parm                       FormatName
c                   Parm                       JobQLib
c                   Parm                       QusEc

 * Process the data from the API

 * Number of jobs in jobq
c     QSpNbrJ       dsply
 * Subsystems jobq is attached to
c     QSpSN         dsply

c                   Eval     *inlr = *on
```

Figure 5.9: This example program uses the Retrieve Job Queue Information (QSPRJOBQ) API (part 2 of 2).

As you have seen in so many of retrieve-type APIs, the first parameter is the receiver variable, while the second parameter describes the length of the receiver variable. Parameter 3 is the format name JOBQ0100, which is the only format name allowed. Remember that the format name is used to describe the data

164

actually returned to the receiver variable in parameter 1. Parameter 4 is the name and library of the job queue that you want information about. And last but not least, parameter 5 is the standard error-handling data structure. If there is such a thing, the Retrieve Job Queue Information API is a plain-vanilla, retrieve-type API. It is nothing fancy, but it gets the job done.

Parameter	Description	Type	Attribute	Size
Table 5.7: Parameters for QSPRJOBQ				
1	The receiver variable.	Output	Char	Varies
2	The receiver length.	Input	Binary	4
3	The job name, which is either the 26-byte qualified job name or the 16-byte internal job name.	Input	Char	Varies

Retrieve System Values API

System values are, in effect, switches that allow you to control how the system controls the flow of work. In other words, system values allow you to control the AS/400's work management. There are literally hundreds of values that you can change to affect the way work is performed on your system. For example, if you change the Controlling Subsystem (QCTLSBSD) value, you change which subsystems get activated when the machine starts up. You might elect to change the Start Up Program system value, changing which program runs automatically when the system IPLs. Many system values could be covered here, but that is not what this book is about. The Work with System Values (WRKSYSVAL) command does a great job of presenting these values to you interactively.

You have already correctly assumed that we are going to show you how to use APIs to inquire about system values from within your program. The Retrieve System Values (QWCRSVAL) API allows you to retrieve any system value you want, and return that value to your program. The parameters for this API are shown in Table 5.8, and an example program is shown in Figure 5.10. This program makes use of QWCRSVAL to retrieve any system value that you pass to the program.

Take a look at the program in Figure 5.10 to see how it (and the Retrieve System Values API) works. The sample program accepts one mandatory parameter: the name of the system value you want to retrieve. It then calls the API, using this system value as parameter 4 on the call.

Table 5.8: Parameters for QWCRSVAL

Parameter	Description	Type	Attribute	Size
1	The receiver variable.	Output	Char	Varies
2	The receiver length.	Input	Binary	4
3	The job name, which is either the 26-byte qualified job name or the 16-byte internal job name.	Input	Char	Varies

```
DName++++++++++ETDsFrom+++To/L+++IDc.Keywords++++++++++++++++++++++
DQWCRDR00       DS
D*                                         Qwc Rsval Data Rtnd
D QWCNSVR            1      4B 0
D*                                         Number Sys Vals Rtnd
D QWCOSVT            5      8B 0
D*
D Data               1       dim(2096)

D QWCSV00        DS        2096
D   QWCSV01             10      OVERLAY(QWCSV00:00001)
D   QWCTD01              1      OVERLAY(QWCSV00:00011)
D   QWCIS03              1      OVERLAY(QWCSV00:00012)
D   QWCLD01             9B 0    OVERLAY(QWCSV00:00013)
D   QWCDATA01         2080      OVERLAY(QWCSV00:00017)

DQUSEC          DS         116      inz
D QUSBPRV             1      4B 0 inz(116)
D QUSBAVL             5      8B 0 inz(0)
D QUSEI               9      15
D QUSERVED           16      16
D QUSED01            17     116

D LockedCon      c                   'System value was locked'
D MoveInd        S            5  0
D NbrOfVals      S           10i 0 Inz(1)
D OutData        s           50
```

Figure 5.10: The Retrieve System Values (QWCRSVAL) API will retrieve system values (part 1 of 2).

```
D ReceiveLen      S              10i 0 Inz(2104)
D SysValue        s              10

DBinaryCvt        DS
D BinaryNbr                 1     4B 0

CLON01Factor1+++++++Opcode&ExtFactor2+++++++Result++++++++Len++D+HiLoEq
c      *entry      Plist
c                  Parm                          SysValue

 * Call the API to get the information you want
C                  Call     'QWCRSVAL'
C                  Parm                          QwcRdr00
C                  Parm                          ReceiveLen
C                  Parm                          NbrofVals
C                  Parm                          SysValue
C                  Parm                          QusEc

 * Process the data from the API
c                  Eval     MoveInd = Qwcosvt - 7
c                  Movea    Data(MoveInd) QwcSV00

c                  Select
 * Value was locked, couldn't get it
c                  When     QwcIs03 = 'L'
c                  Movel    LockedCon     OutData
 * Character data
c                  When     QwcTd01 = 'C'
c                  Movel    QwcData01     OutData
 * Binary data
c                  When     QwcTd01 = 'B'
c                  Movel    QwcData01     BinaryCvt
c                  Movel    BinaryNbr     OutData

c                  Endsl

 * Display system value
c     OutData      dsply

c                  Eval     *inlr = *on
```

Figure 5.10: The Retrieve System Values (QWCRSVAL) API will retrieve system values (part 2 of 2).

Once again, the first parameter is the receiver variable, and the second parameter describes the length of the receiver variable named in the first. The third parameter is the number of system values you want the API to retrieve. Since this example is only retrieving one system value at a time, a one is passed in the third parameter. The fourth parameter is an array of the names of the system values you want to retrieve. Again, since only one system value is being retrieved, you can pass the name of the system value that was passed to the program. Parameter 5 is the standard error-handling data structure.

Chapter 1 covers the method for calling the API twice to determine the proper length of the receiver variable. However, using this method to get the length of the receiver variable doesn't work for this retrieve API. Instead, you have to calculate the length of the variable in advance. The following formula may be used for calculating the length of the receiver variable:

For each system value, get the length and add 24. Then, add four to the final total.

Since this sample program is designed to be able to retrieve any system value, you don't really know the length of the system value that will be passed into the program. So, just to be safe, take the largest system value that you can find, which is the local path name. The length of the local path name happens to be 2,080 bytes long. Therefore, that is the value used to calculate the length of the variable. It's fine if the receiver variable is a little longer than the actual data returned by the API. After all, what is a little unused memory, among friends? Once the API has been called, the receiver variable will contain the system value you requested. Figure 5.11 shows the general layout of the receiver variable. The actual layout will vary depending on how many system values you request when you call the API.

As shown in Figure 5.11, the first field in the receiver variable is a 4-byte binary field that contains the number of system values returned. This field will be followed by exactly that many 4-byte fields, each containing an offset pointer to a system-value information table. This offset value is relative to the start of the receiver variable. The actual system-data tables immediately follow these fields.

Since each system value can be a different size, it is necessary to wrap some fields that describe the system value around the actual data itself. This combination of system-value descriptive fields and system-value data is called a *system-value information table*. The layout for the system-value information table is shown in Table 5.9.

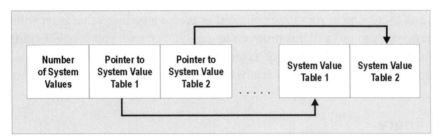

Figure 5.11: The receiver format from Receive System Value (QWCRSVAL) API shows the location of the retrieved system value.

Table 5.9: System-Value Information Table Layout

Description	Attribute	Size
The system value name.	Char	10
The type of data, which is one of three codes: • C—Character data. • B—Binary data. • BLANK—No value is available.	Char	1
The information status code, which is one of the following: • BLANK—The information is available. • L—The information is not available because the value is locked.	Char	1
The length of the data that follows.	Binary	4
The system value data.	Varies	Varies

The only remaining task left for the program is to process the data in the receiver variable, using the pointers to the system value information tables. Since we are only using one system value at a time, this is very easy to do. The only problem to avoid involves dealing with the system values that are stored as binary numbers. Since this program is written as a generic system-value handler, the data fields must be defined as character. When binary data is returned, the data must be translated by moving it to a character data structure with a binary subfield. You can then move the subfield back to a character field to be displayed on the screen.

That's all there is to it. Any time you need to access a system value from within a program, you can just call this program to get it. Of course, you should modify this program to pass the data back as a parameter, or better yet, make a subprocedure out of it, so it will return the system value to the calling program.

Summary

Throughout this book, we try to show that APIs have many practical uses in everyday programming tasks. Work-management APIs can be used to help you work with and mange your system. We encourage you to "hit the books" and find other work-management APIs that might work for you. The information is there. All you need to do is find out how to get it. And as usual, APIs are one of your best resources.

6

MESSAGE APIs

Messages are a way of life on the AS/400. Every time you start, hold, or cancel a job, the system issues a message. While your job is executing, the system sends messages to the job log. If the system needs human intervention (such as pressing the Start button on a printer or loading a tape on a tape drive), the system notifies the interested parties by sending a message.

Another type of message is an application error message, designed to notify program operators of a problem with what they are trying to do. For example, if your program presents the operator with a screen asking for input, and the operator enters erroneous information, your program must issue an error message to tell the bozo (um…operator, that is) that he or she has made a mistake.

There are many ways for your applications to issue error messages. This chapter explores the relevant APIs, including the Send Program Message API and the Remove Program Messages API. The Send Program Message (QMHSNDPM) API lets you send error messages to any job in the job stack. The QMHSNDPM examples in this chapter show you how to "wrap" a subprocedure around the API, and then use it to issue error messages with variable information embedded in them.

If you are going to send error messages to a jobs message queue, you need to be able to delete messages from the queue. You'll see how to use the Remove Program Messages (QMHRMVPM) API for this, once again "wrapped" in a subprocedure.

One very useful byproduct of message handling in your programs is the ability to get the names of the program in your job stack. Why would retrieving the program name be useful? It is a logical question, with a not-so-obvious answer. Retrieving the program name is important when using database trigger programs. If you have worked with trigger programs, you might already know that they have a "blind spot." A trigger program does not tell you what program caused the trigger to fire. This information can be critical, depending on what your trigger was designed to do. You will learn how to use the Receive Program Message (QMHRCVPM) API to retrieve the program name and use a procedure that can get the job done.

Sending Error Messages

The error subfile has been with RPG almost since the beginning (or at least as long as we can remember, which is pretty much the same thing). The concept is rather simple. The user fills in multiple fields on a screen, and presses Enter. The program then validates all of the entries and writes an error message to the job log for each error found. The program redisplays the screen, along with a subfile of all errors that were written to the job log.

This sounds simple enough, but as you know, the devil is in the details. What if you want the erroneous data shown as part of the error message, such as "Customer number 12345 is invalid"? One way to send messages with embedded data is by using the Send Program Message (QMHSNDPM) API. This API sends a message to the job log along with any necessary message data, but it can be cumbersome to use. It has 10 parameters (nine required and one optional), which can seem intimidating at first glance. This is one of those instances where appearances can be deceiving, however. If you glance ahead to the code in Figure 6.3, you will see that the procedures being covered in the next two examples are really very easy to use.

Figure 6.1 shows the code for the **SndErrMsg** procedure. (Note that the terms *subprocedure* and *procedure* are used interchangeably throughout this book.) Take a minute to review the code. As with any procedure, it starts with the procedure interface. The first keyword is the Operational Descriptor, OPDESC. This tells the system that information about the parameters will be accessible to the procedure via the Retrieve Operational Descriptor (CEEDOD) API. You'll see more about this later.

```
HNOMAIN
 *
 *  procedure name:    SndErrMsg
 *
 *  procedure function: Send a program message wrapper 4 QMHSNDPM api.

 * SndErrMsg prototype
DName++++++++++ETDsFrom+++To/L+++IDc.Keywords++++++++++++++++++++++
d SndErrMsg       PR                      opdesc
d PMsgId                          10      const
d PMsgData                     32766      const options(*varsize:*nopass)
d PMsgInType                      10      const options(*nopass)
d PMsgFile                        10      const options(*nopass)
d PMsgLib                         10      const options(*nopass)

PName++++++++++..T.................Keywords++++++++++++++++++++++++
P SndErrMsg       B                       export

DName++++++++++ETDsFrom+++To/L+++IDc.Keywords++++++++++++++++++++++
d SndErrMsg       PI                      opdesc
d MsgInId                         10      const
d MsgInData                    32766      const options(*varsize:*nopass)
d MsgInType                       10      const options(*nopass)
d MsgFile                         10      const options(*nopass)
d MsgLib                          10      const options(*nopass)

d DefMsgFile      s               10      inz('QCPFMSGF  ')
d DefMsgLib       s               10      inz('QSYS      ')
d DefMsgType      s               10      inz('*DIAG     ')
d MsgFileLib      s               20
d MsgData         s                       like(MsgInData)
d MsgDtaLen       s                6  0
d MsgId           s               10
d MsgKey          s                9b 0
d MsgQueue        s               10
d MsgQueNbr       s                9b 0
```

Figure 6.1: The Send Error Message procedure sends messages with embedded message data (part 1 of 3).

```
d  MsgType        s           10
d  Release        s           10

D  ErrorDs        DS                    INZ
D  BytesProv              1     4B 0 inz(116)
D  BytesAval              5     8B 0
D  MessageId              9    15
D  Err###               16    16
D  MessageDta           17   116
  *_____*
  * Prototype for CEEDOD (Retrieve operational descriptor)
  *_____
D  CEEDOD        PR
D  ParmNum                    10I 0 CONST
D                             10I 0
D                             10I 0
D                             10I 0
D                             10I 0
D                             10I 0
D                             12A    OPTIONS(*OMIT)

  * Parameters passed to CEEDOD
D  DescType      S            10I 0
D  DataType      S            10I 0
D  DescInfo1     S            10I 0
D  DescInfo2     S            10I 0
D  InLen         S            10I 0
D  HexLen        S            10I 0
  *


CLON01Factor1+++++++Opcode&ExtFactor2+++++++Result++++++++Len++D+HiLoEq
c                     move      MsgInId       MsgId

  * Get size of message data field if passed to program
c                     if        %parms > 1
c                     callp     CEEDOD(2          :DescType:DataType:
c                                 DescInfo1 : DescInfo2: Inlen:
c                                 *OMIT)
c                     clear                   MsgData
c                     move      Inlen         MsgDtaLen
c                     eval      MsgData = %subst(MsgInData:1:MsgDtaLen)
c                     else
c                     clear                   MsgDtaLen
c                     clear                   MsgData
c                     endif

  * If message type passed to program, use it
c                     if        %parms >= 3
```

Figure 6.1: The Send Error Message procedure sends messages with embedded message data (part 2 of 3).

```
C                       eval        MsgType = MsgIntype
C                       else
C                       eval        MsgType = DefMsgType
C                       endif

 * If message file passed to program, use it
C                       if          %parms >= 4
C                       movel       MsgFile         MsgFileLib
C                       else
C                       movel       DefMsgFile      MsgFileLib
C                       endif

 * If message file library passed to program, use it
C                       if          %parms >= 5
C                       move        MsgLib          MsgFileLib
C                       else
C                       move        DefMsgLib       MsgFileLib
C                       endif

 * Call API to send message to caller of procedure
C                       CALL        'QMHSNDPM'
C                       PARM                        MsgId
C                       PARM                        MsgFileLib
C                       PARM                        MsgData
C                       PARM                        MsgDtaLen
C                       PARM                        MsgType
C                       PARM        '*'             MsgQueue
C                       PARM        1               MsgQueNbr
C                       PARM                        MsgKey
C                       PARM                        ErrorDs

C                       return

PName+++++++++++..T.................Keywords+++++++++++++++++++++++++++
P  SndErrMsg       E
```

Figure 6.1: The Send Error Message procedure sends messages with embedded message data (part 3 of 3).

Notice that every parameter has the CONST keyword. This means that the parameters are *constant*, and the procedure will not change any of those parameters. It also tells the system that the calling program can pass the parameters with literals as well as fields. Now take a look at the **PmsgData** parameter. The parameter has two keywords, *VARSIZE and *NOPASS. The *NOPASS keyword indicates that this parameter does not have to be passed to this procedure. The *VARSIZE keyword indicates that the length of the field being passed for this parameter is variable in size and can be of any length. Taken together, these two keywords tell the system that you don't have to pass any message data with the error message, but if you do, the message data can be of any length.

The three remaining parameters (type of error message, error file name, and error file library) also contain the *NOPASS keyword and are therefore not required parameters. The variables **DefMsgFile** and **DefMsgLib** contain the default error-message file name and library that the program uses if you do not pass in these parameters. For this application, these defaults are set to QCPFMSG/QSYS. If your application uses your own message file, however, you should change these fields to your own defaults, or always pass them when you call the procedure. The default message type is contained in the field **DefMsgType**.

Now consider what **SndErrMsg** actually does. If you have passed message data to the procedure, it will know that because the %PARMS built-in-function indicates that more than one parameter was passed. When this is the case, the procedure will need to know the length of the message data that was passed. To retrieve the length, the Retrieve Operational Descriptor (CEEDOD) API is called. This API retrieves information about parameters passed to the calling program; that is, the program containing the call to CEEDOD.

We feel that CEEDOD could use some serious work by IBM to improve its flexibility and functionality. Currently, about all CEEDOD is good for is retrieving the length of a parameter. Table 6.1 outlines the parameters for this API. The first parameter is a number that corresponds to the parameter order that was passed to this procedure.

In our example, we have coded the number *2*, indicating that information about the second parameter should be passed to this program. The second parameter in the example happens to be message data. The next four parameters return some basic information about the type of data being passed. Since we are not interested in the type of data, only the length, these parameters can be ignored. The sixth parameter, INLEN, gives the length of the data being passed. The last parameter is an optional feedback code indicating errors. This parameter is omitted altogether in the example.

Table 6.1: Retrieve Operational Descriptor API (CEEDOD)

Parameter	Description	Type	Attribute	Size
1	The ordinal position of the parameter about which you want information.	Input	Integer	4
2	The descriptor type, which is one of the following values: • 1—Escape. • 2—Element. • 3—Array. • 4—Structure.	Output	Integer	4
3	The data type, which is one of the following values: • 1—An element descriptor type that is not one of the others. • 2—SBCS character string. • 3—SBCS zoned character string. • 4—SBCS variable-length field with a 2-byte character count field. • 5—SBCS variable-length field with a 4-byte character count field. • 6—A string of bits. • 7—A variable-length string of bits with a 2-byte count field. • 8—A variable-length string of bits with a 4-byte count field. • 9—DBCS character string. • 10—DBCS zoned character string. • 11—DBCS variable field with a 2-byte count field. • 12—DBCS variable field with a 4-byte count field.	Output	Integer	4
4	The binary value of the first descriptor field. It is zero if omitted by the descriptor.	Output	Integer	4
5	The binary value of the second descriptor field. It is zero if omitted by the descriptor.	Output	Integer	4
6	The length of the data that is passed.	Output	Integer	4

177

Now that CEEDOD has retrieved the length of the message data being passed, the procedure can call the Send Program Message (QMHSNDPM) API. This API actually sends the error message to the message queue of the calling program. Table 6.2 shows the details for the parameters to this API. If you look closely at the parameters, you will see that the first five roughly correspond to the procedure interface for the **SndErrMsg** procedure. For example, the message data length that has been retrieved is parameter 4 for the API.

The message file and library make up one parameter for the API. The information is simply passed on to this API, using either the established default values, or the values passed to this procedure as parameters. The last four parameters (message queue, message queue number, message key, and error data structure) are ones that the user of the procedure does not need to know about. Values are supplied for those parameters that make the **SndErrMsg** procedure work. Thus, some of the complexity of the API is hidden from the user of the procedure. This technique is generally referred to as *wrapping*.

Table 6.2: Send Program Message API (QMHSNDPM) (part 1 of 2)				
Parameter	**Description**	**Type**	**Attribute**	**Size**
1	An identifying code for the predefined message or blanks.	Input	Char	7
2	The message file name, where the first 10 characters contain the file name, and the second 10 are the library name where the file resides. It can be blank for immediate messages that don't use message files.	Input	Char	20
3	Substitution data for the message being sent. If blanks are used for the message field, this data is the complete text of the message being sent.	Input	Char	Varies
4	The length of the message data field. Valid values are zero to 32,767 for message data, and zero to 6,000 for immediate text.	Input	Binary	4

Table 6.2: Send Program Message API (QMHSNDPM) (part 2 of 2)

Parameter	Description	Type	Attribute	Size
5	The message type, as follows: • *COMP—Completion. • *DIAG—Diagnostic. • *ESCAPE—Escape. • *INFO—Informational. • *INQ—Inquiry. • *NOTIFY—Notification. • *RQS—Request. • *STATUS—Status.	Input	Char	10
6	The call stack entry to send the message to or to begin counting using the stack counter (parameter 7).	Input	Char (or Pointer)	Varies
7	The number of entries up the stack, relative to the call stack entry, to send the message to.	Input	Binary	4
8	The message key, which is assigned by the API for any message type except status.	Output	Char	4
Optional Group 1				
9	A standard error code structure.	In/Out	Char	Varies

Removing Error Messages

One of the difficulties that can occur when presenting subfile error messages is removing the last error message that is displayed. For instance, suppose you present a screen, edit the entries, and display an error message. The user corrects the error, but makes another error in a different field. You edit that field and want to display only the new error. When you display the subfile, however, both the old and new errors are in the subfile.

To eliminate this problem, you need to remove messages from the message queue after you have displayed them. The Remove Program Messages

(QMHRMVPM) API does just that. Table 6.3 shows the parameters for this API. We have wrapped a procedure around this API and named it **RmvErrMsg**. All you have to do is call the procedure after displaying your input screen.

Table 6.3: Remove Program Message API (QMHRMVPM)				
Parameter	**Description**	**Type**	**Attribute**	**Size**
1	The call stack entry; that is, the message queue from which messages are to be removed, or from which counting is to begin using the stack counter parameter.	Input	Char	Varies
2	The number of entries up the stack, starting from the call stack entry, to which messages are to be sent.	Input	Binary	4
3	The message key. If the message to remove has the parameter *BYKEY or *SCOPE, this is the key of the single message to delete.	Input	Char	4
4	The messages to remove, as follows: • *ALL—Remove all messages. • *BYKEY—Remove the single message in the message key parameter. • *KEEPRQS—Remove all but request messages. • *NEW—Remove all new messages. • *OLD—Remove all old messages. • *SCOPE—Remove the scope message specified in the message key.	Input	Char	10
Optional Group 1				
5	A standard error data structure.	In/Out	Char	Varies

The code for this procedure is shown in Figure 6.2. The procedure accepts one optional parameter, the message ID that you want to remove. The default value for this is *ALL, which means remove all messages from the message queue.

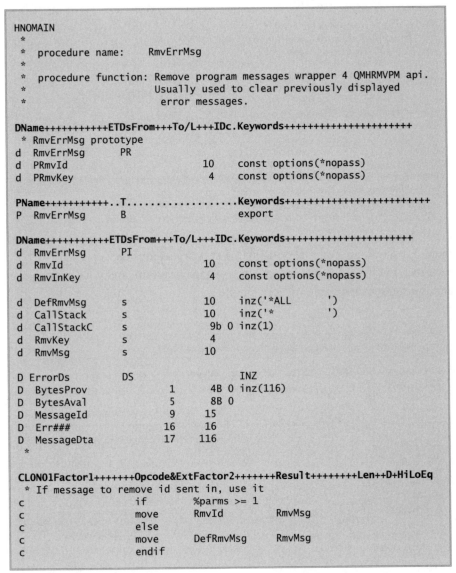

```
HNOMAIN
*
*    procedure name:    RmvErrMsg
*
*    procedure function: Remove program messages wrapper 4 QMHRMVPM api.
*                        Usually used to clear previously displayed
*                        error messages.

DName+++++++++++ETDsFrom+++To/L+++IDc.Keywords++++++++++++++++++++++
*  RmvErrMsg prototype
d   RmvErrMsg       PR
d   PRmvId                      10      const options(*nopass)
d   PRmvKey                      4      const options(*nopass)

PName+++++++++++..T.................Keywords++++++++++++++++++++++++
P   RmvErrMsg       B                   export

DName+++++++++++ETDsFrom+++To/L+++IDc.Keywords++++++++++++++++++++++
d   RmvErrMsg       PI
d   RmvId                       10      const options(*nopass)
d   RmvInKey                     4      const options(*nopass)

d   DefRmvMsg       s           10      inz('*ALL      ')
d   CallStack       s           10      inz('*         ')
d   CallStackC      s            9b 0   inz(1)
d   RmvKey          s            4
d   RmvMsg          s           10

D ErrorDs           DS                  INZ
D   BytesProv               1    4B 0   inz(116)
D   BytesAval               5    8B 0
D   MessageId               9   15
D   Err###                 16   16
D   MessageDta             17  116
*

CLON01Factor1+++++++Opcode&ExtFactor2+++++++Result+++++++Len++D+HiLoEq
*  If message to remove id sent in, use it
c                   if        %parms >= 1
c                   move      RmvId         RmvMsg
c                   else
c                   move      DefRmvMsg     RmvMsg
c                   endif
```

Figure 6.2: The RmvErrMsg procedure removes messages from the message queue (part 1 of 2).

```
 * If message key sent in, use it
c                    if         %parms = 2
c                    move       RmvInKey        RmvKey
c                    else
c                    clear                      RmvKey
c                    endif

 * Call API to remove messages from message queue
C                    CALL       'QMHRMVPM'
C                    PARM                       CallStack
C                    PARM                       CallStackC
C                    PARM                       RmvKey
C                    PARM                       RmvMsg
C                    PARM                       ErrorDs

c                    return

PName+++++++++++..T.................Keywords++++++++++++++++++++++++
P   RmvErrMsg        E
```

Figure 6.2: The RmvErrMsg procedure removes messages from the message queue (part 2 of 2).

Figure 6.3 shows an example of using the two procedures SndErrMsg and RmvErrMsg. Put these two procedures in a service program, and your error-handling routines will become very simple.

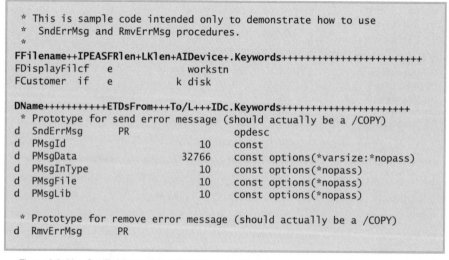

```
 * This is sample code intended only to demonstrate how to use
 *  SndErrMsg and RmvErrMsg procedures.
 *
FFilename++IPEASFRlen+LKlen+AIDevice+.Keywords++++++++++++++++++++++++
FDisplayFilcf   e              workstn
FCustomer   if  e          k disk

DName++++++++++++ETDsFrom+++To/L+++IDc.Keywords++++++++++++++++++++++++
 * Prototype for send error message (should actually be a /COPY)
d  SndErrMsg      PR                  opdesc
d  PMsgId                      10     const
d  PMsgData                 32766     const options(*varsize:*nopass)
d  PMsgInType                  10     const options(*nopass)
d  PMsgFile                    10     const options(*nopass)
d  PMsgLib                     10     const options(*nopass)

 * Prototype for remove error message (should actually be a /COPY)
d  RmvErrMsg      PR
```

Figure 6.3: Use SndErrMsg and RmvErrMsg procedures to make error-handling easy (part 1 of 2).

```
d   PRmvId                    10     const options(*nopass)
d   PRmvKey                    4     const options(*nopass)

CLON01Factor1+++++++Opcode&ExtFactor2+++++++Result++++++++Len++D+HiLoEq
c                   Dou        *in61 = *off
 * Display the messages in the subfile
c                   WRITE      MSGCTL

 * Display a screen for the user to enter information. User enters
 *  a customer number that is not on file in the Customer file
c                   exfmt      format4

 * Remove any previously displayed messages from the job log
c                   callp      RmvErrMsg

 * If customer does not exist, issue error message and pass customer
 *  number to display in error message
c     @CustNbr      Chain      Customer                            61
c                   if         *in61
c                   callp      SndErrMsg('USR0453':@CustNbr)
c                   endif
c                   enddo
```

Figure 6.3: Use SndErrMsg and RmvErrMsg procedures to make error-handling easy (part 2 of 2).

APIs with Database Triggers

The Receive Program Message (QMHRCVPM) API is also used for message handling. This API is the opposite of the Send Program Message API. It receives the messages sent to a message queue and makes the message data available to your program. Perhaps even more advantageous, this API also receives information about the message retrieved.

Among the information that can be retrieved about a message is the name of the program that received the message. Wait a gosh darn minute, you say! If you sent the message, don't you know who it was sent to? Not necessarily. Since you can use the call stack and call-stack-counter parameters to send a message somewhere up the stack to some calling program, you don't need to know the name of the program.

At this point, you might be scratching your head and asking yourself, "If I don't need to know the name of the program I sent the message to, then why is it a useful bit of information"? If you're a fan of *Hitchhiker's Guide to the Galaxy*, you might be satisfied that "the answer to your question is 42." Otherwise, the answer to your question is database triggers. A database trigger is a very good way to assign a monitoring program to a file. Whenever the file is modified, the system calls your trigger program, passing the before and after buffers of the record being changed. The system also passes information to your trigger program like who modified the file and when. What the system does *not* pass to your trigger program is the name of the program that caused the trigger program to be invoked.

We find this oversight pretty amazing. IBM went through a lot of trouble to devise this elaborate and very useful technique of tracking changes to a file. It doesn't matter what tool you use to modify the data in the file, the trigger will fire and you can monitor the change. For some reason, though, IBM did not think it necessary to know the name of the program that caused the trigger to fire! Was the culprit DFU, SQL, or a program? Who knows? This omission makes triggers pretty worthless for debugging database problems.

Once again, it's APIs to the rescue! You can use the QMHSNDPM API in a trigger program to send a message up the stack to whatever program initiated the trigger. You can then use the QMHRCVPM API to get the name of the program that received the message you sent. This calling program obviously must be the program that caused the trigger to fire. Figure 6.4 shows the code for a trigger program that performs this important function. The details for QMHRCVPM are shown in Table 6.4.

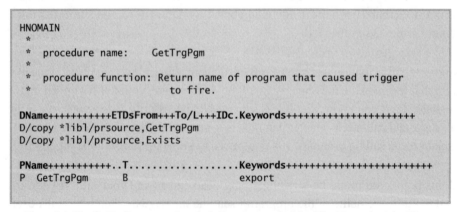

```
HNOMAIN
*
*   procedure name:     GetTrgPgm
*
*   procedure function: Return name of program that caused trigger
*                             to fire.

DName++++++++++ETDsFrom+++To/L+++IDc.Keywords++++++++++++++++++++++
D/copy *libl/prsource,GetTrgPgm
D/copy *libl/prsource,Exists


PName++++++++++..T.................Keywords++++++++++++++++++++++++
P  GetTrgPgm       B                 export
```

Figure 6.4: The GetTrgPgm procedure finds the program that fired the trigger (part 1 of 3).

```
DName++++++++++ETDsFrom+++To/L+++IDc.Keywords++++++++++++++++++++++
d   GetTrgPgm        PI              20

d   MsgAction        s               10
d   MsgData          s                9
d   MsgDtaLen        s                6  0 inz(%size(MsgData))
d   MsgFileLib       s               20
d   MsgId            s               10
d   MsgKey           s                9b 0
d   MsgQueue         s               10
d   MsgQueNbr        s                9b 0
d   MsgType          s               10
d   RcvData          s             1000
d   RcvDtaLen        s                6  0 inz(%size(RcvData))
d   RcvFormat        s                8
d   RcvKey           s                9b 0 inz
d   StackNbr         s                6  0 inz(3)
d   TestPgm          s               10
d   WaitTime         s                9b 0
d   WhoCalled        s               20
    *

D   ErrorDs          DS                       INZ
D   BytesProv               1        4B 0 inz(116)
D   BytesAval               5        8B 0
D   MessageId               9       15
D   Err###                 16       16
D   MessageDta             17      116

CLON01Factor1+++++++Opcode&ExtFactor2+++++++Result++++++++Len++D+HiLoEq
c                   dou       WhoCalled <> *blanks
c                   movel     'QCPFMSG  '  MsgFileLib
c                   move      'QSYS     '  MsgFileLib
C                   CALL      'QMHSNDPM'
C                   PARM                   MsgId
C                   PARM                   MsgFileLib
C                   PARM                   MsgData
C                   PARM                   MsgDtaLen
C                   PARM      '*RQS'       MsgType
C                   PARM      '*'          MsgQueue
C                   PARM      StackNbr     MsgQueNbr
C                   PARM                   RcvKey
C                   PARM                   ErrorDs

    * cpf2904 call stack not found
c                   if        MessageId = 'CPF2904'
c                   eval      WhoCalled = MessageId
c                   endif
```

Figure 6.4: The GetTrgPgm procedure finds the program that fired the trigger (part 2 of 3).

```
c                 if        WhoCalled = *blanks
c                 move      RcvKey        MsgKey
C                 CALL      'QMHRCVPM'
C                 PARM                    RcvData
C                 PARM                    RcvDtaLen
C                 PARM      'RCVM0200'    RcvFormat
C                 PARM      '*'           MsgQueue
C                 PARM      StackNbr      MsgQueNbr
C                 PARM      '*RQS'        MsgType
C                 PARM                    MsgKey
c                 parm      0             WaitTime
c                 parm      '*REMOVE'     MsgAction
C                 PARM                    ErrorDs

c                 eval      StackNbr = StackNbr + 1
c                 eval      TestPgm = %subst(RcvData:111:10)
c                 if        Exists(TestPgm:'*PGM':'QSYS') = 'Y' OR
c                           Exists(TestPgm:'*MOD':'QSYS') = 'Y' OR
c                           Exists(TestPgm:'*PGM':'QPDA') = 'Y' OR
c                           Exists(TestPgm:'*MOD':'QPDA') = 'Y'
c                 iter
c                 endif
c                 eval      WhoCalled = TestPgm
c                 endif
c                 enddo

c                 return    WhoCalled

PName+++++++++++..T...............Keywords++++++++++++++++++++++++++++
P  GetTrgPgm       E
```

Figure 6.4: The GetTrgPgm procedure finds the program that fired the trigger (part 3 of 3).

When you review the code in Figure 6.4, you need you to be aware of a certain idiosyncrasy regarding the "who fired the trigger?" program. When it attempts to rise through the job stack searching for the program in question, interspersed among all the valid, useful user programs is some unknown IBM stuff! So, the first program up the stack might not actually be the program that called you, but rather IBM's program that is handling the call request.

To "sort the wheat from the chaff," a program is ignored if it resides in a system library (either QSYS or QPDA). A procedure called EXISTS is used to see if the program exists in either of these two libraries. (This procedure is described in detail in chapter 8.) If it is a system program, the procedure sends a message to its caller and checks again. This loop continues until it finds the program that fired the trigger. The resulting program is named "Shooter."

Table 6.4: Receive Program Messages (QMHRCVPM) (part 1 of 2)				
Parameter	Description	Type	Attribute	Size
1	The message information, a variable that gets the message received.	Output	Char	Varies
2	The length of the variable receiving the message. The minimum length is 8 bytes.	Input	Binary	4
3	The format name, as follows: • RCVM0100—Brief message information. • RCVM0200—All message information. • RCVM0300—All message information, plus information on the sender of the message.	Input	Char	8
4	The call stack entry from whose message queue messages are to be received.	Input	Char	Varies
5	The call stack counter; that is, how many calls up the stack, from the call stack entry, to actually send the message.	Input	Binary	4
6	The message type, as follows: • *COMP—Completion. • *DIAG—Diagnostic. • *ESCAPE—Escape. • *INFO—Informational. • *INQ—Inquiry. • *NOTIFY—Notification. • *RQS—Request. • *STATUS—Status.	Input	Char	10
7	The key to the message being received.	Input	Char	4

Table 6.4: Receive Program Messages (QMHRCVPM) (part 2 of 2)				
Parameter	Description	Type	Attribute	Size
8	The length of time to wait for a message to arrive on the message queue. Zero means don't wait at all, -1 means wait forever, and any other number means wait this specified time.	Input	Binary	4
9	The message action, which is one of the following: • *OLD—Keep the message in the queue and mark it as old. • *REMOVE—Remove the message. • *SAME—Keep the message without changing its status. This allows you to receive the message again.	Input	Char	10
10	A standard error structure.	I/O	Char	Varies
Optional Group 1				
11	The length of the call stack entry.	Input	Binary	4
12	The call stack entry's qualification.	Input	Char	20
Optional Group 2				
13	The call stack entry's data type.	Input	Char	10
14	A coded character-set identifier.	Input	Binary	4

Summary

There are many more APIs that deal with message handling. This chapter covers the basics of sending, removing, and receiving messages using APIs. It provides some tools and examples that show how you can put these APIs to good use, but it barely scratches the surface of all that is available.

Be sure to explore the message APIs on your own. If you come up with a useful tool (and expert that you now are, we're sure you will), let us know. Maybe you could just send us a message....

7

SECURITY APIs

$\mathbf{W}$e feel extremely privileged to have worked on the AS/400 since its birth. We have watched our beloved box reinvent itself over and over again: from OPM to ILE, from CISC to RISC, and from being a box that ran RPG almost exclusively to one that efficiently runs applications designed for other operating systems. All the while, the AS/400 has managed to remain backward-compatible. Do you know of any other system that comes close to making those claims? Neither do we.

Recently, the AS/400 has once again been reborn because of the explosive growth rate of the Internet. AS/400 customers have become accustomed to just standing the system in the corner by itself and forgetting about it while it ran their business forever. Now they can stand it in a corner, connect it to the Internet, and forget about it while it runs their business forever—but that's not a very good idea. If you attach anything to the Internet, including your beloved AS/400, you need to pay attention to security.

You can live safely in a connected world, but you cannot naively leave your windows open and your doors unlocked at night. On the Internet, predators are everywhere.

This doesn't mean you should lock your AS/400 up tight and ignore the technological revolution occurring around you. Hook your AS/400 up to the Internet! There are far too many advantages to being connected. Proceed with caution, however, by using a quality firewall, taking advantage of the AS/400's fully integrated object-level security, and (last but not least) taking advantage of security APIs.

If you are a veteran in this business, you will remember when security was never an issue. The AS/400 used to ship with security level 10 as the default. How restrictive was that security level? Well, you did have to turn the machine on before you could gain access to it, but that was all there was to it. Those days are long gone. Security level 10 is not even supported any more. The AS/400 now ships with security level 30 as the default. It is strongly recommended that you bump the security level to 40 or 50, especially if you are going to attach your box to the Internet.

This is not all bad news, however. The AS/400 is one of the most secure boxes around. It's never been sick a day in its life. The fact that it seems to be immune to today's computer viruses is probably due to the unique nature of its architecture more than anything else. Hackers, like criminals everywhere, are generally looking for a quick strike. If it seems troublesome to have to break into a box, they are far more likely to move on to easier pickings. Learning a foreign operating system seems to be a considerable hindrance to the average hacker. Why go through the trouble? After all, there are plenty of NT and UNIX boxes out there....

You can control security on the AS/400 in several different ways. From access passwords to object-level security, OS/400 does a good job of keeping your system secure. It even supports level 50 security, which is often required in high-security government installations. As complete as OS/400's security is, however, there are still occasions when you need a little something extra. That is where the security APIs come into play.

This chapter starts off with a look at the Retrieve Encrypted Password (QSYRUPWD) API and its complement API, Set Encrypted Password (QSYSUPWD). Together, these two APIs enable you to more easily maintain identical user profiles on separate systems.

While on the subject of user profiles, it's worthwhile to take a look at how to retrieve any information you want about a user profile (except the password, of course). The Retrieve User Information (QSYRUSRI) API will deliver "the goods" on demand.

You'll see how to put this all together with two programs that use these APIs. One program is called whenever a new user profile is created, and it communicates this fact to a DDM data queue. The other program (residing on another AS400) reads the data queue and creates a copy of the user profile on that machine—password and all!

The chapter closes with a look at another type of security object: the authorization list. You will learn how to store encrypted passwords in an authorization list so that you can verify a correct user-and-password combination. This capability lets you secure your own applications with encrypted passwords.

Retrieving Encrypted Passwords

Passwords are stored in user profiles using an *encryption algorithm*. Encryption has been around for as long as secrets have been kept. It is the process of encoding and decoding a password or message so that prying eyes cannot see it. They might see the result of the encryption, but that result is impossible to decipher without the key to the encryption code.

Since everything done on your AS/400 is tracked by user profile, it's very important that access to each user's profile be secure. Only the owner of the user profile must know his or her password. The first sample program in this chapter shows you how an encrypted password may be retrieved—but not deciphered. It is retrieved in its fully encrypted state. You might be wondering why encoded information like this would have any value. It is valuable because, even in its encrypted state, you can use a password to keep your security consistent across several AS/400 systems. An example will explore this scenario.

As you can see from the code in Figure 7.1, the Retrieve Encrypted Password (QSYRUPWD) API is one of the simpler retrieve APIs. As you have seen in previous chapters, the API is actually called twice, first to determine the length of the data that will be retrieved, and then again to actually retrieve the data. The parameters for the Retrieve Encrypted Password API are listed in Table 7.1.

```
HNOMAIN
   *   procedure name:    RtvEncPwd
   *
   *   procedure function: Retrieve encrypted password for given user
   *
DName++++++++++++ETDsFrom+++To/L+++IDc.Keywords++++++++++++++++++++++++
d  RtvEncPwd       PR            38
d    PmProfile                   10   const

PName+++++++++++++..T.................Keywords++++++++++++++++++++++++++
P  RtvEncPwd       B                  export

DName++++++++++++ETDsFrom+++To/L+++IDc.Keywords++++++++++++++++++++++++
d  RtvEncPwd       PI            38
d    PmProfile                   10   const

   * Local Variables

DQSYD0100          DS                     Based(ReceivePtr)
D*                                        Qsy RUPWD UPWD0100
D QSYBRTN04                1    4B 0
D*                                        Bytes Returned
D QSYBAVL04                5    8B 0
D*                                        Bytes Available
D QSYPN06                  9    18
D*                                        Profile Name
D PassWord                19    38

D Receiver1          DS
D   BytesRtn1                   10i 0
D   BytesAvl1                   10i 0

DQUSEC             DS           116   inz
D QUSBPRV                  1    4B 0 inz(116)
D QUSBAVL                  5    8B 0 inz(0)
D QUSEI                    9    15
D QUSERVED                16    16
D QUSED01                 17    116

D FormatName         S             8   Inz('UPWD0100')
D InProfile          S            10
D ReceiveLen         S            10i 0
```

Figure 7.1: Use the Retrieve Encrypted Password (QSYRUPWD) to get an encrypted password (part 1 of 2).

```
CLON01Factor1+++++++Opcode&ExtFactor2+++++++Result++++++++Len++D+HiLoEq
c                 Eval      InProfile = PmProfile
 * Call the API to get the information you want
C                 Call      'QSYRUPWD'
C                 Parm                      Receiver1
C                 Parm      8               ReceiveLen
C                 Parm                      FormatName
C                 Parm                      InProfile
C                 Parm                      QusEc
 * Allocate enough storage for receiver
c                 Alloc     BytesAvl1       ReceivePtr
 * Call the API to get the information you want
C                 Call      'QSYRUPWD'
C                 Parm                      QsyD0100
C                 Parm      BytesAvl1       ReceiveLen
C                 Parm                      FormatName
C                 Parm                      InProfile
C                 Parm                      QusEc

c                 Return    QsyD0100

PName+++++++++++..T.................Keywords++++++++++++++++++++++++++
P  RtvEncPwd      E
```

Figure 7.1: Use the Retrieve Encrypted Password (QSYRUPWD) to get an encrypted password (part 2 of 2).

Table 7.1: Retrieve Encrypted Password (QSYRUPWD)

Parameter	Description		Type	Attribute	Size
1	The receiver variable, returned in this format:		Output	Char	Varies
	Position	**Description**			
	1 to 4	Bytes returned.			
	5 to 8	Bytes available.			
	9 to 18	Profile name.			
	19 to ???	Encrypted password.			
2	The length of the receiver variable.		Input	Binary	4
3	The format name, which must be UPWD0100.		Input	Char	8
4	The user profile name.		Input	Char	10

Setting Encrypted Passwords

Suppose you need to maintain identical user profiles on several different AS/400s. Both user profiles represent the same person and need to have the same password. Why should the company security officer have to bounce through the various systems, duplicating identical user profiles on multiple machines? Instead, the Set Encrypted Password (QSYSUPWD) API can be used in conjunction with the Retrieve Encrypted Password API to perform this function.

The idea for this exercise is to create a user profile and then use the Set Encrypted Password (QSYSUPWD) API to set its password. You already saw how to use QSYSRUPWD to retrieve the original password on one AS/400 (call it *System A*). The sample program shown in Figure 7.2 uses QSYSUPWD to establish the password on the second AS/400 (*System B*). The parameters for the Set Encrypted Password API are listed in Table 7.2.

Table 7.2: Set Encrypted Password (QSYSUPWD)				
Parameter	**Description**	**Type**	**Attribute**	**Size**
1	The encrypted password structure (received from the Retrieve Encrypted Password API), which must be in the original format, with no changes allowed. Its format is as follows: <table><tr><td>**Position**</td><td>**Description**</td></tr><tr><td>1 to 4</td><td>Bytes returned.</td></tr><tr><td>5 to 8</td><td>Bytes available.</td></tr><tr><td>9 to 18</td><td>Profile name.</td></tr><tr><td>19 to ???</td><td>Encrypted password.</td></tr></table>	Input	Char	Varies
Parameter	**Description**	**Type**	**Attribute**	**Size**
2	The length of parameter 1.	Input	Binary	4
3	The format name, which must be UPWD0100.	Input	Char	8
4	The user profile name.	Input	Char	10

```
HNOMAIN
 *   procedure name:     SetEncPwd
 *
 *   procedure function: Set encrypted password for given user
 *
DName++++++++++++ETDsFrom+++To/L+++IDc.Keywords++++++++++++++++++++++
d  SetEncPwd      PR
d    PwdStruct                    38

PName++++++++++++..T.................Keywords+++++++++++++++++++++++++
P  SetEncPwd      B                     export

DName++++++++++++ETDsFrom+++To/L+++IDc.Keywords++++++++++++++++++++++
d  SetEncPwd      PI
d    QSYSD0100                    38

DQSYD0100        DS                                Qsy RUPWD UPWD0100
D*
D QSYBRTN04                 1      4B 0
D*                                                Bytes Returned
D QSYBAVL04                 5      8B 0
D*                                                Bytes Available
D QSYPN06                   9      18
D*                                                Profile Name
D PassWord                 19      38

DQUSEC           DS               116      inz
D QUSBPRV                   1      4B 0 inz(116)
D QUSBAVL                   5      8B 0 inz(0)
D QUSEI                     9      15
D QUSERVED                 16      16
D QUSED01                  17      116

D FormatName      S                 8      Inz('UPWD0100')
D InProfile       S                10
D ReceiveLen      S                10i 0

CL0N01Factor1+++++++Opcode&ExtFactor2+++++++Result++++++++Len++D+HiLoEq
 * Call the API to get the information you want
C                     Call      'QSYSUPWD'
C                     Parm                      QsyD0100
C                     Parm      QsyBAvl04       ReceiveLen
C                     Parm                      FormatName
C                     Parm                      InProfile
C                     Parm                      QusEc

c                     Return

PName++++++++++++..T.................Keywords+++++++++++++++++++++++++
P  SetEncPwd      E
```

Figure 7.2: Using Set Encrypted Password (QSYSUPWD) helps to maintain identical user profiles on different AS/400s.

You have now seen how to use APIs to capture a password in its encrypted state, and how to use that encrypted password to update an existing user profile. Our stated reason for using these APIs, however, is to maintain user profiles for the same user on different AS/400s. How do you get the user profile from System A to System B? Clearly, there's more work to do. For one thing, you need to retrieve more information about a user than just the password. You need all of the other information that goes along with that user profile. That is exactly what the next section is about.

Retrieving User Information

When you want to know something about a user, where do you go to get it? You call the Retrieve User Information (QSYRUSRI) API. This API will tell you everything there is to know about a user.

The Retrieve User Information API is not only useful when you want to know something about a user, but when you are maintaining two identical systems and need to duplicate user profiles. Figure 7.3 shows a program that uses this powerful API. Table 7.3 lists the necessary parameters.

```
DName+++++++++++ETDsFrom+++To/L+++IDc.Keywords+++++++++++++++++++++++
DQSYI0300          DS                    Based(ReceivePtr)
D*                                       Qsy USRI0300
D QSYBRTN02             1      4B 0
D*                                       Bytes Returned
D QSYBAVL02             5      8B 0
D*                                       Bytes Available
D QSYUP03               9     18
D*                                       User Profile
D QSYPS00              19     31
D*                                       Previous Signon
D QSYRSV103            32     32
D*                                       Reserved 1
D QSYSN00              33     36B 0
D*                                       Signon Notval
D QSYUS02              37     46
D*                                       User Status
D QSYPD02              47     54
D*                                       Pwdchg Date
```

Figure 7.3: The Retrieve User Information (QSYRUSRI) API retrieves information from a user profile (part 1 of 6).

```
D QSYNP00                    55    55
D*                                            No Password
D QSYRSV203                   56    56
D*                                            Reserved 2
D QSYPI01                     57    60B 0
D*                                            Pwdexp Interval
D QSYPD03                     61    68
D*                                            Pwdexp Date
D QSYPD04                     69    72B 0
D*                                            Pwdexp Days
D QSYPE00                     73    73
D*                                            Password Expired
D QSYUC00                     74    83
D*                                            User Class
D  QSYAOBJ01                  84    84
D*                                            All Object
D  QSYSA05                    85    85
D*                                            Security Admin
D  QSYJC01                    86    86
D*                                            Job Control
D  QSYSC01                    87    87
D*                                            Spool Control
D  QSYSS02                    88    88
D*                                            Save System
D  QSYRVICE01                 89    89
D*                                            Service
D  QSYAUDIT01                 90    90
D*                                            Audit
D  QSYISC01                   91    91
D*                                            Io Sys Cfg
D  QSYERVED10                 92    98
D*                                            Reserved
D QSYGP02                     99    108
D*                                            Group Profile
D QSYOWNER01                  109   118
D*                                            Owner
D QSYGA00                     119   128
D*                                            Group Auth
D QSYAL04                     129   138
D*                                            Assistance Level
D QSYCLIB                     139   148
D*                                            Current Library
D  QSYNAME14                  149   158
D*                                            Name
D  QSYBRARY14                 159   168
D*                                            Library
D  QSYNAME15                  169   178
D*                                            Name
D  QSYBRARY15                 179   188
D*                                            Library
```

Figure 7.3: The Retrieve User Information (QSYRUSRI) API retrieves information from a user profile (part 2 of 6).

197

```
D QSYLC00            189   198
D*                               Limit Capabilities
D QSYTD              199   248
D*                               Text Description
D QSYDS00            249   258
D*                               Display Signon
D QSYLDS             259   268
D*                               Limit DeviceSsn
D QSYKB              269   278
D*                               Keyboard Buffering
D QSYRSV300          279   280
D*                               Reserved 3
D QSYMS              281   284B 0
D*                               Max Storage
D QSYSU              285   288B 0
D*                               Storage Used
D QSYSP              289   289
D*                               Scheduling Priority
D   QSYNAME16        290   299
D*                               Name
D   QSYBRARY16       300   309
D*                               Library
D QSYAC              310   324
D*                               Accounting Code
D   QSYNAME17        325   334
D*                               Name
D   QSYBRARY17       335   344
D*                               Library
D QSYMD              345   354
D*                               Msgq Delivery
D QSYRSV4            355   356
D*                               Reserved 4
D QSYMS00            357   360B 0
D*                               Msgq Severity
D   QSYNAME18        361   370
D*                               Name
D   QSYBRARY18       371   380
D*                               Library
D QSYPD05            381   390
D*                               Print Device
D QSYSE              391   400
D*                               Special Environment
D   QSYNAME19        401   410
D*                               Name
D   QSYBRARY19       411   420
D*                               Library
D QSYLI              421   430
D*                               Language Id
D QSYCI              431   440
D*                               Country Id
```

Figure 7.3: The Retrieve User Information (QSYRUSRI) API retrieves information from a user profile (part 3 of 6).

```
D QSYCCSID00              441    444B 0
D*                                        CCSID
D  QSYSK00                445    445
D*                                        Show Keywords
D  QSYSD00                446    446
D*                                        Show Details
D  QSYFH00                447    447
D*                                        Fullscreen Help
D  QSYSS03                448    448
D*                                        Show Status
D  QSYNS00                449    449
D*                                        Noshow Status
D  QSYRK00                450    450
D*                                        Roll Key
D  QSYPM00                451    451
D*                                        Print Message
D  QSYERVED11             452    480
D*                                        Reserved
D  QSYNAME20              481    490
D*                                        Name
D  QSYBRARY20             491    500
D*                                        Library
D QSYOBJA18               501    510
D*                                        Object Audit
D  QSYCMDS00              511    511
D*                                        Command Strings
D  QSYREATE00             512    512
D*                                        Create
D  QSYELETE00             513    513
D*                                        Delete
D  QSYJD01                514    514
D*                                        Job Data
D  QSYOBJM07              515    515
D*                                        Object Mgt
D  QSYOS00                516    516
D*                                        Office Services
D  QSYPGMA00              517    517
D*                                        Program Adopt
D  QSYSR00                518    518
D*                                        Save Restore
D  QSYURITY00             519    519
D*                                        Security
D  QSYST00                520    520
D*                                        Service Tools
D  QSYSFILD00             521    521
D*                                        Spool File Data
D  QSYSM00                522    522
D*                                        System Management
D  QSYTICAL00             523    523
D*                                        Optical
```

Figure 7.3: The Retrieve User Information (QSYRUSRI) API retrieves information from a user profile (part 4 of 6).

```
D  QSYERVED12              524    574
D*                                                  Reserved
D  QSYGAT00                575    584
D*                                                  Group Auth Type
D  QSYSG000                585    588B 0
D*                                                  Supp Group Offset
D  QSYSGNBR02              589    592B 0
D*                                                  Supp Group Number
D  QSYUID                  593    596B 0
D*                                                  UID
D  QSYGID                  597    600B 0
D*                                                  GID
D  QSYHDO                  601    604B 0
D*                                                  HomeDir Offset
D  QSYHDL                  605    608B 0
D*                                                  HomeDir Len
D  QSYLJA                  609    624
D*                                                  Locale Job Attributes
D  QSYLO                   625    628B 0
D*                                                  Locale Offset
D  QSYLL                   629    632B 0
D*                                                  Locale Len
D  QSYGMI03                633    633
D*                                                  Group Members Indicator
D  QSYDCI                  634    634
D*                                                  Digital Certificate Indi
D  QSYCC                   635    644
D*                                                  Chrid Control
D*QSYSGN02                 645    654    DIM(00001)
D*
D*                                       Varying length
D*QSYPI02                  655    655
D*
D*                                       Varying length
D*QSYLI00                  656    656
D*
D*                                          Varying length

D Receiver1       DS
D  BytesRtn1                      10i 0
D  BytesAvl1                      10i 0

DQUSEC            DS             116    inz
D QUSBPRV                  1       4B 0 inz(116)
D QUSBAVL                  5       8B 0 inz(0)
D QUSEI                    9      15
D QUSERVED                16      16
D QUSED01                 17     116

D FormatName      S                8    inz('USRI0300')
```

Figure 7.3: The Retrieve User Information (QSYRUSRI) API retrieves information from a user profile (part 5 of 6).

```
D UsrProfile      s            10
D ReceiveLen      S            10i 0
D SgDsp           s            10
D OI              S             4 0

CLON01Factor1+++++++Opcode&ExtFactor2+++++++Result++++++++Len++D+HiLoEq
C     *entry      Plist
C                 Parm                        UsrProfile

* Call the API to get the information you want
C                 Call      'QSYRUSRI'
C                 Parm                        Receiver1
C                 Parm      8                 ReceiveLen
C                 Parm                        FormatName
C                 Parm                        UsrProfile
C                 Parm                        QusEc

* Allocate enough storage for receiver
C                 Alloc     BytesAvl1         ReceivePtr

* Call the API to get the information you want
C                 Call      'QSYRUSRI'
C                 Parm                        QSYI0300
C                 Parm      BytesAvl1         ReceiveLen
C                 Parm                        FormatName
C                 Parm                        UsrProfile
C                 Parm                        QusEc

* Process the data from the API

* Limit capabilities ?
C     QsyLC00     dsply
* Group profile
C     QsyGP02     dsply
C                 z-add     qsysgo00          oi
C                 do        qsysgnbr02
C                 eval      sgdsp = %subst(QsyI0300:OI:10)
* Supplemental group profile
C     sgdsp       dsply
C                 eval      oi = oi + 10
C                 enddo

C                 Eval      *inlr = *on
```

Figure 7.3: The Retrieve User Information (QSYRUSRI) API retrieves information from a user profile (part 6 of 6).

By now, you should be able to read this type of program easily—it is a standard retrieve-type API program. It accepts the user profile as a parameter and passes it along as one of the parameters to the API, using the "double-call" technique to find the correct size of the receiver variable. You have seen this technique throughout the book, starting in chapter 1.

The first parameter that QSYRUSRI uses is the receiver variable, while the second parameter describes the length of the receiver variable named in parameter 1. The third parameter is the record format name describing the data that will be returned into the receiver variable. Parameter 4 is the name of the user profile in question, while parameter 5 is the standard error-handling data structure.

Table 7.3: Retrieve User Information (QSYRUSRI)

Parameter	Description	Type	Attribute	Size
1	The receiver variable, a variable to receive the output from the API. Its format depends on the record format name specified in parameter 3.	Output	Char	Varies
2	The length of parameter 1.	Input	Binary	4
3	The format name, which is one of the following: • USRI0100—Signon and password information. • USRI0200—Authority information. • USRI0300—All information.	Input	Char	8
4	The name of the user profile to retrieve information about. The special value *CURRENT returns information about the current user.	Input	Char	10
4	A standard error data structure.	I/O	Char	Varies

The calls to QSYRUSRI are coded using format name QSYI0300. This is the format that returns the most information about the user, and therefore is the slowest to execute. The sample program then uses the DSPLY opcode to display some of the information to the screen, demonstrating that the code is working properly.

The wildcard in this API involves group profiles. More than one group profile might be associated with a user profile. Therefore, a loop has been coded to display any supplemental group profiles that the user profile has specified.

Duplicating User Profiles (with Passwords)

Now that you have the all the pieces of the puzzle, you're ready for a sample program that puts them all together. The diagram in Figure 7.4 illustrates the flow of the sample program, shown in Figure 7.5. It copies user-profile information from System A to System B.

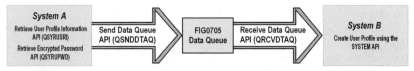

Figure 7.4: This diagram illustrates the duplication of user profiles from one system to another.

The sample program takes the user profile name and calls the Retrieve User Information API to get all the pertinent information from the profile. This information is passed along to the other computer in order to create a duplicate user profile. Once again, the double-call technique determines the length of the receiver variable and then allocates an opcode to define the correct amount of storage for the variable. Next, the encrypted password information structure is retrieved by calling the **RtvEncPwd** procedure. The **RtvEncPwd** procedure, at the bottom of Figure 7.5, calls the Retrieve Encrypted Password (QSYRUPWD) API to get the password data structure of the user profile.

Last, but not least, the receiver variable and the encrypted password structure are concatenated to form one field that is written to the FIG0705 data queue in library QGPL. The data is written to the data queue using the QSNDDTAQ API. In this example, the data queue is named FIG0705. (Send/receive data-queue APIs are covered in chapter 8.)

```
DName+++++++++++ETDsFrom+++To/L+++IDc.Keywords++++++++++++++++++++++
d  RtvEncPwd      PR             38
d   PmProfile                    10     const

DPassWordDs       DS             38
```

Figure 7.5: This program retrieves user-profile information and sends it to a remote data queue (part 1 of 8).

```
DCrtP0100        DS              38
D                                20
D                                 8
D UsrProfile                     10

DQSYI0300        DS                    Based(ReceivePtr)
D*                                     Qsy USRI0300
D QSYBRTN02               1      4B 0
D*                                     Bytes Returned
D QSYBAVL02               5      8B 0
D*                                     Bytes Available
D QSYUP03                 9     18
D*                                     User Profile
D QSYPS00                19     31
D*                                     Previous Signon
D QSYRSV103              32     32
D*                                     Reserved 1
D QSYSN00                33     36B 0
D*                                     Signon Notval
D QSYUS02                37     46
D*                                     User Status
D QSYPD02                47     54
D*                                     Pwdchg Date
D QSYNP00                55     55
D*                                     No Password
D QSYRSV203              56     56
D*                                     Reserved 2
D QSYPI01                57     60B 0
D*                                     Pwdexp Interval
D QSYPD03                61     68
D*                                     Pwdexp Date
D QSYPD04                69     72B 0
D*                                     Pwdexp Days
D QSYPE00                73     73
D*                                     Password Expired
D QSYUC00                74     83
D*                                     User Class
D  QSYAOBJ01             84     84
D*                                     All Object
D  QSYSA05               85     85
D*                                     Security Admin
D  QSYJC01               86     86
D*                                     Job Control
D  QSYSC01               87     87
D*                                     Spool Control
D  QSYSS02               88     88
D*                                     Save System
D  QSYRVICE01            89     89
```

Figure 7.5: This program retrieves user-profile information and sends it to a remote data queue (part 2 of 8).

```
D*                                    Service
D  QSYAUDIT01        90      90
D*                                    Audit
D  QSYISC01          91      91
D*                                    Io Sys Cfg
D  QSYERVED10        92      98
D*                                    Reserved
D QSYGP02            99     108
D*                                    Group Profile
D QSYOWNER01        109     118
D*                                    Owner
D QSYGA00           119     128
D*                                    Group Auth
D QSYAL04           129     138
D*                                    Assistance Level
D QSYCLIB           139     148
D*                                    Current Library
D  QSYNAME14        149     158
D*                                    Name
D  QSYBRARY14       159     168
D*                                    Library
D  QSYNAME15        169     178
D*                                    Name
D  QSYBRARY15       179     188
D*                                    Library
D QSYLC00           189     198
D*                                    Limit Capabilities
D QSYTD             199     248
D*                                    Text Description
D QSYDS00           249     258
D*                                    Display Signon
D QSYLDS            259     268
D*                                    Limit DeviceSsn
D QSYKB             269     278
D*                                    Keyboard Buffering
D QSYRSV300         279     280
D*                                    Reserved 3
D QSYMS             281     284B 0
D*                                    Max Storage
D QSYSU             285     288B 0
D*                                    Storage Used
D QSYSP             289     289
D*                                    Scheduling Priority
D  QSYNAME16        290     299
D*                                    Name
D  QSYBRARY16       300     309
D*                                    Library
D QSYAC             310     324
```

Figure 7.5: This program retrieves user-profile information and sends it to a remote data queue (part 3 of 8).

```
D*                                        Accounting Code
D  QSYNAME17          325    334
D*                                        Name
D  QSYBRARY17         335    344
D*                                        Library
D QSYMD               345    354
D*                                        Msgq Delivery
D QSYRSV4             355    356
D*                                        Reserved 4
D QSYMS00             357    360B 0
D*                                        Msgq Severity
D  QSYNAME18          361    370
D*                                        Name
D  QSYBRARY18         371    380
D*                                        Library
D QSYPD05             381    390
D*                                        Print Device
D QSYSE               391    400
D*                                        Special Environment
D  QSYNAME19          401    410
D*                                        Name
D  QSYBRARY19         411    420
D*                                        Library
D QSYLI               421    430
D*                                        Language Id
D QSYCI               431    440
D*                                        Country Id
D QSYCCSID00          441    444B 0
D*                                        CCSID
D  QSYSK00            445    445
D*                                        Show Keywords
D  QSYSD00            446    446
D*                                        Show Details
D  QSYFH00            447    447
D*                                        Fullscreen Help
D  QSYSS03            448    448
D*                                        Show Status
D  QSYNS00            449    449
D*                                        Noshow Status
D  QSYRK00            450    450
D*                                        Roll Key
D  QSYPM00            451    451
D*                                        Print Message
D  QSYERVED11         452    480
D*                                        Reserved
D  QSYNAME20          481    490
D*                                        Name
D  QSYBRARY20         491    500
```

Figure 7.5: This program retrieves user-profile information and sends it to a remote data queue (part 4 of 8).

```
D*                                              Library
D QSYOBJA18               501    510
D*                                              Object Audit
D   QSYCMDS00             511    511
D*                                              Command Strings
D   QSYREATE00            512    512
D*                                              Create
D   QSYELETE00            513    513
D*                                              Delete
D   QSYJD01               514    514
D*                                              Job Data
D   QSYOBJM07             515    515
D*                                              Object Mgt
D   QSYOS00               516    516
D*                                              Office Services
D   QSYPGMA00             517    517
D*                                              Program Adopt
D   QSYSR00               518    518
D*                                              Save Restore
D   QSYURITY00            519    519
D*                                              Security
D   QSYST00               520    520
D*                                              Service Tools
D   QSYSFILD00            521    521
D*                                              Spool File Data
D   QSYSM00               522    522
D*                                              System Management
D   QSYTICAL00            523    523
D*                                              Optical
D   QSYERVED12            524    574
D*                                              Reserved
D QSYGAT00                575    584
D*                                              Group Auth Type
D QSYSGO00                585    588B 0
D*                                              Supp Group Offset
D QSYSGNBR02              589    592B 0
D*                                              Supp Group Number
D QSYUID                  593    596B 0
D*                                              UID
D QSYGID                  597    600B 0
D*                                              GID
D QSYHDO                  601    604B 0
D*                                              HomeDir Offset
D QSYHDL                  605    608B 0
D*                                              HomeDir Len
D QSYLJA                  609    624
D*                                              Locale Job Attributes
D QSYLO                   625    628B 0
```

Figure 7.5: This program retrieves user-profile information and sends it to a remote data queue (part 5 of 8).

```
D*                                      Locale Offset
D QSYLL                  629     632B 0
D*                                      Locale Len
D QSYGMI03               633     633
D*                                      Group Members Indicator
D QSYDCI                 634     634
D*                                      Digital Certificate
Indicato
D QSYCC                  635     644
D*                                      Chrid Control
D*QSYSGN02               645     654    DIM(00001)
D*
D*                              Varying length
D*QSYPI02                655     655
D*
D*                      Varying length
D*QSYLI00                656     656
D*
D*                              Varying length

D Receiver1      DS
D  BytesRtn1                    10i 0
D  BytesAvl1                    10i 0

DQUSEC          DS            116    inz
D QUSBPRV              1        4B 0 inz(116)
D QUSBAVL              5        8B 0 inz(0)
D QUSEI                9       15
D QUSERVED            16       16
D QUSED01             17      116

d Data           S          1000
d DataQue        S            10              inz('FIG0705')
d DataQueLib     S            10              inz('QGPL ')
d DataLength     S             5  0           inz(1000)
D FormatName     S             8    inz('USRI0300')
D InData         S            38
d Key            S             4              inz('0000')
d KeyLength      S             3  0           inz(4)
D OI             S             4  0
D ReceiveLen     S            10i 0

CLON01Factor1+++++++Opcode&ExtFactor2+++++++Result++++++++Len++D+HiLoEq
c       *entry       Plist
c                    Parm                      InData
c                    eval      CrtP0100 = InData

* Call the api to get the information you want
```

Figure 7.5: This program retrieves user-profile information and sends it to a remote data queue (part 6 of 8).

```
C               Call       'QSYRUSRI'
C               Parm                    Receiver1
C               Parm       8            ReceiveLen
C               Parm                    FormatName
C               Parm                    UsrProfile
C               Parm                    QusEc

* Allocate enough storage for receiver
c               Alloc      BytesAvl1    ReceivePtr

* Call the api to get the information you want
C               Call       'QSYRUSRI'
C               Parm                    QSYI0300
C               Parm       BytesAvl1    ReceiveLen
C               Parm                    FormatName
C               Parm                    UsrProfile
C               Parm                    QusEc

* Retrieve the encrypted password data
c               Eval       PassWordDs = RtvEncPwd(UsrProfile)
c               Eval       DataLength = BytesAvl1 + 38
c               Eval       Data = PassWordDs + Qsyi0300

* Write the information to the DDM data queue
c               CALL       'QSNDDTAQ'
C               PARM                    DataQue
C               PARM                    DataQueLib
C               PARM                    DataLength
C               PARM                    Data
C               PARM                    KeyLength
C               PARM                    Key

c               Eval       *inlr = *on
*******************************************************************
*   procedure name:   RtvEncPwd
*
*   procedure function: Retrieve encrypted password for given user
*
PName++++++++++..T.................Keywords++++++++++++++++++++++++
P  RtvEncPwd    B                  export

DName+++++++++++ETDsFrom+++To/L+++IDc.Keywords++++++++++++++++++++++
d  RtvEncPwd    PI            38
d  PmProfile                  10    const

* Local Variables

DQSYD0100        DS                 Based(ReceivePtr)
```

Figure 7.5: This program retrieves user-profile information and sends it to a remote data queue (part 7 of 8).

```
D*                                          Qsy RUPWD UPWD0100
D QSYBRTN04              1       4B 0
D*                                          Bytes Returned
D QSYBAVL04              5       8B 0
D*                                          Bytes Available
D QSYPN06               9      18
D*                                          Profile Name
D PassWord             19      38

D Receiver1     DS
D  BytesRtn1                   10i 0
D  BytesAvl1                   10i 0

DQUSEC          DS           116     inz
D QUSBPRV                1       4B 0 inz(116)
D QUSBAVL                5       8B 0 inz(0)
D QUSEI                 9      15
D QUSERVED             16      16
D QUSED01              17     116

D FormatName    S                8     Inz('UPWD0100')
D InProfile     S               10
D ReceiveLen    S               10i 0

CLON01Factor1+++++++Opcode&ExtFactor2+++++++Result++++++++Len++D+HiLoEq
c                     Eval      InProfile = PmProfile
 * Call the api to get the information you want
C                     Call      'QSYRUPWD'
C                     Parm                    Receiver1
C                     Parm      8             ReceiveLen
C                     Parm                    FormatName
C                     Parm                    InProfile
C                     Parm                    QusEc
 * Allocate enough storage for receiver
c                     Alloc     BytesAvl1     ReceivePtr
 * Call the api to get the information you want
C                     Call      'QSYRUPWD'
C                     Parm                    QsyD0100
C                     Parm      BytesAvl1     ReceiveLen
C                     Parm                    FormatName
C                     Parm                    InProfile
C                     Parm                    QusEc

c                     Return    QsyD0100
PName+++++++++++..T.................Keywords+++++++++++++++++++++++++++
P   RtvEncPwd     E
```

Figure 7.5: This program retrieves user-profile information and sends it to a remote data queue (part 8 of 8).

Knowing When to Invoke Authority

So, the concept seems cool, but how do you know when to call this program? It might seem that you would call it whenever a new user profile was added to the main machine. You could run reports (weekly, daily, or hourly) that list all user profiles on your system and then compare them for additions. For every addition, you would call the program.

However, this would be manually intensive, and it would defeat the entire purpose of automating the task. You really want to run the program immediately, and *automatically*, whenever a new user profile was added. You can use a special technique called an *exit point program* to accomplish this.

To employ this method, all you have to do is register the sample program as an exit point program. The program will then be invoked whenever a new user profile is created. In our example, the program has already been coded to accept the parameters that this exit point function will pass. So, to register this program as an exit point program, run the command below:

```
ADDEXITPGM EXITPNT(QIBM_QSY_CRT_PROFILE) FORMAT(CRTP0100) PGMNBR(*LOW)
PGM(XXXLIB/FIG0705)
```

Note that you must have authority to the command before proceeding with this procedure. After executing the command, whenever a user profile is added to the system, program FIG0705 in library XXXLIB will be called. The format of the data passed to the program can be seen in data structure CRTP0100 (in Figure 7.5). The data structure consists of three subfields: a 20-byte field containing the exit point name, an 8-byte field containing the format name, and a 10-byte field contain the user profile name. This is not a lot of information, but because of the power of APIs, all you really need is the user profile name.

Now the sample program has been established as an exit point program. The exit point program will be invoked each time a user profile is added. It will write the data to the FIG0705 data queue. Where did the data queue come from? You need to create it, of course. To do that, execute this command:

```
CRTDTAQ DTAQ(QGPL/FIG0705) TYPE(*DDM) MAXLEN(1000) SEQ(*KEYED)
KEYLEN(4) RMTDTAQ(QGPL/FIG0705S) RMTLOCNAME(RMTNAME)
```

Did you notice the type parameter used on the Create Data Queue (CRTDTAQ) command? It is specified as a type of *DDM* (which stands for *Distributed Data Management*). As the name implies, the DDM value for the type parameter tells your AS/400 that the data queue being created is really just a "pointer" to a data queue located on a different system. When a DDM data queue is created, you must specify the name of the other computer, using the RMTLOCNAME parameter. In the CRTDTAQ command example, the other computer is called RMTNAME.

Just as the RMTLOCNAME parameter tells the system what computer the remote data queue resides on, the RMTDTAQ parameter tells your AS/400 the physical name and location of the data queue as it is defined on the remote system. In other words, this is where you specify the name of the data queue on the other computer that the DDM "pointer" connects with.

You also need to create the standard (non-DDM) data queue on the other computer. It must use the same name and location as specified on the RMTDTAQ parameter. For the purposes of the example, the data queue on the remote computer needs to be named FIG0705S. The Create Data Queue command below shows how to create the standard data queue on the remote system. Obviously, the command must be run while you are signed on to the remote system specified in the RMTLOCNAME parameter of the CRTDTAQ command.

```
CRTDTAQ DTAQ(QGPL/FIG0705S) MAXLEN(100) SEQ(*KEYED)
```

There are two sides to every equation. You have now seen everything that is required for *sending* the information to the remote system, but what needs to be done on the remote system? What setup, in addition to creating the data queue, is required to allow user profiles on System A to be automatically written to System B? The code in Figure 7.6 shows another sample program that represents the receiving side of the equation. This program reads the remote data queue, creates the duplicative user profile on System B, and then sets the password for the newly created user profile. The password on System B is exactly the same as the password on System A.

```
*
*  To create:
*     CRTBNDRPG PGM(XXXLIB/FIG0706) DFTACTGRP(*NO) BNDDIR(QC2LE)
*
DName+++++++++++ETDsFrom+++To/L+++IDc.Keywords+++++++++++++++++++++++
d System           PR                10i 0 extproc('system')
d  Cmd                                *     value options(*string)
d CpfMsgId          s                 7     import('_EXCP_MSGID')
d FormatCmd         PR             1000
d  UsrProfile                       10     const
d  SetEncPwd        PR
d   PwdStruct                       38

DPassWordDs        DS              38
DReceiveDs         DS            1000
d ProfData                    39 1000

DQSYI0300          DS
D QSYUP03                       9   18
D*                                         User Profile
D QSYUS02                      37   46
D*                                         User Status
D QSYPD02                      47   54
D*                                         Pwdchg Date
D QSYNP00                      55   55
D*                                         No Password
D QSYRSV203                    56   56
D*                                         Reserved 2
D QSYPI01                      57   60B 0
D*                                         Pwdexp Interval
D QSYPD03                      61   68
D*                                         Pwdexp Date
D QSYPD04                      69   72B 0
D*                                         Pwdexp Days
D QSYPE00                      73   73
D*                                         Password Expired
D QSYUC00                      74   83
D*                                         User Class
D  QSYAOBJ01                   84   84
D*                                         All Object
D  QSYSA05                     85   85
D*                                         Security Admin
D  QSYJC01                     86   86
D*                                         Job Control
D  QSYSC01                     87   87
D*                                         Spool Control
D  QSYSS02                     88   88
D*                                         Save System
D  QSYRVICE01                  89   89
```

Figure 7.6: This program creates a duplicate user profile with password (part 1 of 7).

```
D*                                          Service
D   QSYAUDIT01              90      90
D*                                          Audit
D   QSYISC01                91      91
D*                                          Io Sys Cfg
D   QSYERVED10              92      98
D*                                          Reserved
D QSYGP02                   99     108
D*                                          Group Profile
D QSYOWNER01               109     118
D*                                          Owner
D QSYGA00                  119     128
D*                                          Group Auth
D QSYAL04                  129     138
D*                                          Assistance Level
D QSYCLIB                  139     148
D*                                          Current Library
D   QSYNAME14              149     158
D*                                          Name
D   QSYBRARY14             159     168
D*                                          Library
D   QSYNAME15              169     178
D*                                          Name
D   QSYBRARY15             179     188
D*                                          Library
D QSYLC00                  189     198
D*                                          Limit Capabilities
D QSYTD                    199     248
D*                                          Text Description
D QSYDS00                  249     258
D*                                          Display Signon
D QSYLDS                   259     268
D*                                          Limit DeviceSsn
D QSYKB                    269     278
D*                                          Keyboard Buffering
D QSYRSV300                279     280
D*                                          Reserved 3
D QSYMS                    281    284B 0
D*                                          Max Storage
D QSYSU                    285    288B 0
D*                                          Storage Used
D QSYSP                    289     289
D*                                          Scheduling Priority
D   QSYNAME16              290     299
D*                                          Name
D   QSYBRARY16             300     309
D*                                          Library
D QSYAC                    310     324
D*                                          Accounting Code
```

Figure 7.6: This program creates a duplicate user profile with password (part 2 of 7).

```
D   QSYNAME17        325    334
D*                                      Name
D   QSYBRARY17       335    344
D*                                      Library
D QSYMD              345    354
D*                                      Msgq Delivery
D QSYRSV4            355    356
D*                                      Reserved 4
D QSYMS00            357    360B 0
D*                                      Msgq Severity
D   QSYNAME18        361    370
D*                                      Name
D   QSYBRARY18       371    380
D*                                      Library
D QSYPD05            381    390
D*                                      Print Device
D QSYSE              391    400
D*                                      Special Environment
D   QSYNAME19        401    410
D*                                      Name
D   QSYBRARY19       411    420
D*                                      Library
D QSYLI              421    430
D*                                      Language Id
D QSYCI              431    440
D*                                      Country Id
D QSYCCSID00         441    444B 0
D*                                      CCSID
D   QSYSK00          445    445
D*                                      Show Keywords
D   QSYSD00          446    446
D*                                      Show Details
D   QSYFH00          447    447
D*                                      Fullscreen Help
D   QSYSS03          448    448
D*                                      Show Status
D   QSYNS00          449    449
D*                                      Noshow Status
D   QSYRK00          450    450
D*                                      Roll Key
D   QSYPM00          451    451
D*                                      Print Message
D   QSYERVED11       452    480
D*                                      Reserved
D   QSYNAME20        481    490
D*                                      Name
D   QSYBRARY20       491    500
D*                                      Library
D QSYOBJA18          501    510
```

Figure 7.6: This program creates a duplicate user profile with password (part 3 of 7).

```
D*                                        Object Audit
D  QSYCMDS00              511    511
D*                                        Command Strings
D  QSYREATE00             512    512
D*                                        Create
D  QSYELETE00             513    513
D*                                        Delete
D  QSYJD01                514    514
D*                                        Job Data
D  QSYOBJM07              515    515
D*                                        Object Mgt
D  QSYOS00                516    516
D*                                        Office Services
D  QSYPGMA00              517    517
D*                                        Program Adopt
D  QSYSR00                518    518
D*                                        Save Restore
D  QSYURITY00             519    519
D*                                        Security

d DataQue        S              10        inz('FIG0904')
d DataQueLib     S              10        inz('QGPL ')
d DataLength     S               5 0      inz(1000)
d Key            S               4        inz('0000')
d KeyLength      S               3 0      inz(4)
d KeyOrder       S               2        inz('EQ')
d SenderInf      S              50
d SenderLen      S               3 0      inz(50)
d WaitLength     S               5 0      inz(-1)

CLON01Factor1+++++++Opcode&ExtFactor2+++++++Result++++++++Len++D+HiLoEq
 * Key '9999' can be put on data queue to end this program
c**                    Dou       Key <> '9999'

 * Read the data queue as entries arrive
c                      CALL      'QRCVDTAQ'
c                      PARM                DataQue
c                      PARM                DataQueLib
c                      PARM                DataLength
c                      PARM                ReceiveDs
c                      PARM                WaitLength
c                      PARM                KeyOrder
c                      PARM                KeyLength
c                      PARM                Key
c                      PARM                SenderLen
c                      PARM                SenderInf
c                      Movel     ReceiveDs PassWordDs
c                      Movel     ProfData  Qsyi0300
```

Figure 7.6: This program creates a duplicate user profile with password (part 4 of 7).

```
 * execute the command to create the user profile
c                    If          System(FormatCmd(QsyUp03)) <> 0
 * If procedure returned not zero, display the error msgid
c     CpfMsgId       dsply
c                    Else

 * Set the password the same as in the original profile
c                    Callp       SetEncPwd(PassWordDs)
c
c                    Endif
c
c                    eval        *inlr = *on
 ********************************************************************
PName+++++++++++..T.................Keywords++++++++++++++++++++++++++++
P FormatCmd         B                 export
DName++++++++++++ETDsFrom+++To/L+++IDc.Keywords++++++++++++++++++++++++++
d  FormatCmd        PI          1000
d   UserProfile                   10       const
d  Cmd              s           1000

CLON01Factor1+++++++Opcode&ExtFactor2+++++++Result++++++++Len++D+HiLoEq
c                    Eval        Cmd = 'CRTUSRPRF +
c                                   USRPRF(' + %trim(UserProfile) +
c                                 ') USRCLS(' + %trim(QsyUC00) +
c                                 ') ASTLVL(' + %trim(QsyAL04) +
c                                 ') CURLIB(' + %trim(QsyCLib) +
c                                 ') LMTCPB(' + %trim(QsyLC00) +
c                                 ') LMTDEVSSN(' + %trim(QsyLDS) +
c                                 ') TEXT(''' + %trim(QsyTD) +
c                                 ''') SPCENV(' + %trim(QsySE) +
c                                 ') GRPPRF(' + %trim(QsyGP02) +
c                                 ') OWNER(' + %trim(QsyOWNER01) +
c                                 ') GRPAUT(' + %trim(QsyGA00) +
c                                 ') PRTDEV(' + %trim(QsyPD05) +
c                                 ')'
c                    If          QsyBrary15 <> *blanks
c                    Eval        Cmd = Cmd +
c                                 ' INLPGM(' + %trim(QsyName15) + '/' +
c                                              %trim(QsyBrary15) + ')'
c                    Else
c                    Eval        Cmd = Cmd +
c                                 ' INLPGM(' + %trim(QsyName15) + ')'
c                    Endif
c                    If          QsyBrary16 <> *blanks
c                    Eval        Cmd = Cmd +
c                                 ' JOBD(' + %trim(QsyName16) + '/' +
c                                            %trim(QsyBrary16) + ')'
c                    Else
```

Figure 7.6: This program creates a duplicate user profile with password (part 5 of 7).

```
C                   Eval      Cmd = Cmd +
C                             ' JOBD(' + %trim(QsyName16) + ')'
C                   Endif
C                   If        QsyBrary18 <> *blanks
C                   Eval      Cmd = Cmd +
C                             ' OUTQ(' + %trim(QsyName18) + '/' +
C                                       %trim(QsyBrary18) + ')'
C                   Else
C                   Eval      Cmd = Cmd +
C                             ' OUTQ(' + %trim(QsyName18) + ')'
C                   Endif
C                   If        QsyBrary19 <> *blanks
C                   Eval      Cmd = Cmd +
C                             ' ATNPGM(' + %trim(QsyName19) + '/' +
C                                         %trim(QsyBrary19) + ')'
C                   Else
C                   Eval      Cmd = Cmd +
C                             ' ATNPGM(' + %trim(QsyName19) + ')'
C                   Endif
* Special authorities
C                   If        QsyAObj01 = 'Y' OR
C                             QsyAudit01 = 'Y' OR
C                             QsyIsc01   = 'Y' OR
C                             QsyJC01    = 'Y' OR
C                             QsySS02    = 'Y' OR
C                             QsySA05    = 'Y' OR
C                             QsyRvice01 = 'Y' OR
C                             QsySC01    = 'Y'
C                   Eval      Cmd = %trim(Cmd) + ' ' + 'SPCAUT('
C                   If        QsyAObj01 = 'Y'
C                   Eval      Cmd = %trim(Cmd) + '*ALLOBJ'
C                   Endif
C                   If        QsyAudit01 = 'Y'
C                   Eval      Cmd = %trim(Cmd) + ' *AUDIT'
C                   Endif
C                   If        QsyISC01 = 'Y'
C                   Eval      Cmd = %trim(Cmd) + ' *IOSYSCFG'
C                   Endif
C                   If        QsyJC01 = 'Y'
C                   Eval      Cmd = %trim(Cmd) + ' *JOBCTL'
C                   Endif
C                   If        QsySS02 = 'Y'
C                   Eval      Cmd = %trim(Cmd) + ' *SAVSYS'
C                   Endif
C                   If        QsySA05 = 'Y'
C                   Eval      Cmd = %trim(Cmd) + ' *SECADM'
C                   Endif
C                   If        QsyRvice01 = 'Y'
C                   Eval      Cmd = %trim(Cmd) + ' *SERVICE'
```

Figure 7.6: This program creates a duplicate user profile with password (part 6 of 7).

```
c                       Endif
c                       If        QsySC01 = 'Y'
c                       Eval      Cmd = %trim(Cmd) + ' *SPLCTL'
c                       Endif

c                       Eval      Cmd = %trim(Cmd) + ')'

c                       Endif

c                       Return    Cmd
PName+++++++++++..T.................Keywords++++++++++++++++++++++++++
P FormatCmd        E
  ********************************************************************
P  SetEncPwd        B                     export
DName++++++++++++ETDsFrom+++To/L+++IDc.Keywords+++++++++++++++++++++++
d  SetEncPwd        PI
d    QSYSD0100                    38

DQUSEC             DS            116      inz
D QUSBPRV                     1    4B 0 inz(116)
D QUSBAVL                     5    8B 0 inz(0)
D QUSEI                       9   15
D QUSERVED                   16   16
D QUSED01                    17  116

D FormatName        S             8       Inz('UPWD0100')

CL0N01Factor1+++++++Opcode&ExtFactor2+++++++Result++++++++Len++D+HiLoEq
 * Call the api to get the information you want
C                       Call      'QSYSUPWD'
C                       Parm                  QsysD0100
C                       Parm                  FormatName
C                       Parm                  QusEc

c                       Return
PName+++++++++++..T.................Keywords++++++++++++++++++++++++++
P  SetEncPwd        E
```

Figure 7.6: This program creates a duplicate user profile with password (part 7 of 7).

The program in Figure 7.6 doesn't need any parameters passed to it because its input comes from the data queue. The program simply needs to be started. It will continue to run until you cancel it, or until it receives a record from the data queue with a key of 9999. Until then, the program will just sit, waiting for information from the data queue.

When an entry is received, the program parses the information into two data structures: **PassWordDs** contains the encrypted password data structure from the Retrieve Encrypted Password API, and QSYI0300 is the format returned from the Retrieve User Information API. The program then "creates" and executes the command to create the user profile.

The program formats the Create User Profile command by executing the **FormatCmd** procedure, passing it the QSYI0300 data structure. This procedure analyses the data structure and creates the CRTUSRPRF command with the information found there. The procedure then returns the formatted CRTUSRPRF command that is used by the system API, which executes the command passed to it. (The system API is covered in chapter 6.) If there is an error with the command, the CPF Message ID will be returned in the field named CPUMSGID, which will be displayed on the screen. If no error occurs, the Set Encrypted Password API is run to change the password on the newly created user profile on System B to match the one on System A.

The program shown here lets you manage duplicate user profiles on multiple systems, but in the interest of brevity, it does not give you the complete picture. You will have to do some work yourself if you want to keep track of changes and deletions to user profiles. There are exit points for these tasks, also. Just enter the command WRKREGINF to get a list of all the exit points on your system. Find the ones that correspond to the function you want to add an exit program to, and away you go! You can use this program as a template for these additions.

Validation Lists

Mission-critical applications are usually secured, requiring that a password be entered before the application may be used. Whether it's for a sensitive application like payroll or for a terminal that happens to be in a busy location intended for many users, a password ensures that the user is authorized to use the function being provided.

Typically, the passwords for these sensitive applications are stored in a database file or even a data area. In turn, these objects (the database file or data area) are usually secured using object security provided by the AS/400. This works well—that is, until someone gets authority to the objects. Then, all of the passwords are readily accessible.

If those passwords were stored in an encrypted state, it would not matter if someone gained authority to the objects. Nobody would be able to view the passwords. This would provide a much higher level of security.

How do you encrypt passwords? You don't have to buy expensive encryption software just to encode a (few, dozen, hundred, or thousand) passwords. You can just use (are you ready for this?) APIs! More specifically, you can use validation-list APIs to encode and decode passwords so that nobody will be able to see them.

A validation list is an object that contains a list of passwords and keys. The object type on the AS/400 is *VLDL. APIs let you add, remove, and, most importantly, verify entries in the validation list. The sample program in Figure 7.7 covers all three of these important functions.

```
****************************************************************************
*   TO COMPILE: (signed on as QSECOFR)
*      CRTBNDRPG PGM(XXXLIB/FIG0707)   SOURCE(XXXLIB/QRPGLESRC)
*      USRPRF(*OWNER) DFTACTGRP(*NO) ACTGRP(QILE) BNDDIR(QC2LE)
****************************************************************************
*
*   ValidRg = Program performs 3 functions:
*      Action code A = Add encrypted password to system
*                  D = Delete encrypted password from system
*                  V = Validate password passed to system
*
DName+++++++++++ETDsFrom+++To/L+++IDc.Keywords+++++++++++++++++++++++
d AddPass         PR              10i 0 ExtProc('QsyAddValidation+
d                                       LstEntry')
d  ListName                       20
d  EntryIdDsH                     18
d  EncriptDsH                     18
d  EntryDSH                       58
d  AtribDsH                       47      options(*omit)

d Action          s               1
d Add             s              10i 0 inz(0)
```

Figure 7.7: This program uses validation-list APIs to encrypt passwords (part 1 of 3).

```
d Description       s              50
d Dlt              s              10i 0 inz(0)
d ErrorText        s              70
d ErrorVal         s              10i 0 based(@errorVal)
d PassWord         s              10
d Rtncode          s               1
d UserId           s              10

 * Validation list name
d  ListNameA       s              20      inz('PWLIST    QGPL     ')

 * Prototype for validation API
d ValidPass        PR             10i 0 ExtProc('QsyVerifyValidation+
d                                      LstEntry')
d  ListName                       20
d  EntryIdDs                      18
d  EncriptDs                      18

 * Prototype for remove API
d DeletePass       PR             10i 0 ExtProc('QsyRemoveValidation+
d                                      LstEntry')
d  ListName                       20
d  EntryIdDs                      18

 * Prototype for error retrieval
d C_Errno          PR              *    extproc('__errno')
d C_Strerror       PR              *    extproc('strerror')
d  errno                          10i 0 value

 * Entry Id list (user profile name or key value)
D EntryIdDs        DS                   INZ
D  IdLength                  1     4b 0 inz(10)
D  CCSIDLen                  5     8b 0 inz(0)
D  EntUserId                 9    18

 * Password to encript
D EncriptDs        DS                   INZ
D  EncripLen                 1     4b 0 inz(10)
D  CCSIDEnc                  5     8b 0 inz(0)
D  EncripData                9    18

 * Free-form description of item
D EntryDs          DS                   INZ
D  EntryLen                  1     4b 0 inz(50)
D  CCSIDEnt                  5     8b 0 inz(0)
D  EntryData                 9    58

CLON01Factor1+++++++Opcode&ExtFactor2+++++++Result++++++++Len++D+HiLoEq
```

Figure 7.7: This program uses validation-list APIs to encrypt passwords (part 2 of 3).

```
c       *entry       plist
c                    parm                      Action
c                    parm                      UserId
c                    parm                      PassWord
c                    parm                      RtnCode
c                    parm                      ErrorText
c                    parm                      Description

c                    eval        EntUserId = UserId
c                    eval        EncripData = Password

c       Action       caseq       'A'           AddPw
c       Action       caseq       'D'           DltPw
c       Action       caseq       'V'           VldPw
c                    endcs

* Trap any errors that may have occurred
c                    eval        @errorval = C_Errno
c                    if          errorval <> 0
c                    if          %parms > 4
c                    eval        ErrorText = %str(C_Strerror(ErrorVal))
c                    eval        RtnCode = 'N'
c                    endif
c                    endif

c                    eval        *inlr = *on

* Add password to system
c       AddPw        Begsr
c                    eval        EntryData = Description
c                    eval        Add = (AddPass(ListnameA:
c                                EntryIdDs:EncriptDs:
c                                EntryDS:*omit))
c                    endsr
* Validate password
c       VldPw        Begsr
c                    If          (ValidPass(ListnameA:
c                                EntryIdDs:EncriptDs)) <> 0
c                    eval        RtnCode = 'N'
c                    endif
c                    endsr
* Delete password
c       DltPw        Begsr
c                    eval        Dlt = (DeletePass(ListnameA:
c                                EntryIdDs))
c                    endsr
```

Figure 7.7: This program uses validation-list APIs to encrypt passwords (part 3 of 3).

The program in Figure 7.7 performs three separate encryption-related functions: add, remove, and verify. It accepts an action code parameter to designate which of the three functions to perform. Each function is a separate subroutine, based on the action code. The other five parameters coming into the program are the user ID, the password to encrypt or verify, a return code to indicate whether the password is valid, an error code, and a description. Let's examine each of these parameters in turn.

When the action code passed to the program is *A*, the **AddPW** subroutine is called. This subroutine calls the **QsyAddValidationLstEntry** API via the **AddPass** prototype statement. This API adds an entry to a validation list. You can see from the prototype statement that the API accepts four mandatory parameters and one optional parameter.

The QsyAddValidationLstEntry API

The parameters to the **QsyAddValidationLstEntry** API are shown in Tables 7.4 and 7.5. The first parameter is the name and library of the validation list where you want the entry added. The validation list must already exist in the specified library. You can add a validation list using the Create Validation List (CRTVLDL) command.

The second parameter is a variable-length data structure that describes a key value. This happens to be a user profile, in this case. The API will associate the password (specified in parameter 3) with the user ID.

The fifth parameter is an optional attribute data structure. The *OMIT keyword is used in the prototype to indicate that this parameter is not needed. The details of this parameter are covered in Table 7.5. As you can see, it is rather complex, full of varying-length structures. The intent of this parameter is to allow you to determine if the encrypted data can be returned with a "find" API. The default (by omitting the parameter) is to not allow a find operation to return encrypted data. This is the most important option regarding security. It allows you to specify that the API only verify the password, not retrieve it. If you want to enable **QsyFindValidationLstEntry** to return the encrypted information, you need to walk through this attribute and set the attribute value to one. In addition, you must check your system values. The Retain Server Security Data (QRETSRVSEC) system value must also be set to one.

Table 7.4: Add Validation List Entry API (QsyAddValidationLstEntry)

Parameter	Description	Type	Attr	Size
1	The name and library of the validation list, where the first 10 characters are the name of the validation list, and the second 10 are the name of the library. Special values for the library portion are *CURLIB and *LIBL.	Input	Char	20
2	The key-data data structure, which cannot exceed 100 bytes. It is formatted as follows: **Position** / **Description** 1 to 4 / The total length of the structure. 5 to 8 / The character-set ID code. Zero means use the CCSID of the current user. 9 to ?? / The key data to store to identify this entry.	Input	Char	Varies
3	The password data structure to be encrypted when stored, which cannot exceed 600 bytes. It is formatted as follows: **Position** / **Description** 1 to 4 / The total length of the structure. 5 to 8 / The character-set ID code. Zero means use the CCSID of the current user. 9 to ?? / The data to encrypt in the validation list.	Input	Char	Varies
4	A free-form description structure that cannot exceed 1,000 bytes. It is formatted as follows: **Position** / **Description** 1 to 4 / The total length of the structure. 5 to 8 / The character-set ID code. 9 to ?? / A description of the entry.	Input	Char	Varies
5	The attribute data structure. It contains attribute information associated with the EntryId data structure and is formatted as follows: **Position** / **Description** 1 to 4 / The number of attributes being added. 5 to ?? / An array of attribute-description structures with the format shown in Table 7.5	Input	Char	Varies

Table 7.5: QsyAddValidationLstEntry Attribute-Description Structures	
Length	**Description**
4 binary	The length of the attribute structure.
4 binary	The location of attribute. Zero means the attribute is stored in the validation list object.
4 binary	The attribute type. Zero indicates a system-defined attribute.
4 binary	The displacement to the attribute ID.
4 binary	The length of the attribute ID.
4 binary	The displacement to the attribute data.
4 binary	The length of the attribute data.
Varies	The Attribute ID. QsyEncryptData is the only valid entry for system-defined attributes.
Varies	The attribute data, with the following format (if stored in the list):

	Length	Description
	4 binary	CCSID of attribute.
	4 binary	Length of attribute.
	8 char	Reserved.
	Varies	Attribute.

That's all there is to the add subroutine. After adding an entry to the validation list, the program returns to the mainline code to see if any errors occurred. It does this by executing the '__errno' API, which checks for a global error value. And yes, the two underscores preceding *errno* are required. If there was an error with the API, the error value would be returned (in field **@errorval**, in this example). The error value code by itself, however, doesn't mean much. Fortunately, you don't have to memorize all of the error-code values that '__errno' supports.

Another API, **strerror**, will translate this code into a character description. It accepts the error code that '__errno' returned as input, and returns a description of the error.

By now it should be obvious that these APIs are a "little bit different." That's because they are C-type APIs. Be sure to use the QC2LE binding directory when compiling a program that uses these types of APIs.

The QsyVerifyValidationLstEntry API

What happens if the action code passed to the sample program happens to be *V* (for *validate*)? The validation subroutine, **VldPW**, is called to verify the password against the key value, both of which were also passed to the program. The validation subroutine calls the **QsyVerifyValidationLstEntry** API to validate the password.

The parameters for this API are shown in Table 7.6. Parameter 1 is the name and library of the validation list that contains the entry to be validated. Parameter 2 is the same variable-length structure that contains the key data used in the Add Validation List Entry API.

Here, however, instead of adding the key data to the list, a lookup is done to find the entry coded in the data structure. If this key is found, its corresponding data is compared with the password in parameter 3. Parameter 3 is the same password structure used in the add routine. If parameter 3 matches the password contained in the list, the API will return a zero. If it does not (or no entry is found), the API will return a non-zero and set the RTNCOD field to *N*. The RTNCOD variable is passed back to the caller of the program, to indicate that the password is not valid.

Table 7.6: Verify Validation List Entry API (QsyVerifyValidationLstEntry)		
Parameter	**Description**	
1	The name and library of the validation list, where the first 10 characters are the name of the validation list and the second 10 are the name of the library.	
2	The key-data data structure, as follows:	
	Position	**Description**
	1 to 4	The total length of the structure.
	5 to 8	The character-set ID code.
	9 to ??	The key data to access the password with.
3	The password data structure, as follows:	
	Position	**Description**
	1 to 4	The total length of the structure.
	5 to 8	The character-set ID code.
	9 to ??	The password used to verify.

The QsyRemoveValidationLstEntry API

Last but not least, what happens when a *D* action code (for *delete*) is passed to the sample program? You guessed it. The delete password subroutine, **DltPW**, is called, which calls the Remove Validation List Entry API (**QsyRemoveValidationLstEntry**). The parameters for this API are listed in Table 7.7. There are only two parameters for this API: the list name and the key data structure indicating the entry to remove from the list. When this API is executed, the indicated entry will be removed.

Table 7.7: QsyRemoveValidationLstEntry		
Parameter	**Description**	
1	The name and library of the validation list, where the first 10 characters are the name of the validation list and the second 10 are the name of the library.	
2	The key-data data structure, as follows:	
	Position	**Description**
	1 to 4	The total length of the structure.
	5 to 8	The character-set ID code.
	9 to ??	The key data to access the password with.

There are a lot of other APIs that deal with validation lists. The Open List of Validation Entries API, for example, opens a list of all the entries in the validation list. There is also the Find Validation List Entry and Change Validation List Entry APIs. In short, there are APIs to do just about anything you want to do with validation lists.

Summary

This chapter examines a variety of APIs that can help you with security issues. You have seen how to maintain identical user profiles on different machines using the Get and Set Encrypted Password APIs. You have also seen how the Retrieve User Information API lets you get the information you need about a user profile.

228

You also saw how to use APIs for validation lists. These unique entities let you store your own encrypted data and secure it with encoded passwords. The ability to use encryption provides you with yet another layer of security within an already secure box. This should help to soothe the fears of even the most paranoid. A little paranoia is not a bad thing in a connected world. In fact, *paranoia* just might be the password of the day.

8

OBJECT APIs

Everything on the AS/400 is an object. If you run the WRKOBJ command and press Help on the type parameter, you will see a listing of 85 different types of objects. Libraries, jobs, and output queues are all objects. If you want to work with an AS/400 object programmatically, then APIs are, without a doubt, your best bet. However, if all of the object APIs were included in this book, you would have to carry it around in a wheelbarrow. Therefore, this chapter limits the exploration of object-related APIs to just a few of the most interesting.

The chapter starts off with Retrieve Object Description (QUSROBJD) API . This tells you everything you want to know about an object, and then some. Ironically, one of our favorite uses for this API involves calling it, but ignoring all of the data that it is capable of returning. We call it just to see if an object exists. You'll learn about this procedure in detail.

Libraries are one of the most common objects on the AS400 because every other kind of object resides in a library. As you are aware, a library object is really nothing more than a directory that binds objects together. That being said, what happens when you want to know what size a library really is? Do you want to know the size of the directory? Of course not. You actually want to know the total size of all of the objects that reside in the library. Unfortunately, if you display the description of the library using IBM's DSPLIBD command, you only get the size of the library itself. A simple solution to this little problem involves the Retrieve Library Description (QLIRLIBDD) API . The sample program provided in this chapter returns the summarized sizes of all objects within a given library.

One of the more unique object types on the AS/400 is the data queue. A data queue is like a pipe. With a pipe, you put water in one end and it comes out the other. With a data queue, you put data in one end (using the Send Data Queue API, QSNDDTAQ) and you get data out the other (using the Receive Data Queue API, QRCVDTAQ). However, a data queue can have many "ends," or more accurately, many programs taking data off the queue. The AS/400 provides you with many ways to attach data queues to a variety of objects, such as display files and spooled files. You'll see an example in this chapter where data queues are used to track jobs on the system.

Finally, you'll look at user indexes. They are created via the Create User Index (QUSCRTUI) API and the Add User Index Entry (QUSADDUI) API . These APIs can be used to sort information returned from other APIs, using the Retrieve User Index (QUSRTVUI) API .

To Exist or Not to Exist, That Is the Question

With apologies to Mr. Shakespeare, the question of whether a given object exists or not is often important when you need to edit operator entries. For example, you might present users with a screen that allows them to enter a printer name or output queue to which the program will send a report. Frequently, a user will mis-key the name of the desired printer or output queue. To avoid indecipherable system errors, it is up to your program to determine if the object keyed really exists on the system.

Figure 8.1 shows the code for a procedure called EXISTS. It uses the Retrieve Object Description (QUSROBJD) API to attempt to retrieve information about a given object. For the purposes of this example, it really doesn't matter what information it finds. We are more interested in what the API does *not* find. If the specified object is not found, the API fills the standard error data structure with an error code, informing you that the object doesn't exist.

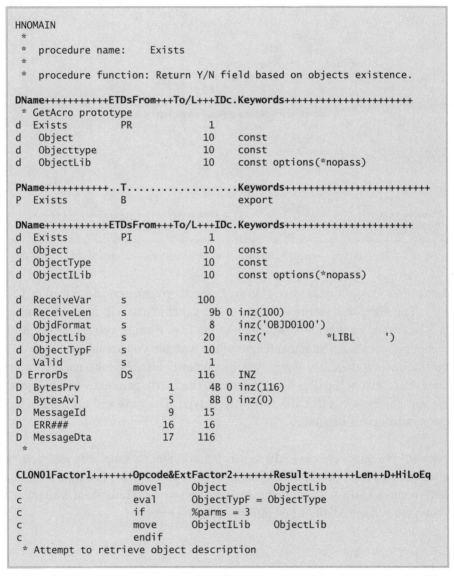

```
HNOMAIN
 *
 *  procedure name:    Exists
 *
 *  procedure function: Return Y/N field based on objects existence.

DName++++++++++++ETDsFrom+++To/L+++IDc.Keywords++++++++++++++++++++++
 * GetAcro prototype
d  Exists         PR            1
d   Object                     10       const
d   Objecttype                 10       const
d   ObjectLib                  10       const options(*nopass)

PName++++++++++++..T.................Keywords++++++++++++++++++++++++
P  Exists         B                     export

DName++++++++++++ETDsFrom+++To/L+++IDc.Keywords++++++++++++++++++++++
d  Exists         PI            1
d   Object                     10       const
d   ObjectType                 10       const
d   ObjectILib                 10       const options(*nopass)

d  ReceiveVar     s           100
d  ReceiveLen     s             9b 0 inz(100)
d  ObjdFormat     s             8      inz('OBJD0100')
d  ObjectLib      s            20      inz('          *LIBL    ')
d  ObjectTypF     s            10
d  Valid          s             1
D  ErrorDs        DS          116      INZ
D   BytesPrv            1        4B 0 inz(116)
D   BytesAvl            5        8B 0 inz(0)
D   MessageId           9       15
D   ERR###             16       16
D   MessageDta         17      116
 *


CLON01Factor1++++++Opcode&ExtFactor2++++++Result++++++++Len++D+HiLoEq
c                   movel     Object        ObjectLib
c                   eval      ObjectTypF = ObjectType
c                   if        %parms = 3
c                   move      ObjectILib    ObjectLib
c                   endif
 * Attempt to retrieve object description
```

Figure 8.1: The EXISTS procedure attempts to retrieve information about a given object (part 1 of 2).

```
C                   CALL      'QUSROBJD'
C                   PARM                    ReceiveVar
C                   PARM                    ReceiveLen
C                   PARM                    ObjdFormat
C                   PARM                    ObjectLib
C                   PARM                    ObjectTypF
C                   PARM                    ErrorDs

c                   select
 * If not authorized, then object exists
c                   when      MessageId = 'CPF9821'
c                   eval      Valid = 'Y'
 * Otherwise, error trying to get object description, means not valid
c                   when      MessageDta <> *blanks
c                   eval      Valid = 'N'
c                   other
c                   eval      Valid = 'Y'
c                   endsl

c                   return    Valid

PName+++++++++++..T.................Keywords++++++++++++++++++++++++++++
P  Exists          E
```

Figure 8.1: The EXISTS procedure attempts to retrieve information about a given object (part 2 of 2).

Take a closer look at QUSROBJD. This API uses six parameters, described in Table 8.1. The first parameter is the name of the variable that will hold the returned data. The second parameter is the length of the first. Be sure you do not define the length greater than the actual length of the variable you are using. If you do, the actual data returned could overflow into other fields. The third parameter describes the format of the data being returned. The fourth parameter is the object name and library, while the fifth is the object type. The sixth and last parameter is the standard error structure.

QUSROBJD is a relatively easy API to use, but don't let its simplicity fool you. It can return some high-powered information. Want to know the last time a file was saved? Want to know who created the object, and when? How about who owns it? This API can return all of this information, and more.

Table 8.1: Retrieve Object Description API (QUSROBJD)

Parameter	Description	Type	Attribute	Size
1	A receiver variable that will contain the output from the API.	Output	Char	Varies
2	The length of parameter 1.	Input	Binary	4
3	The name of the record format (supplied by the API) that will describe the format of the returned data in parameter 1. Possible values are as follows: • OBJD0100—Basic information. • OBJD0200—Similar to PDM information. • OBJD0300—Service information. • OBJD0400—Full information.	Input	Char	8
4	The object name (the first 10 characters), followed by the library name of the object (the second 10 characters).	Input	Char	20
5	The object type.	Input	Char	10
6	A standard error structure.	I/O	Char	Varies

An Alternative to DSPLIBD

What do you want to see when you display a library description? IBM's Display Library Description (DSPLIBD) command shows the size of the library, not the size of all the objects in it. That information probably does not help you much. You probably want to see a summary of the size of all objects in the library.

There is an API, of course, that will give you this essential information: the Retrieve Library Description (QLIRLIBD) API. This API tells you everything there is to know about a library. Sometimes, however, you might be looking for object information; things like who owns the library, when it was created, and when it was last saved.

You already know that the Retrieve Object Description (QUSROBJD) API can be used to retrieve information common to all objects. A program that uses the

Retrieve Library Description API and the Retrieve Object Description API will show you library information that is considerably more useful than IBM's DSPLIBD command. The output from such a program is shown in Figure 8.2. It combines object information with specific library information to present a panel with more pertinent information.

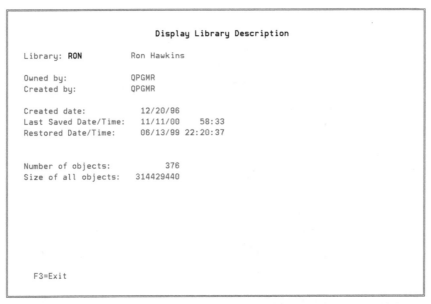

```
                           Display Library Description

        Library: RON          Ron Hawkins

        Owned by:             QPGMR
        Created by:           QPGMR

        Created date:         12/20/96
        Last Saved Date/Time: 11/11/00      58:33
        Restored Date/Time:   06/13/99 22:20:37


        Number of objects:           376
        Size of all objects:   314429440







         F3=Exit
```

Figure 8.2: This Display Library Description screen presents the number and size of objects in a library.

The code for this display file is shown in Figure 8.3, while the program itself is shown in Figure 8.4.

```
AAN01N02N03T.Name++++++RLen++TDpBLinPosFunctions+++++++++++++++++++++++
A                                       DSPSIZ(24 80 *DS3)
A                                       CF03
A           R FORMAT1
A             OBJDSP        1A  P
A             WAITDSP       1A  P
A                                     1 29'Display Library Description'
A                                       DSPATR(HI)
A                                     3  2'Library:'
```

Figure 8.3: The display file is used by the LIBDSP program (part 1 of 2).

```
A           LIB         10A  O  3 11DSPATR(HI)
A                             14  2'Size of all objects:'
A                                  DSPATR(&OBJDSP)
A           TOTSIZ      10Y 00 14 24EDTCDE(Z)
A                             13  2'Number of objects:'
A                                  DSPATR(&OBJDSP)
A           TOTOBJ      10Y 00 13 24EDTCDE(Z)
A                             23  4'F3=Exit'
A                                  COLOR(BLU)
A           TXTDSC      50A  O  3 24
A                              6  2'Created by:'
A           CRTBY       10A  O  6 24
A                              8  2'Created date:'
A           CRTDTE      10A  O  8 24
A                              5  2'Owned by:'
A           OWNEDBY     10A  O  5 24
A                              9  2'Last Saved Date/Time:'
A           LSTSVDDT    10A  O  9 24
A           LSTSVDTM     6Y 00  9 35EDTWRD('  :  :  ')
A                             10  2'Restored Date/Time:'
A           RSTDTE      10A  O 10 24
A           RSTTIM       6Y 00 10 35EDTWRD('  :  :  ')
A                             12  2'Now gathering information rega
A                                  g number and size of objects.'
A                                  DSPATR(HI)
A                                  DSPATR(&WAITDSP)
```

Figure 8.3: The display file is used by the LIBDSP *program (part 2 of 2).*

```
FFilename++IPEASFRlen+LKlen+AIDevice+.Keywords++++++++++++++++++++++++
FFig0803   CF   E               WORKSTN
F                                       infds(info)

DName+++++++++++ETDsFrom+++To/L+++IDc.Keywords++++++++++++++++++++++
D F03         c                    const(x'33')
D Info        ds
D   key                 369    369

D Cymd        s                7  0
D DateFld     s                 d  inz
D GetObjInf   s                 1
D Lib         s               10
d NonDisplay  s                1  inz(x'27')
d Normal      s                1  inz(x'20')
d ObjdFormat  s                8  inz('OBJD0400')
d ObjectLib   s               20  inz('          QSYS      ')
d ObjectTypF  s               10  inz('*LIB')
```

Figure 8.4: A program that displays library descriptions has several uses (part 1 of 5).

```
d ObjRcvLen        s             9b 0 inz(460)
D ReceiveLen       s            10i 0 inz(56)


D ReceiverDs       DS
D   RcvBytRtn                    10i 0
d   RcvBytAvl                    10i 0
D   RcvRcdRtn                    10i 0
d   RcvRcdAvl                    10i 0
d   LenRtnDta                    10i 0
d   RcvKey                       10i 0
d   FldSize                      10i 0
d   LibSize                      10i 0
d   LibMult                      10i 0
d   InfoStat                      1
d   Reserve3                      3
d   LenRtnDta2                   10i 0
d   RcvKey2                      10i 0
d   FldSize2                     10i 0
d   NbrOfObjs                    10i 0

D AttrArray        DS                   INZ
D   NbrOfKeys                    10i 0 inz(2)
d   Key1                         10i 0 inz(6)
d   Key2                         10i 0 inz(7)

DQUSD0400          DS
D*                                         Qus OBJD0400
D QUSBRTN09                1     4B 0
D*                                         Bytes Returned
D QUSBAVL10                5     8B 0
D*                                         Bytes Available
D QUSOBJN03                9    18
D*                                         Object Name
D QUSOBJLN02              19    28
D*                                         Object Lib Name
D QUSOBJT03               29    38
D*                                         Object Type
D QUSRL04                 39    48
D*                                         Return Lib
D QUSASP07                49    52B 0
D*                                         Aux Storage Pool
D QUSOBJ007               53    62
D*                                         Object Owner
D QUSOBJD07               63    64
D*                                         Object Domain
D QUSCDT16                65    77
D*                                         Create Date Time
D QUSCDT17                78    90
D*                                         Change Date Time
```

Figure 8.4: A program that displays library descriptions has several uses (part 2 of 5).

```
D QUSEOA07                   91    100
D*                                         Extended Obj Attr
D QUSTD14                   101    150
D*                                         Text Description
D QUSSFILN09                151    160
D*                                         Source File Name
D QUSSFLN09                 161    170
D*                                         Source File Lib Name
D QUSSFMN05                 171    180
D*                                         Source File Mbr Name
D QUSSFUDT04               181    193
D*                                         Source File Update Date
D QUSOSDT03                 194    206
D*                                         Object Saved Date Time
D QUSORDT03                 207    219
D*                                         Object Restored Date Tim
D QUSCUP04                  220    229
D*                                         Creator User Profile
D QUSSOBJC04               230    237
D*                                         System Object Creation
D QUSRD02                   238    244
D*                                         Reset Date
D QUSSS05                   245    248B 0
D*                                         Save Size
D QUSSSNBR03               249    252B 0
D*                                         Save Sequence Number
D QUSORAGE05               253    262
D*                                         Storage
D QUSSCMD03                 263    272
D*                                         Save Command
D QUSSVID03                 273    343
D*                                         Save Volume ID
D QUSSD05                   344    353
D*                                         Save Device
D QUSSFILN10                354    363
D*                                         Save File Name
D QUSSFLN10                 364    373
D*                                         Save File Lib Name
D QUSSL09                   374    390
D*                                         Save Label
D QUSSL10                   391    399
D*                                         System Level
D QUSPILER04               400    415
D*                                         Compiler
D QUSOBJL05                 416    423
D*                                         Object Level
D QUSUC04                   424    424
D*                                         User Changed
D QUSLPGM04                 425    440
D*                                         Licensed Program
```

Figure 8.4: A program that displays library descriptions has several uses (part 3 of 5).

```
D QUSPTF04                441      450
D*                                            PTF
D QUSAPAR04               451      460
D*                                            APAR
D QUSLUD                  461      467
D*                                            Last Used Date
D QUSUIU01                468      468
D*                                            Usage Information Update
D QUSDUC01                469      472B 0
D*                                            Days Used Count
D QUSOBJS00               473      476B 0
D*                                            Object Size
D QUSOBJSM00              477      480B 0
D*                                            Object Size Multiplier
D QUSOBJCS04              481      481
D*                                            Object Compress Status
D QUSAC04                 482      482
D*                                            Allow Change
D QUSCBPGM04              483      483
D*                                            Changed By Program
D QUSUDA05                484      493
D*                                            User Defined Attr
D QUSOASPI00              494      494
D*                                            Overflow ASP Indicator
D QUSSADT02               495      507
D*                                            Save Active Date Time
D QUSOBJAV04              508      517
D*                                            Object Audit Value
D QUSPG03                 518      527
D*                                            Primary Group
 * Standard Error Code data structure
dQUSEC           DS                116
d QUSBPRV                   1       4B 0      inz(116)

CLON01Factor1+++++++Opcode&ExtFactor2+++++++Result++++++++Len++D+HiLoEq
C     *ENTRY     PLIST
C                PARM                         Lib
C                PARM                         GetObjInf

c                movel     Lib                ObjectLib
 * Retrieve object description
C                CALL      'QUSROBJD'
C                PARM                         QUsd0400
C                PARM                         ObjRcvLen
C                PARM                         ObjdFormat
C                PARM                         ObjectLib
C                PARM                         ObjectTypF
C                PARM                         QusEc

c                Eval      CrtBy = QUSCUP04
```

Figure 8.4: A program that displays library descriptions has several uses (part 4 of 5).

```
C                       Eval        TxtDsc = QUStd14

 * Creation date
C                       if          QusCDT16 <> *blanks
C                       movel       QUSCDT16        Cymd
C         *CYMD         move        Cymd            DateFld
C         *MDY          move        DateFld         CrtDte
C                       endif

 * Restore date
C                       if          QusORDt03 <> *blanks
C                       movel       QUSORDt03       Cymd
C                       move        QUSORDt03       RstTim
C         *CYMD         move        Cymd            DateFld
C         *MDY          move        DateFld         RstDte
C                       endif
 * Last saved date
C                       if          QusOsDt03 <> *blanks
C                       movel       QUSOsDt03       Cymd
C                       move        QUSOsDt03       LstSvdTm
C         *CYMD         move        Cymd            DateFld
C         *MDY          move        DateFld         LstSvdDt
C                       endif

C                       move        QusObjo07       OwnedBy
C                       eval        ObjDsp = NonDisplay

C                       if          %parms > 1
C                       Write       Format1

 * Retrieve library description getting size (and number) of all
 * objects in the library
C                       CALL        'QLIRLIBD'
C                       PARM                        ReceiverDs
C                       PARM                        ReceiveLen
C                       PARM                        Lib
C                       PARM                        AttrArray
C                       PARM                        QusEc

C                       Z-add       NbrOfObjs       TotObj
C         LibSize       Mult        LibMult         TotSiz
C                       Eval        ObjDsp = Normal
C                       Endif

C                       eval        WaitDsp = NonDisplay
C                       Exfmt       Format1

C                       Eval        *inlr = *on
```

Figure 8.4: A program that displays library descriptions has several uses (part 5 of 5).

The first thing the program in Figure 8.4 does is call QUSROBJD to get information about the object. Table 8.1 shows all the parameters for this API. The program uses format OBJD0400, which returns all information about the object. This format gives everything you need except the total number and size of all the objects in the library. For that data, the QLIRLIBD API is used.

Depending on the number of objects in the library, the QLIRLIBD API can take quite some time to run. Rather than subject the operator to unnecessary delays, the program makes calling QLIRLIBD optional. If you pass a second parameter to the program, QLIRLIBD is called, and the total number of objects and total size will display on the screen, as in Figure 8.2.

If you choose to show the total size and number of objects, a status message is submitted to the screen that says, "Now gathering total information...." When QLIRLIBD finishes tallying the totals, they are written to the screen.

QLIRLIBD accepts five parameters, described in Table 8.2. The parameters are pretty standard for retrieve-type APIs. The first is the name of the variable that will hold the information being returned, while the second is the length of the first. Parameter 3 is the name of the library that the API is to retrieve information about. Parameter 4 is an array of keys.

Where most retrieve APIs have a record format name that describes the format of the data being returned, this API uses a method we refer to as the *key method*. Simply put, the API assigns a key value to each piece of information that it is willing to return to you. You give it a list of keys, and it returns the corresponding value that each of the keys represent.

Take a look at the definition of the ATTRARRAY data structure in Figure 8.4. You will see three fields defined within the data structure. The first field, **NbrOfKeys**, tells the API how many keys (or pieces of information) you want returned. Since this field is initialized with a value of two, two more fields follow, **Key1** and **Key2**. These two fields have been initialized to 6 and 7, respectively. If you look in Table 8.2 for the description of parameter 4, you will see that key 6 corresponds to the total size of all the objects in the library, and key 7 corresponds to the total number of all the objects in the library. The last parameter of the API is the standard error code data structure that you should be very familiar with by now.

Table 8.2: Retrieve Library Description API (QLIRLIBD)

Parameter	Description	Type	Attribute	Size
1	A variable receiver. A receiver variable to hold output from the API.	Output	Char	Varies
2	The length of variable receiver. The length of parameter 1.	Input	Binary	4
3	The library name. The name of the library to retrieve information about.	Input	Char	10
4	Attribute array 1, as follows:	Input	Char	Varies

Length	Type	Description
4	Binary	The number of keys in the array.
4	Binary	A key indicating the attribute to retrieve. This field repeats for each key in the array.

Valid key values:

Key	Length	Type	Description
1	1	Char	The type of library.
2	4	Binary	ASP.
3	10	Char	Create authority.
4	10	Char	Create object auditing.
5	50	Char	Description.
6	12	Char	Library size information.
7	4	Binary	The number of objects in a library.

Optional Parameter Group 1

Parameter	Description	Type	Attribute	Size
5	A standard error data structure.	I/O	Char	Varies

The program in Figure 8.4 is simple, yet powerful. The APIs it uses enable you to retrieve information that normally would not be available to you. APIs allow you to create shortcuts to information, circumventing IBM's consistency constraints. In other words, IBM will not show object information when viewing a library description or a file description. If you want object information, you must run the appropriate WRKOBJ command, and then you get *only* object information. While this is great for consistency (one of the strengths of the AS/400), it's also nice to be able to create your own versions of commands that show you what you think is important to see. APIs put you in control of the information you want to see, when you want to see it.

Queuing Your Data

A data queue is a fast method of passing data between programs. You use tools on the system to put the data on the queue, and one or more programs can take data off via the Receive Data Queue (QRCVDTAQ) API. There are a variety of methods available to put data in the queue, as you will see a little later. Pulling data from a data queue usually involves one or more programs, which continually monitor the data queue and take data off it. The information may be retrieved either as it arrives, or at a later time.

Now for the standard question, "Data queue APIs: What can you do with them?" This is a great question to ask of any API, but it is especially pertinent regarding data queues because for most RPG shops, the data queue is a bit of an enigma. It is one of those objects on the AS/400 that was designed to enhance program communications.

For starters, you can use a data queue to communicate between two programs, consolidating many program calls into a single one. For instance, suppose you have a data-entry program that allows the user to press a function key to print out a bill on demand. Conventional wisdom would dictate that the print function be a separate program that gets called when the function key is pressed. However, if this program is called often, the overhead on the system could get quite taxing.

The overhead required to initialize a program can be a big performance hit, especially if the program uses more than one or two database files. If that program is called, and therefore initialized, over and over again, the overall system performance can be dramatically affected.

A better approach in this case would be to have the print program running all the time, waiting on a data queue. When the user presses the function key, instead of calling a program, the program puts data on the data queue using the Send Data Queue (QSNDDTAQ) API. As soon as data is put on the queue, the print program wakes up and prints the information. The overall resources needed by the machine are a lot less because the program is initialized only once, and then is always in memory.

Another good use for data queues involves passing data from one system to another. Using the remote data queue feature, you can create a data queue with one end sitting on one system and the other end sitting on another. You write to the data queue from one system, and read the data off the queue from the other. This method is another example how data queues can be used to enhance program-to-program communications.

Both of the preceding scenarios involve programs that write data to the data queue. As mentioned earlier, however, data queues are all about communication. You can attach data queues to numerous objects on your AS/400, and the system will write information onto the queue for you. For instance, if you attach a data queue to a spooled file, the system will write information to the queue every time a spooled file goes to Ready status. This might be useful, for example, in a server program that automatically moves spooled files among a select group of printers. It would allow you to design print jobs that would share the load and get the overall throughput to print more quickly.

Attaching Data Queues to Jobs

You know that data queues are all about communication and that data queues can be attached to many AS/400 objects. It should come as no surprise, therefore, that you can also attach data queues to jobs. More to the point, you can attach a data queue to a job as an exit point, so that job information will be put in the data queue whenever a job is started, ended, or submitted to a job queue. This lets you monitor jobs on the system.

When would this ability be useful? Just use your imagination. How about a chance to get even with that guy on the loading docks who had the audacity to talk bad about your system *and* your favorite team? Want to know whenever he signs on? Want to change the run priority of his jobs to 90 each time? Better yet, *randomly* change his priority! Of course, you could also make more constructive use of this ability, like being notified every time QSECOFR signs on your system.

In any case, that's the example we're going to show using data queues: how to set the system up to monitor so that anytime a job is submitted to your system, the job name is written to a data queue. (We'll leave up to you the decision as to what action to take for a particular user.)

The Receive Data Queue (QRCVDTAQ) API is used to read the data queue. Table 8.3 shows the parameters for the Receive Data Queue API in detail. Despite its initial appearance, this API is not very complicated. The API looks for the data queue name in parameter 1 and the data queue library name in parameter 2. Parameter 3 specifies the length of the data you are pulling off the data queue and Parameter 4 is the variable that you put the data into.

A word of warning is warranted here. You need to make sure that parameters 3 and 4 match. If you say the size of the variable is 100 bytes, then the size of the variable had better be 100 bytes. If it is not, unpredictable results can occur. If you say the variable is 100 bytes but only define it as 50, the "extra" 50 bytes returned by the API might overflow and corrupt data fields that are defined directly after the variable field! While this might fly in the face of conventional programming, it is not all that uncommon in the world of APIs. The boundaries for APIs are not as clear-cut as they are with RPG code. One other word of warning: Make sure that this length is the same length as the maximum length (MAXLEN) parameter on the Create Data Queue (CRTDTAQ) command you use to create the data queue. (You'll see more about creating the data queue later.)

Table 8.3: Receive Data Queue API (QRCVDTAQ)

Parameter	Description	Type	Attribute	Size
1	The name of the data queue from which to receive data.	Input	Char	10
2	The name of the library where the data queue resides.	Input	Char	10
3	The length of the data to be received from the data queue and put into parameter 4.	Input	Packed	5
4	The name of the variable to receive the data from the data queue.	Output	Char	Varies
5	The wait length, which is one of the following: • -1—Wait indefinitely. • 0—Do not wait at all. • +Number—Wait the specified number of seconds.	Input	Packed	5
Optional Group 1				
6	The key order, which is one of the following: • EQ—Equal. • LT—Less than. • GT—Greater than. • LE—Less than or equal to. • GE—Greater than or equal to.	Input	Char	2
7	The length of the key field specified in parameter 8.	Input	Packed	3
8	The key value to compare data received against. The key order will be applied against this field, and only records that meet the criteria will be received.	Input	Char	Varies
Optional Group 2				
9	The length of the sender information specified in parameter 10.	Input	Packed	3
10	Information about the user who put the data on the data queue.	Output	Char	Varies

Another important parameter is parameter number 5, the data queue wait length. This parameter is where you specify how long you want the API to wait to receive data on the data queue. If there is no data on the queue, do you want it to wait continually until data is put on the queue? If so, put a negative one in this parameter. That number will never be reached, so your program will wait forever. On the other hand, if you specify zero, the API will not wait at all, or you can put the number of seconds you want to elapse before the API continues without getting any data off the queue.

In many cases, the next six parameters are optional. This example program, however, needs to use them. These parameters are all about keyed data queues, and that is the type of queue you must employ to track a job's starting and ending. Parameter 6 is the type of comparison being done on the key (GT, LT, EQ, etc.), and parameter 7 is the length of the key specified in parameter 8. The key specifies what type of information you are pulling off the queue (job starts, job ends, both starts and ends, etc.). Parameters 9 and 10 deal with recording the sender information. Parameter 9 is where you specify the length of the send information you want the system to put in parameter 10.

Despite outward appearances, this API is relatively simple. As a matter of fact, so is the program that uses it. You simply set up a loop to continually call the Receive Data Queue (QRCVDTAQ) API until the data read from the queue is '0000'. The API will sit on the call to QRCVDTAQ until there is some data to get. It will then bring that data into the variable called DATA, where you can parse it to get the user of the job. Sending '0000' to the data queue terminates the program at the end of the day. Another program uses the Send Data Queue (QSNDDTAQ) API to accomplish this task.

There are a few more details you need to know in order to put this program to work. The monitoring program takes data off the data queue, but you need to tell the system that you want it to put information on the queue. Technically, this technique is called using a *job-notification exit point*. So, the first thing you have to do to make it work is to register the exit point with the system.

You register job-notification exit points using the Add Exit Program (ADDEXITPGM) command, as shown in Figure 8.5. Of course, you must have adequate authority to run this command.

```
ADDEXITPGM EXITPNT(QIBM_QWT_JOBNOTIFY) FORMAT(NOTIFY01) PGMNBR(10)
PGM(DATQLIB/DATQNAME) PGMDTA(*JOB 200 '0007*ANY        *ANY')
```

Figure 8.5: Registering an exit program with the system might require a change of the program number on your system.

Enter the command in Figure 8.5, but note that you might need to change the program number on your system. The program number is simply used for identification by the system. Essentially, it is just a sequence number to keep the entries separate. If you are not sure which number to use, run the Work with Registration Information (WRKREGINF) command to view the QIBM_QWT_JOBNOTIFY entry, and look for an unused program number.

Take another look at the command in Figure 8.5. The PGMDTA parameter is comprised of five entries. The first entry (*JOB) is the CCSID parameter. The next entry is the length of the data being put on the queue. The third entry is a code indicating what information will be logged to the data queue. The last two entries indicate the subsystem and library that you want to monitor. In this example, *ANY is used for these two entries, indicating that all subsystems should be used. If a subsystem has already been started, entries will not be put on the data queue until the next time the subsystem is started. The registration facility is only checked when the subsystem starts up. Also, each subsystem is limited to using a maximum of eight data queues.

The next step in this process is to create the data queue. Enter the command in Figure 8.6 to accomplish this task. For the purposes of this example, the data queue must be a keyed data queue, with a key length of 4 bytes and a minimum entry length of at least 74 (200 is used in this example).

```
CRTDTAQ DTAQ(DATAQLIB/DATQNAME) MAXLEN(200) SEQ(*KEYED) KEYLEN(4)
SENDERID(*YES)
```

Figure 8.6: Enter a command to create a data queue.

You have now laid all the necessary groundwork and are ready to submit the program shown in Figure 8.7. The program should be submitted, since it's going to wait forever on the data queue. Otherwise, your terminal will be tied up for a long time. You should also submit it to a queue where other jobs are not going to "stack up" behind it.

```
DName+++++++++++ETDsFrom+++To/L+++IDc.Keywords+++++++++++++++++++++++++
d DataQue         S              10          inz('WATCH')
d DataQueLib      S              10          inz('QGPL ')
d DataLength      S               5 0        inz(200)
d Key             S               4          inz('0001')
d KeyLength       S               3 0        inz(4)
d KeyOrder        S               2          inz('LE')
d SenderInf       S              50
d SenderLen       S               3 0        inz(50)
d WaitLength      S               5 0        inz(-1)

d Data            ds            200
d   MgdIdent                    10
d   MsgFormat                    2
d   InternalID                 16
d   JobName                    10
d   PrfName                    10
d   JobNumber                   6
d   CurentName                 10

CLON01Factor1+++++++Opcode&ExtFactor2+++++++Result++++++++Len++D+HiLoEq
 * Key '0000' is put there by the ENDWATCH request program
c                   Dou       Key = '0000'

 * Read the data queue as entries arrive
c                   CALL      'QRCVDTAQ'
c                   PARM                    DataQue
c                   PARM                    DataQueLib
c                   PARM                    DataLength
c                   PARM                    Data
c                   PARM                    WaitLength
c                   PARM                    KeyOrder
c                   PARM                    KeyLength
c                   PARM                    Key
c                   PARM                    SenderLen
c                   PARM                    SenderInf

c                   Select
```

Figure 8.7: The job-monitoring program uses the QRCVDTAQ command (part 1 of 2).

```
* Key '0000' is the end request record
c                   When        Key = '0000'
c                   leave

c                   When        PrfName = 'BIGAL'
* Take whatever action you want here
c                   endsl

c                   enddo

c                   eval        *inlr = *on
```

Figure 8.7: The job-monitoring program uses the QRCVDTAQ command (part 2 of 2).

Now that you have the monitoring program running in the background, you'll need a way to end it. The answer is the program in Figure 8.8. This program uses the Send Data Queue (QSNDDTAQ) API to write an entry with a key value of 0000. The monitoring program is coded to end itself when it reads an entry with this key. Table 8.4 shows the parameters for QSNDDTAQ.

```
DName+++++++++++ETDsFrom+++To/L+++IDc.Keywords+++++++++++++++++++++
d Data            S              200
d DataQue         S               10            inz('WATCH')
d DataQueLib      S               10            inz('QGPL ')
d DataLength      S                5 0          inz(200)
d Key             S                4            inz('0000')
d KeyLength       S                3 0          inz(4)

CLON01Factor1+++++++Opcode&ExtFactor2+++++++Result+++++++Len++D+HiLoEq
 * Send a '0000' key to queue to request the monitoring program to end
c                   CALL        'QSNDDTAQ'
C                   PARM                      DataQue
C                   PARM                      DataQueLib
C                   PARM                      DataLength
C                   PARM                      Data
C                   PARM                      KeyLength
C                   PARM                      Key

c                   eval        *inlr = *on
```

Figure 8.8: Use the QSNDDTAQ command to end the monitoring program.

Table 8.4: Send Data Queue API (QSNDDTAQ)				
Parameter	**Description**	**Type**	**Attribute**	**Size**
1	The name of the data queue to send data to.	Input	Char	10
2	The name of the library where the data queue resides.	Input	Char	10
3	The length of data to send to the data queue and put into parameter 4.	Input	Packed	5
4	The name of the variable containing the data to be placed on the data queue.	Output	Char	Varies
Optional Group 1				
7	The length of the key field specified in parameter 8.	Input	Packed	3
8	The key value to assign to data being put on the queue.	Input	Char	Varies

User Indexing

Let's continue examining object APIs by looking at another type of object, the user index. A user index is an object that lets you store and sort information. It is similar in function to a database file, but a user index is faster if your table is larger than a thousand entries. It provides quick table lookups, cross-referencing, and sequencing of data.

One of our favorite uses for a user index is to sort information retrieved from APIs. All APIs return their information into a user space or a receiver variable. You process the data returned from the API, just as you normally would. Instead of printing or displaying the data immediately, however, you add the data to a user index. Once you have processed all of the data from the API, you set up a loop to retrieve the data from the user index in the sequence you want.

The sequence in which the information comes back from the user index depends on the key value specified when the index is created. In other words, it comes back sorted by the field specified as the key. You specify the key length when you create the user index, and you specify the value for the key when you add an entry to the index. The following APIs deal with user indexes:

- Create User Index, **QusCrtUI**.
- Add User Index, **QusAddUI**.
- Retrieve User Index, **QusRtvUI**.

Figure 8.9 shows a program that uses all three of these APIs, and more. Its purpose is to list all of the programs in a given library, sequencing them in order of date-last-used. It also shows the activation group that each program uses.

```
****************************************************************
* To Create:
*       CRTBNDRPG PGM(XXX/FIG0807) SRCFILE(XXXLIB/SOURCEFILE)
*       DFTACTGRP(*NO) ACTGRP(ILE) TGTRLS(V4R4M0)
****************************************************************
FFilename++IPEASFRlen+LKlen+AIDevice+.Keywords+++++++++++++++++++++++++
fQsysprt   o   f  132        printer oflind(*inof)

DName++++++++++++ETDsFrom+++To/L+++IDc.Keywords++++++++++++++++++++++++
D CrtUsrSpc       PR            *
D   CrtSpcName                20        const

d Author          s           10        inz('*ALL')
d ChangeDate      s            6 0
d CYMD            s            7
d DateField       s            d
d EntLLN          s           10i 0 inz(408)
d EntryAttr       s            1        inz('F')
d EntryLen        s           10i 0 inz(%size(IndexEntry))
d Extend          s           10
D FormatName      S            8
D ImediateUp      S            1        inz('1')
D InDateFmt       S           10
D IndexName       S           20        inz('INDEX0807 QTEMP      ')
d InLib           s           10
d IndRecLen       S           10i 0
d InsTyp          S           10i 0
d KeyIns          s            1        inz('1')
d KeyLength       s           10i 0 inz(18)
D ListFormat      S            8
d LUDate          s            7 0
d MaximumEnt      S           10i 0
D MemberName      S           10
d NbrAdd          S           10i 0
```

Figure 8.9: This program lists all of the programs in a given library (part 1 of 8).

```
d NbrEntry        S              10i 0
d NbrReturnd      S              10i 0
D ObjNamLIb       S              20     inz('*ALL        *LIBL    ')
D ObjType         S              10
D Optimize        S               1     inz('1')
D OutDateFmt      S              10
D Pass8           S               8
d PrintDate       s               6  0
d ReceiveLen      S              10i 0
D Replace         S              10     inz('*YES')
D ReturnLib       S              10
D Search          S              30
d SearchLen       S              10i 0
d SearchOff       S              10i 0
d SearchType      S              10i 0
D SpacePtr        S               *
d TextD           s              50
d TotCtr          s               5  0
d Ui              s               7  0
D UserSpace       S              20     inz('SPACE0807 QTEMP')
d X               s               7  0

D IndexEntry      DS            131     INZ
D  KeyData               1       18
D  DSIndex              19      131
D  SfObj                        10     overlay(DsIndex:*Next)
D  SfLstd                        6  0 overlay(DsIndex:*Next)
D  SfCrtd                        6  0 overlay(DsIndex:*Next)
D  SfOwnr                       10     overlay(DsIndex:*Next)
D  SfObserve                     1     overlay(DsIndex:*Next)
D  SfText                       50     overlay(DsIndex:*Next)
D  SfActGrp                     30     overlay(DsIndex:*Next)

D PgmReceive      DS            502
D  Observable           105     105
D  ActGroup             473     502

D GetReceive      DS              8
D  GetRtnd               1        4B 0
D  GetAvl                5        8B 0
D IndReceive      DS           32000   based(IndRcvPtr)
D EntLof          DS            408
D  Aof                           8     DIM(51)
D  Lao            DS            300
D  El                    1        4B 0
D  Eo                    5        8B 0

 * General Header Data structure
```

Figure 8.9: This program lists all of the programs in a given library (part 2 of 8).

```
DQUSHO300        DS          576     Based(GenDsPoint)
D QUSISO0              104    104
D*                                   Information Status
D QUSOLD00             125    128B 0
D*                                   Offset List Data
D QUSSLD00             129    132B 0
D*                                   Size List Data
D QUSNBRLE00          133    136B 0
D*                                   Number List Entries
D QUSSEE00            137    140B 0
D*                                   Size Each Entry

D*Type Definition for the OBJL0700 format.
D*******************************************************************
DQUSL0700         DS          588                based(ListPoint)
D*                                               Qus OBJL0700
D QUSOBJNU05            1     10
D*                                   Object Name Used
D QUSOLNU05            11     20
D*                                   Object Name Used
D PgmAndLib             1     20
D*                                   Program and Library
D QUSOBJTU05           21     30
D*                                   Object Type Used
D QUSISO06             31     31
D*                                   Information Status
D QUSTD11              42     91
D*                                   Text Description
D QUSOBJO03           113    122
D*                                   Object Owner
D QUSCDT08            125    132
D*                                   Create Date Time
D QUSCDT09            133    140
D*                                   Change Date Time
D QUSLUDT00           533    540
D*                                   Last Used Date Time

 * Standard Error Code data structure
DQUSEC            DS          116
D QUSBPRV               1      4B 0  inz(116)
D QUSBAVL               5      8B 0


CLON01Factor1+++++++Opcode&ExtFactor2+++++++Result+++++++Len++D+HiLoEq
C      *entry      Plist
C                  Parm                   InLib
C                  move       InLib       ObjNamLib

 *  Create user space for file list information
C                  Eval       SpacePtr = CrtUsrSpc(UserSpace)
```

Figure 8.9: This program lists all of the programs in a given library (part 3 of 8).

```
 *   Create user index
 C                  Call      'QUSCRTUI'
 C                  Parm                      IndexName
 C                  Parm                      Extend
 C                  Parm                      EntryAttr
 C                  Parm                      EntryLen
 C                  Parm                      KeyIns
 C                  Parm                      KeyLength
 C                  Parm                      ImediateUp
 C                  Parm                      Optimize
 C                  Parm                      Author
 C                  Parm                      TextD
 C                  Parm                      Replace
 C                  Parm                      QusEc

 C                  If        QusBAvl = 0
 *   List program names to user space
 C                  Call      'QUSLOBJ'
 C                  Parm                      UserSpace
 C                  Parm      'OBJL0700'      ListFormat
 C                  Parm                      ObjNamLib
 C                  Parm      '*PGM'          ObjType
 C                  Parm                      QusEc

 *   Load the general data structure
 c                  Eval      GenDsPoint = SpacePtr

 *   If the list API was complete or partially complete
 c                  if        QuSISO0 = 'C' OR
 c                            QuSISO0 = 'P'
 *   Load the list data structure
 c                  Eval      ListPoint = GenDsPoint + QusOLD00

 C                  Do        QusNbrLE00

 *   If the list entry has no problems, otherwise ignore it
 c                  if        QuSISO6 = ' '

 C                  Call      'QCLRPGMI'
 C                  Parm                      PgmReceive
 C                  Parm      502             ReceiveLen
 C                  Parm      'PGMI0200'      FormatName
 C                  Parm                      PgmAndLib
 C                  Parm                      QusEc
 C        PRTHED    IFEQ      *BLANKS
 C                  EXCEPT    HEADNG
 C                  MOVE      'N'             PRTHED          1
 C                  ENDIF
```

Figure 8.9: This program lists all of the programs in a given library (part 4 of 8).

```
C                       Call      'QWCCVTDT'
C                       Parm      '*DTS'          InDateFmt
C                       Parm                      QusCdt08
C                       Parm      '*YMD'          OutDateFmt
C                       Parm                      CYMD
C                       Parm                      QusEc
c                       move      CYMD            PrintDate

c                       If        QusLUDT00 <> x'0000000000000000'
C                       CALL      'QWCCVTDT'
C                       PARM      '*DTS'          InDateFmt
C                       Parm                      QusLUDT00
C                       PARM      '*YMD'          OutDateFmt
C                       PARM                      CYMD
C                       PARM                      QusEc
c                       move      CYMD            LUDate
c                       else
c                       move      *zeros          CYMD
c                       move      *zeros          LUDate
c                       endif
C                       Move      QusObjNU05      SfObj
C                       Move      PrintDate       SfCrtD
C                       Move      LUDate          SfLstD
C                       Move      QusTD11         SfText
C                       Move      QusObj003       SfOwnr
C                       Move      Observable      SfObserve
C                       Move      ActGroup        SfActGrp
C                       Movel     CYMD            KeyData
C                       Move      QusObjNU05      KeyData
 *   Add to user index
C                       Call      'QUSADDUI'
C                       Parm                      ReturnLib
C                       Parm                      NbrAdd
C                       Parm                      IndexName
C                       Parm      2               InsTyp
C                       Parm                      IndexEntry
C                       Parm                      EntryLen
C                       Parm                      Pass8
C                       Parm      1               NbrEntry
C                       Parm                      QusEc
c                       endif

c                       Eval      ListPoint = ListPoint + QusSEE00

c                       EndDo

C     NbrReturnd        DouLT     MaximumEnt
 * Retrieve size of receiver variable needed
C                       Call      'QUSRTVUI'
```

Figure 8.9: This program lists all of the programs in a given library (part 5 of 8).

```
C                     Parm                      GetReceive
C                     Parm        8             IndRecLen
C                     Parm                      EntLof
C                     Parm        408           EntLLN
C                     Parm                      NbrReturnd
C                     Parm                      ReturnLib
C                     Parm                      IndexName
C                     Parm        'IDXE0100'    FormatName
C                     Parm        50            MaximumEnt
C                     Parm        4             SearchType
C                     Parm                      Search
C                     Parm        30            SearchLen
C                     Parm        0             SearchOff
C                     Parm                      QusEc
 *  Allocate needed storage so field will be large enough
C                     Alloc       GetAvl        IndRcvPtr
 *  Retrieve user index
C                     Call        'QUSRTVUI'
C                     Parm                      IndReceive
C                     Parm        GetAvl        IndRecLen
C                     Parm                      EntLof
C                     Parm        408           EntLLN
C                     Parm                      NbrReturnd
C                     Parm                      ReturnLib
C                     Parm                      IndexName
C                     Parm        'IDXE0100'    FormatName
C                     Parm        50            MaximumEnt
C                     Parm        4             SearchType
C                     Parm                      Search
C                     Parm        30            SearchLen
C                     Parm        0             SearchOff
C                     Parm                      QusEc
C        KeyLength    ADD         1             UI
c                     Clear                     x
 *  Do for the number of entries returned from QUSRTVUI
C        2            Do          NbrReturnd    X
 *  Move the lengths and offsets array to binary length and offset field
C                     Movea       Aof(X)        Lao
 *  Add the offset field to index field
C                     Add         Eo            Ui
c                     Eval        DsIndex = %subst(IndReceive:UI:
c                                 %len(DsIndex))
C                     Except      Print
C                     Add         1             TotCtr
C                     EndDo
 *  Set up search request for next 50 entries from QUSRTVUI
c                     Eval        Search = %subst(IndReceive:Ui-KeyLength:
c                                 %len(Search))
C                     EndDo
```

Figure 8.9: This program lists all of the programs in a given library (part 6 of 8).

```
c                     Endif
c                     Endif

c                     Except    Last
c                     eval      *inlr = *on
 *
OFilename++DF..N01N02N03Excnam++++B++A++Sb+Sa+...................
OQSYSPRT   E              HEADNG          1 02
O          OR    OF
O                                        40 'Program Listing'
o                                       120 'Page:'
o                         PAGE        z  130
O          E              HEADNG          2
O          OR    OF
O                                        29 'LIBRARY -'
O                         InLib          39
O          E              HEADNG          1
O          OR    OF
O                                         7 'PROGRAM'
O                                        21 'CREATED'
O                                        31 'LAST USD'
O                                        37 'OWNER'
O                                        48 'OBSERVE'
O                                        60 'TEXT'
O                                       111 'ACT GROUP'
O          EF             PRINT           1
O                         SfObj          11
O                         SfCrtD      Y  21
O                         SfLstd      Y  31
O                         SfOwnr         42
O                         SfObserve      45
O                         SfText        100
O                         SfActGrp      132
O          E              LAST          2 1
O                                        18 'TOTAL PRINTED'
O                         TotCtr      Z  25
 *
 *  Procedure to create extendable user space, return pointer to it.
 *
PName+++++++++++..T.................Keywords++++++++++++++++++++++++
P CrtUsrSpc       B              export
DName++++++++++++ETDsFrom+++To/L+++IDc.Keywords+++++++++++++++++++++
d CrtUsrSpc       PI              *
d   CrtSpcName                   20     const

 * Local Variables
D PasSpcName      DS             20
D  SLib                    11     20
```

Figure 8.9: This program lists all of the programs in a given library (part 7 of 8).

```
D ChgAttrDs       DS            13
D  NumberAttr                    9B 0 inz(1)
D  KeyAttr                       9B 0 inz(3)
D  DataSize                      9B 0 inz(1)
D  AttrData                      1    inz('1')
D ListPtr         S              *
D SpaceAttr       S             10    inz
D SpaceAuth       S             10    INZ('*CHANGE')
D SpaceLen        S              9B 0 INZ(2048)
D SpaceReplc      S             10    INZ('*YES')
D SpaceText       S             50
D SpaceValue      S              1

CLON01Factor1+++++++Opcode&ExtFactor2+++++++Result++++++++Len++D+HiLoEq
 * Create the user space
C                   move        CrtSpcName      PasSpcName
C                   CALL        'QUSCRTUS'
C                   PARM                        PasSpcName
C                   PARM                        SpaceAttr
C                   PARM                        SpaceLen
C                   PARM                        SpaceValue
C                   PARM                        SpaceAuth
C                   PARM                        SpaceText
C                   PARM        '*YES'          SpaceReplc
C                   PARM                        QusEc
 * Get pointer to user space
C                   CALL        'QUSPTRUS'
C                   PARM                        PasSpcName
C                   PARM                        ListPtr
 * Change user space to be extendable
C                   CALL        'QUSCUSAT'
C                   PARM                        Slib
C                   PARM                        PasSpcName
C                   PARM                        ChgAttrDs
C                   PARM                        QusEc

C                   return      ListPtr
PName++++++++++..T.................Keywords+++++++++++++++++++++++++++
P CrtUsrSpc        E
```

Figure 8.9: This program lists all of the programs in a given library (part 8 of 8).

The first thing the program does is call **CrtUsrSpc** to create an expandable user space for other APIs to use. (For more information on user spaces, refer to chapter 1.)

Next, a user index is created by calling the Create User Index (QUSCRTUI) API. This API has 10 mandatory and four optional parameters. Don't let the sheer number of parameters deter you from using user indexes. The capability provided by these APIs is well worth the effort it takes to understand them. Besides, if you are from the old school and happen to use the 3C method of programming (Cut, Copy, and Clone), once you have a working copy of the API, it's easy to use in other programs.

Table 8.5 shows these parameters in detail, but the important points are as follows:

- Parameter 1 is the name (and library) of the index you want to create.

- Parameter 2 is the extended attribute of the user index you are creating. Leave this parameter blank because there isn't an extended attribute for a user index.

- Parameter 3 tells the API whether to use fixed length data (F) or variable length data (V). In this case, fixed-length entries are used.

- Parameter 4 specifies the length of each entry that will be put in the index.

- Parameter 5 indicates whether keys will be used to add and retrieve records from the index. A zero indicates no keys will be used, while a one (which is used for this example) indicates that keys will be used to insert records into the index.

- Parameter 6 is the length of the data that is the key to the index. The key will be defined starting at the beginning of the data being put in the index and will continue for the length specified in this parameter.

- The next two parameters, 7 and 8, deal with performance issues of the API itself. Parameter 7 indicates whether entries added to the index are to be written to auxiliary storage immediately (one) or written later (zero). Indexes that are written immediately take longer to process than those that are written later. Parameter 8 indicates what type of optimization you want the API tuned for. A zero indicates that you are mainly going to be accessing the index randomly, one record at a time. A one indicates that you will be accessing the index sequentially.

- The next parameter is the authority level to be granted to users of the index, and the last required parameter is a text description of the index.

Table 8.5: Create User Index API (QUSCRTUI) (part 1 of 2)

Parameter	Description	Type	Attribute	Size
1	The name and library of the user index to create, where the first 10 characters are the user name, and the next 10 are the library name. It accepts *CURLIB.	Input	Char	20
2	An extended attribute to be given to the user index. It must be a valid *NAME.	Input	Char	10
3	An entry-length attribute that indicates whether entries will be of a fixed (F) or variable (V) length.	Input	Char	1
04	The length of each index entry. If fixed length, valid values are one to 2,000. If variable, valid values are zero or negative one. A zero indicates a maximum of 120 bytes. A negative one indicates a maximum of 2,000 bytes.	Input	Binary	4
5	The key insertion, either a zero if no key is used or a one if a key is used.	Input	Char	1
6	The length of key portion of the index entry. The key begins in position 1.	Input	Binary	4
7	Immediate update; a zero means no immediate update, while a one means every add or remove is written to auxiliary storage immediately.	Input	Char	1
8	Optimization; a zero means optimize for random, while a one means optimize for sequential processing.	Input	Char	1
9	Public authority; the authority to give to a user of the index who does not have specific authority.	Input	Char	10
10	A description of the user index.	Input	Char	50

Optional parameters exist, starting with parameter 10. This parameter indicates whether an existing index should be replaced with the new one you are creating. It is followed by the standard error-data-structure parameter. These two parameters form the first optional parameter grouping. Since the error parameter should be included, you must also include the Replace Yes/No parameter.

Parameter	Description	Type	Attribute	Size
Table 8.5: Create User Index API (QUSCRTUI) (part 2 of 2)				
Optional Group 1				
11	Replace, which is one of the following: • *NO—Do not replace an index if it already exists. Issue an error instead. • *YES—Replace an existing index of the same name and library.	Input	Char	10
12	A standard error data structure.	I/O	Char	Varies
Optional Group 2				
13	The domain into which the user index is to be created, which is one of the following: • *DEFAULT—The system decides which domain. • *SYSTEM—Put in the system domain. • *USER—Put in the user domain.	Input	Char	10
Optional Group 3				
14	Usage tracking, which provides better availability to the index. If tracking is on (indicated by a one) checkpoints are kept while changing. If a partial change is found, the index is flagged as damaged.	Input	Char	1

Let's consider parameter groupings for a minute. An optional parameter grouping is a group of parameters that are included or excluded together. If you want to use one parameter in a grouping, you must use all of them. Conversely, if you want to omit one of the parameters, you must omit all of them. There are often multiple optional parameter groupings for an API, like the three for the Create User Index API.

The other optional groupings in this API deal with usage tracking and what domain to place the index in. Both of these options are ignored in this example.

Now that the user space and user index are built, it's time to generate the list of programs in the library. The List Objects (QUSLOBJ) API accomplishes this task. This API, covered earlier in this chapter, puts the list of programs into the user space. Using pointers, data structures are overlaid on the user space, thus populating the data fields with the information in the list.

As the loop extracts each program name from the list of programs, we want a little more information than the QUSLOBJ API gives. We want to show if the program has its observable information removed, and the activation group attribute that the programs use. The Retrieve Program Information (QCLRPGMI) API can access both of these items of information.

The parameters for QCLRPGMI are shown in Table 8.6. Since it's a standard receive-type API, the first parameter is the receiver variable to hold the output from the API, and the second parameter is the length of the first. Parameter 3 describes the format of the data being returned. Parameter 4 is the name and library of the program to get more information about. The last parameter is the standard error data structure.

Table 8.6: Retrieve Program Information API (QCLRPGMI)				
Parameter	**Description**	**Type**	**Attribute**	**Size**
1	The name of the receiver variable to receive the output of the API.	Output	Char	Varies
2	The length of parameter 1.	Input	Binary	4
3	The format name; the name of the API-supplied record format describing the format of the data being returned.	Input	Char	8
4	The program name and library, where the first 10 characters are the program name and the second 10 are the library name.	Input	Char	20
5	A standard error data structure	I/O	Char	Varies

You now have all the information you want about each program in the library, but there is a small problem with two of the fields that were retrieved using the List Objects API. The "create date" and the "last used date" are in system timestamp format. This is a 64-bit binary field that needs to be converted to a more user-friendly format. There is an API to accomplish this, of course. It is called the Convert Date and Time Format (QWCCVTDT) API. The details for the parameters to this API are given in Table 8.7.

Table 8.7: Convert Date and Time Format API (QWCCVTDT)				
Parameter	**Description**	**Type**	**Attribute**	**Size**
1	The format of the date in parameter 2, as follows:	Input	Char	10

Value	Description
*CURRENT	Machine clock time
*DTS	System timestamp
*JOB	DATFMT job attribute
*SYSVAL	QDATFMT system value
*YMD	Year/month/date
*YYMD	YYYYMMDD
*MDY	Month/day/year
*MDYY	MMDDYYYY
*DMY	Day/month/year
*DMYY	DDMMYYYY
*JUL	Julian format
*LONGJUL	*YYYYDDD*

2	The data to be converted.	Input	Char	Varies
3	The format of the output variable.	Input	Char	10
4	The output variable. Formatted output.	Output	Char	Varies
5	A standard error data structure.	I/O	Char	Varies

The first parameter of QWCCVTDT indicates the format of the date to be converted. In this case, *DTS indicates that you are converting from a system timestamp format. The second parameter is the actual date field to convert. Parameters 3 and 4 are the output format and the output date. Because *YMD is specified as the format, the first position of the date returned will contain a century indicator. A value of zero indicates the 20th century, while a one indicates the 21st century.

If you were going to print the listing in the order that the List Object API returned (alphabetically), you would be ready to print a detail line at this point. This report should not print in that sequence, however; it should print the programs in ascending order by date of last use. So, instead of printing a detail line at this point, the program adds an entry to the user index. This entry will contain the data that we will eventually print on the report.

To add an entry to the user index, call the Add User Index Entry (QUSADDUI) API. This API has nine parameters, listed in detail in Table 8.8. The first parameter returned is the library name where the API found the index that it is adding an entry to. The second parameter is the number of entries that were successfully added to the index. This field is useful if you are adding multiple entries to the index with one call to the API and an error occurs. You can interrogate this field to see how many indexes were actually added. In this example, only one is added at a time, so you can pretty much ignore this parameter for now.

Parameter 3 is the name of the index that the program is adding an entry to. Parameter 4 is a code telling the API what type of insert (add) is to be done. Code 2, used in the example, means if an entry already exists in the index with the same key as the one being added, update the entry with the data portion that we are adding.

Parameter 5 is the actual data and key being added to the index. Since a fixed-length entry is used in the example, it is a data structure in the form of key fields followed by data fields. The length of the key field was specified on the Create User Index API. The total length of the entry being added is specified in parameter 6.

If you were using a variable-length entry, you would fill parameter 7 with a data structure that contained binary fields indicating the length and position of the information being added. Since a fixed-length entry is being used, parameter 7 is blank. Parameter 8 indicates the number of entries being added to the index with this call to the API. In this case, only one is being added at a time. The last parameter is the standard error data structure.

Table 8.8: Add User Index API (QUSADDUI)

Parameter	Description	Type	Attribute	Size
1	The name of the library that the index entry was added to.	Output	Char	10
2	The number of index entries added.	Output	Binary	4
3	The name and library of the user index to create. The first 10 characters are the user name, and the next 10 are the library name. *CURLIB is accepted.	Input	Char	20
4	The insert type code, which is one of the following: • 1—Insert a unique argument. • 2—Insert with replacement, which updates the data portion of the existing key. • 3—Insert without replacement. This is add only. If an entry exists with the key value, an error is issued.	Input	Binary	4
5	The entry or entries to be added to the index.	Input	Char	Varies
6	The length of each index entry. If it is fixed length, valid values are one to 2,000. If it is variable, valid values are zero or negative one. Zero indicates a maximum of 120 bytes. Negative one indicates a maximum of 2,000.	Input	Binary	4
7	A multiple occurring data structure of two 4-byte binary fields containing the lengths and offset pointers to data in the index entry parameter. This parameter is ignored if entries are of a fixed length.	Input	Char	Varies
8	The number of index entries contained in parameter 5 that are to be added to the index.	Input	Binary	4
9	A standard error data structure with a description of the user index.	I/O	Char	Varies

You have now seen how to process an item from the list generated by the List Object (QUSLOBJ) API and add it to a user index using the Add User Index (QUSADDUI) API. Next, the program increments the pointer to get the next item in the list and starts processing it. When every entry on the list has been processed, it's time to think about printing the report.

To print the report, the program sets up another loop calling the Retrieve User Index Entries (QUSRTVUI) API repeatedly until it has retrieved every entry on the user index. Each time QUSRTVUI is called, it returns a field indicating the number of entries that were returned, and another field indicating the maximum number of entries that could be returned with each call. A loop is set up using these two fields. If the number of entries returned is less than the maximum number of entries that could be returned, the loop ends.

Since QUSRTVUI is a retrieve-type API that can potentially return a tremendous amount of data, the double-call technique is used to determine the proper size of the receiver variable. (This technique is discussed in detail in chapter 1.)

QUSRTVUI has 14 required parameters. By now, the number of parameters should not deter you; most of them are easy to use and are documented in Table 8.9. They are also summarized in the following list:

- Parameter 1 is the receiver variable that will contain the results of calling the API.

- Parameter 2 is the length of parameter 1. This is standard retrieve-type API processing.

- Parameter 3 is a multiple occurring data structure with one occurrence for each entry retrieved from the index. The structure contains entry lengths and offsets pointing to each entry put in the receiver variable. You use this structure to parse out the data returned in the receiver variable. This is different from the normal processing of retrieve-type APIs, but it is necessary because each entry in the index can be of variable size, so you can't be sure where the data is going to be in the receiver variable even when you use a format name to describe the data. Still, it's not much different from the techniques used to process data returned into user spaces.

- Parameter 4 is simply the length of parameter 3.

- Parameter 5 is the number of index entries that were returned into the receiver variable. This number is used to control the processing loop. When it is less that the maximum number of possible entries that can be returned (parameter 9), the last batch of entries has been received.

- Parameter 6 is the library where the user index was found.

- Parameter 7 is the name of the user index.

- Parameter 8 is the format name describing the format of the data returned in parameter 1.

- Parameter 9 is the maximum number of entries that can be returned with each call to the API.

- The next four parameters deal with the search criteria used to retrieve index entries. The first of these (parameter 10) is a code describing the type of index search to be made (GT, LT, EQ, etc). The example uses code 4, which means do a greater-than-or-equal-to type of search. In other words, find the index entries that are greater than or equal to the search criteria entered in the next parameter (11).

- Parameter 11 is the search value to compare against. Parameter 12 is the length of parameter 11.

The last search parameter is the offset of the second search element from the beginning of the search field. If you are using two search fields concatenated together into the search parameter, this field indicates where the second search field begins. In the case of the example, you are not comparing two search fields with each other to determine which records to read, so the value of this field is zero.

The last parameter to specify is the standard error data structure. The rest of the code simply parses out the data in the receiver variable and prints each entry that it gets. The result is a report printed in last-used-date sequence. This is a prime example of the power of APIs at work!

Table 8.9 Retrieve User Index Entry API (QUSRTVUI) (part 1 of 2)				
Parameter	Description	Type	Attribute	Size
1	A variable that holds the user index entries returned by the API. Data will be in the following format: 	Size	Description	 4 binary	Bytes returned. 4 binary	Bytes available. Varies	Entries that satisfied search criteria.	Output	Char	Varies
2	The length of the receiver variable in parameter 1. For entries specified on QUSCRTUI, the length should be the maximum length (in parameter 9) plus eight.	Input	Binary	4
3	A multiple occurring data structure of two 4-byte binary fields containing lengths and offset pointers to data in the index entry parameter. This parameter is ignored if entries are of a fixed length. It is used to process the variable-length entries returned.	Output	Char	Varies
4	The length of the receiver variable in parameter 3.	Input	Binary	4
5	The number of index entries that satisfied the search criteria.	Output	Binary	4
6	The library name from which user indexes are retrieved.	Output	Char	10
7	The name and library of the user index from which to retrieve indexes. The first 10 characters are the user name, and the next 10 are the library name. *CURLIB is accepted.	Input	Char	20
8	The format name, describing format of the data returned. It must be IDXE0100.	Input	Char	8
9	The maximum number of entries to return. Valid entries are one to 4,095.	Input	Binary	4

Table 8.9 Retrieve User Index Entry API (QUSRTVUI) (part 2 of 2)				
Parameter	Description	Type	Attribute	Size
10	The search type, a code indicating the type of compare to perform against the search criteria field. The code is one of the following: **Code** Description • 1—Equal to. • 2—Greater than. • 3—Less than. • 4—Greater than or equal to. • 5—Less than or equal to. • 6—First. • 7—Last. • 8—Between.	Input	Binary	4
11	The criteria used to search the index, to determine what entries to return.	Input	Char	Varies
12	The length of parameter 11. This parameter is ignored if the search type is 6 (first) or 7 (last).	Input	Binary	4
13	The offset of the second search element from the beginning of the search criteria. It is only used for search type 8 (between).	Input	Binary	4
13	A standard error data structure describing the user index.	I/O	Char	Varies

Summary

In this chapter, you discovered that object APIs are some of the most useful APIs there are. You found that the Retrieve Object Description and List Object Description APIs can be used to provide a plethora of information about any object on your system. You saw that testing for the existence of an object is a common programming task, which the QUSROBJD API handles easily.

You also saw how data queues can provide quick solutions to many programming problems, and that they can eliminate a lot of system overhead when used with a properly designed system. Similarly, user indexes can also be used for a lot of solutions, such as sorting the output of other APIs. Or they can be used to sort subfiles. Yet another use is to provide fast lookups of records on files that are being chained to regularly.

Since everything on the AS/400 is an object, it stands to reason that object APIs are extremely powerful. If you are going to be your organization's designated API guru, take the time to learn about object APIs. It will be time well spent.

9

Socket APIs

Almost every building that you have ever been in has electrical sockets, but they are so commonplace that you walk right by them every day without even noticing. Underappreciated and overworked, without them, you would not be able to run any electrical device. Electrical sockets enable the appliances in your home to connect to the power grid. You plug the appliance into the socket and forget about it. Whenever you want what your appliance supplies, you simply turn it on, and the power grid supplies the needed energy.

Similarly, your AS/400 has API sockets that enable programs on the AS/400 to communicate with programs on a PC. How do they do that? Well, you start up a server socket program on your AS/400, and whenever the program on your PC wants information your AS/400 supplies, the program posts its request, and the API socket program supplies the required information. It's not a perfect analogy, of course, because your AS/400 could act as either the power grid or the appliance. Nevertheless, socket APIs allow RPG programs to exchange information with PC-based programs. The most common use for socket APIs is in a client/server application. Although a server is typically one system and the clients are others, in fact, both functions can reside on the same machine.

This chapter shows you a sockets program for communicating with a PC voice-response system. The process begins when a customer calls the support center. The voice-response system on the PC answers the call and prompts the caller to enter an account number. That account number is then passed to the AS/400 via a socket connection. The application on the AS/400 determines the status of the account and sends that information back to the voice-response system on the PC. The information passed via the socket's connection includes the account balance and the date and amount of the last payment. The voice-response system then "reads" that data back to the customer who made the call. The entire process is slick and fast. The really good news is that the program is also easy to write.

Delivering the Goods

Figure 9.1 shows the APIs used in the sockets program needed for the voice-response system.

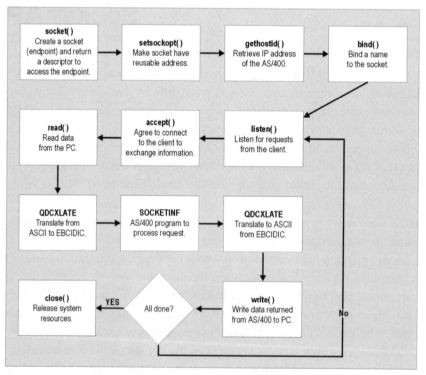

Figure 9.1: The sockets program shown in Figure 9.2 follows this flow.

Figure 9.2 shows that there are only 11 basic functions in this program, each accomplished via an API. Although many other socket APIs are available, the ones in this sample program are sufficient to exchange information between the PC and your AS/400.

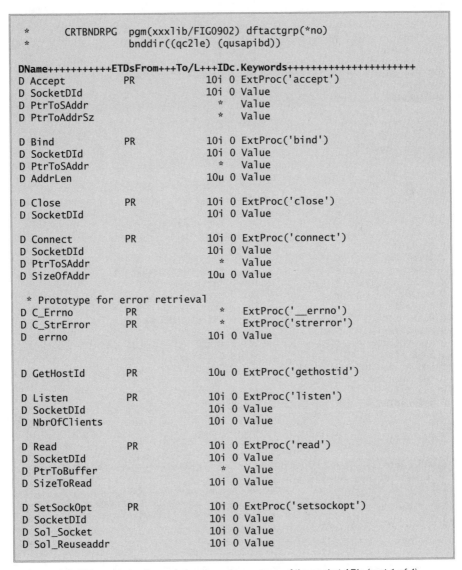

```
 *       CRTBNDRPG  pgm(xxxlib/FIG0902) dftactgrp(*no)
 *                  bnddir((qc2le) (qusapibd))

DName++++++++++ETDsFrom+++To/L+++IDc.Keywords++++++++++++++++++++++
D Accept          PR            10i 0 ExtProc('accept')
D SocketDId                     10i 0 Value
D PtrToSAddr                      * Value
D PtrToAddrSz                     * Value

D Bind            PR            10i 0 ExtProc('bind')
D SocketDId                     10i 0 Value
D PtrToSAddr                      * Value
D AddrLen                       10u 0 Value

D Close           PR            10i 0 ExtProc('close')
D SocketDId                     10i 0 Value

D Connect         PR            10i 0 ExtProc('connect')
D SocketDId                     10i 0 Value
D PtrToSAddr                      * Value
D SizeOfAddr                    10u 0 Value

 * Prototype for error retrieval
D C_Errno         PR              * ExtProc('__errno')
D C_StrError      PR              * ExtProc('strerror')
D  errno                        10i 0 Value

D GetHostId       PR            10u 0 ExtProc('gethostid')

D Listen          PR            10i 0 ExtProc('listen')
D SocketDId                     10i 0 Value
D NbrOfClients                  10i 0 Value

D Read            PR            10i 0 ExtProc('read')
D SocketDId                     10i 0 Value
D PtrToBuffer                     * Value
D SizeToRead                    10i 0 Value

D SetSockOpt      PR            10i 0 ExtProc('setsockopt')
D SocketDId                     10i 0 Value
D Sol_Socket                    10i 0 Value
D Sol_Reuseaddr                 10i 0 Value
```

Figure 9.2: This example of a socket program uses many of the socket APIs (part 1 of 4).

```
D PtrToOn                             *  Value
D SizeOfOn                          10u 0 Value

D Socket            PR              10i 0 ExtProc('socket')
D Af_Inet                          10i 0 Value
D Sock_Stream                      10i 0 Value
D                                  10i 0 Value

D Write             PR              10i 0 ExtProc('write')
D SocketDId                         10i 0 Value
D PtrToBuffer                       *  Value
D SizeToRead                        10i 0 Value

D sockaddr          DS
D   sa_family                       5u 0
D   sa_data                        14a
D serveraddr        DS
D   sin_family                      5i 0
D   sin_port                        5u 0 inz(2510)
D   sin_addr                       10u 0
D    sin_addrA                      4a    Overlay(sin_addr)
D   sin_zero                        8a

D Af_Inet           C                     Const(2)
D AS/400sid         S              10i 0 inz
D DataLen           S               5P 0 inz
d ErrorText         s              80
d ErrorVal          s              10i 0 based(@errorVal)
D On                S              10u 0 inz(1)
D PcSId             S              10i 0 inz
D RqsBuffer         S              60A    inz
D RqsBfrLen         C                     %SIZE(RqsBuffer)
D RspBuffer         S              60A    inz
D ReturnCode        S              10i 0 inz(0)
D Sock_Stream       C                     Const(1)
D Sol_Reuseaddr     C                     Const(55)
D Sol_Socket        C                     Const(-1)
D svaddrlen         S              10u 0 inz
D NbrReadIn         S              10i 0 inz
D Unused            C                     Const(0)
D Table             S              10A    inz
D TableLib          S              10A    inz('QSYS')

CLON01Factor1+++++++Opcode&ExtFactor2+++++++Result++++++++Len++D+HiLoEq
 * Create socket descriptor
C                   Eval      AS/400sid = Socket(Af_Inet
C                                               :Sock_Stream
C                                               :Unused)
C                   If        (AS/400sid > 0)
```

Figure 9.2: This example of a socket program uses many of the socket APIs (part 2 of 4).

```
***** Set socket descriptor to be reuseable.
C                Eval       ReturnCode = SetSockOpt(AS/400sid
C                           :Sol_Socket:Sol_Reuseaddr
C                           :%addr(On):%size(On))
C                If         (ReturnCode < 0)
C                Eval       @errorval = C_Errno
C                Eval       ErrorText = %str(C_Strerror(ErrorVal))
C                Endif

C                Eval       sin_family = Af_Inet
C                Eval       sin_port = 2510

* retrieve as/400 ip address
C                Eval       sin_addr = GetHostId
C                Eval       sin_zero = X'0000000000000000'
C                Eval       svaddrlen = %size(serveraddr)
C                Eval       ReturnCode = Bind(AS/400sid
C                           :%addr(serveraddr):svaddrlen)
C                If         (ReturnCode < 0)
C                Eval       @errorval = C_Errno
C                Eval       ErrorText = %str(C_Strerror(ErrorVal))
C                Else

* Listen for connection requests from client
C                Eval       ReturnCode = Listen(AS/400sid:10)
C                If         (ReturnCode < 0)
C                Eval       @errorval = C_Errno
C                Eval       ErrorText = %str(C_Strerror(ErrorVal))
C                Else
* Accept new requests to communicate with client.
*   We need to accept each new request before we can read it
C                Dow        (RqsBuffer <> '*STOPSVR')
C                Eval       ReturnCode = Accept(AS/400sid
C                           :%addr(serveraddr):%addr(svaddrlen))
C                If         (ReturnCode < 0)
C                Eval       @errorval = C_Errno
C                Eval       ErrorText = %str(C_Strerror(ErrorVal))
C                Leave
C                Endif

C                Eval       PcSId      = ReturnCode

C                Dow        (ReturnCode > 0)
* Process data received from client
C                Eval       NbrReadIn = Read(PcSId
C                           :%addr(RqsBuffer):rqsBfrLen)

* If error reading records in, go back to accepting connections
C                If         (NbrReadIn < *zeros)
C                Eval       ReturnCode = Close(PcSId)
```

Figure 9.2: This example of a socket program uses many of the socket APIs (part 3 of 4).

```
C                 Leave
C                 Endif

* translate from ASCII to EBCDIC
C                 Call(e)   'QDCXLATE'
C                 Parm      rqsbfrlen    DataLen
C                 Parm                   RqsBuffer
C                 Parm      'QEBCDIC'    Table
C                 Parm                   TableLib
C                 If        %Error
C                 Eval      ReturnCode = Close(PcSId)
C                 Leave
C                 Endif

* Process the request
C                 Call      'SOCKETINF'
C                 Parm                   RqsBuffer
C                 Parm                   RspBuffer

C                 Call(e)   'QDCXLATE'
C                 Parm      rqsbfrlen    DataLen
C                 Parm                   RspBuffer
C                 Parm      'QASCII '    Table
C                 Parm                   TableLib
C                 If        %Error
C                 Eval      ReturnCode = Close(PcSId    )
C                 Leave
C                 Endif

* Send data back to client     .
C                 Eval      ReturnCode = Write(PcSId
C                           :%addr(RspBuffer):rqsbfrlen)
C                 If        (ReturnCode < 0)
c                 Eval      @errorval = C_Errno
c                 Eval      ErrorText = %str(C_Strerror(ErrorVal))
C                 Leave
C                 Endif

C                 Enddo
C                 Enddo

C                 Endif
C                 Endif
C                 Endif

C                 Eval      ReturnCode = Close(AS/400sid)
C                 Eval      *Inlr = *on
```

Figure 9.2: This example of a socket program uses many of the socket APIs (part 4 of 4).

The first function the program in Figure 9.2 needs to perform is creating a socket. A socket is an endpoint for communications, just as an electrical socket is an endpoint for electricity. Once you have established the socket, all you have to do is plug something in, and you are ready to go. The **Socket()** API is used to create the socket. The parameters for this API are given in Table 9.1.

Table 9.1: Parameters for the Create Socket API, Socket()					
Parameter	**Description**		**Type**	**Attr**	**Size**
Returns	An integer that has one of the following values: • -1—An error occurred. • A value other than −1—A number representing the socket descriptor.		Output	Integer	10
1	The address family, as follows:		Input	Integer	10
	Code	**Value**	**Description**		
	AF_INET	2	Internet domain communications.		
	AF_NS	6	Novel or Xerox protocol definitions.		
	AF_UNIX	1	UNIX domain communications.		
	AF_TELEPHONY	99	ISDN telephony domain communications.		
2	The type of communication to establish, as follows:		Input	Integer	10
	Code	**Value**	**Description**		
	SOCK_DGRAM	2	Datagram socket.		
	SOCK_SEQPACKET	5	Full-duplex sequenced packet.		
	SOCK_STREAM	1	Full-duplex stream socket.		
	SOCK_RAW	3	Communicate directly with network protocols.		
3	The protocol to be used on the socket. A zero means to use the default protocol that matches the type of communication.		Input	Integer	10

279

The next step is to establish the socket attributes. This is done with a call to the Set Socket Option API, **SetSockOpt()**. The parameters to this API are shown in Table 9.2. The Set Socket Option API can be used to set many options on a socket connection, but for the purposes of this example, it sets the socket to be reusable.

Table 9.2: Parameters for the Set Socket Options API, SetSockOpt() (part 1 of 2)					
Parameter	**Description**		**Type**	**Attr**	**Size**
1	The descriptor of the socket whose options are to be changed.		Input	Integer	10
2	The level of option to be changed, that is, does request apply to the socket or to the underlying protocol? One of the following:		Input	Integer	10
	Code	**Value**	**Description**		
	IPPROTO_IP	2	IP protocol layer.		
	IPPROTO_TCP	5	TCP protocol layer.		
	NNSPROTO_IPX	1	IPX protocol layer.		
	NNSPROTO_SPX	3	SPX protocol layer.		
	SOL_SOCKET	-1	Applies to socket.		
3	The option name, as follows:		Input	Integer	10
	Name	**Value**	**Description**		
	SO_BROADCAST	5	Allow broadcast messages.		
	SO_DONTROUTE	15	Just use interface addresses.		
	SO_ERROR	20	Socket error status.		
	SO_KEEPALIVE	25	Connections kept alive with periodic messages.		
	SO_LINGER	30	Socket lingers on close.		
	SO_OOBINLINE	35	Out-of-band data is received inline.		
	SO_RCVBUF	40	Receive buffer size.		

Table 9.2: Parameters for the Set Socket Options API, SetSockOpt() (part 2 of 2)

Parameter	Description				Type	Attr	Size
3, cont.	**Name**	**Value**	**Description**				
	SO_RCVLOWAT	45	Receive low water mark.				
	SO_RVCTIMEO	50	Receive timeout value.				
	SO_REUSEADDR	55	Allow local address reuse.				
	SO_SNDBUF	60	Send buffer size.				
	SO_SNDLOWAT	65	Send low water mark.				
	SO_SNDTIMEO	70	Send timeout value.				
	SO_TYPE	75	Socket type.				
	SO_LOOPBACK	80	Sender receives a copy of each message transmitted.				
4	A pointer to the value of the option to set, where zero means off and one means on. Other values are valid depending on the option being set.				Input	Pointer	16
5	The length of the value in parameter 4.				Input	Integer	10

After the socket attributes are set, the program needs the IP address of the AS/400. The GetHostId() API is used to get it. The parameter for this API is shown in Table 9.3.

Table 9.3: Parameters for the Get Host Id API, GetHostId()

Parameter	Description	Type	Attr	Size
Returns	A 32-bit IP address; an integer represents the address.	Output	Integer	10

The previous step identified the address of the AS/400, but since two-way communication is being performed, the program needs to have addresses for both parties concerned. Therefore, the next thing to do is to get the local address for the socket that was just created. To do that, the program uses the Bind() API, whose parameters are shown in Table 9.4.

When you look at Bind(), you can see that it uses a server-address data structure aptly named **serveraddr**. Embedded within that structure is a field called **sin_port**. This is the port number that the PC will use to talk to the program. This example uses port 2510. We chose that port number because it was the port that the PC program was coded to use.

Table 9.4: Parameters for the Set Local Address API, Bind()

Parameter	Description	Type	Attr	Size
Returns	An integer indicating the following: • -1—An error occurred. • 0—The procedure was successful.	Output	Integer	10
1	The descriptor of the socket to be bound.	Input	Integer	10
2	A pointer to the address structure, with the following format: • 5u—The address family. • 14—The address.	Input	Pointer	16
3	The length of the address in parameter 2.	Input	Integer	10

Next, the sockets program goes into listening mode, using the Listen() API. This API tells the socket to accept incoming connection requests. Failure to run Listen() would result in a sockets program that would ignore all incoming communication requests. Table 9.5 shows the parameters for this API.

Table 9.5: Parameters for the Listen API, Listen()

Parameter	Description	Type	Attr	Size
Returns	An integer indicating the following: • -1—An error occurred. • 0—The procedure was successful.	Output	Integer	10
1	The descriptor of the socket to use to listen.	Input	Integer	10
2	Backlog; the maximum number of requests that can be queued before the system begins rejecting requests.	Input	Pointer	16

So, the sockets program will be accepting input, but what initiates the action? Well, the Accept() API monitors the socket connection. This causes the program to take the first connection request and create a connection between the server (AS/400) and the client (PC). The program will then just sit on this API until a connection request is received. Table 9.6 lists the parameters for this API.

Table 9.6: Parameters for the Accept Input API, Accept()				
Parameter	**Description**	**Type**	**Attr**	**Size**
Returns	An integer indicating the following: • -1—An error occurred. • 0—The procedure was successful.	Output	Integer	10
1	The descriptor of the socket.	Input	Integer	10
2	A pointer to the address structure, with the following format: • 5u—The address family. • 14—The address.	Input	Pointer	16
3	The length of the address in parameter 2.	Input	Integer	10

The last two steps caused a connection to be made, so now the program needs to get the data coming through the connection. For that, it uses the Read() API. Table 9.7 lists the parameters for this API.

Table 9.7: Parameters for the Read Data API, Read()				
Parameter	**Description**	**Type**	**Attr**	**Size**
Returns	An integer indicating the following: • -1—An error occurred. • *n*—The number of bytes returned in the buffer.	Output	Integer	10
1	The descriptor of the file.	Input	Integer	10
2	A pointer to the buffer that contains the request data.	Output	Pointer	16
3	The number of bytes to read into buffer.	Input	Integer	10

But PCs talk in ASCII format, and your AS/400 talks in EBCDIC. The QDCXLATE API acts as an interpreter, so that the two systems understand each other. Since the data coming from the PC is in ASCII format, we need to translate it into EBCIDIC. The parameters for QDCXLATE are listed in Table 9.8.

Table 9.8: Parameters for the Translate Data API (QDCXLATE)				
Parameter	**Description**	**Type**	**Attr**	**Size**
1	The length of data to translate (the size of parameter 2).	Input	Dec	5
2	The data to translate.	Input	Char	Varies
3	The translation table.	Input	Char	10
4	The name of the library that contains the translation table.	Input	Char	10

Now that the data is in a format that the AS/400 likes, you can do anything you want with it. For the purposes of this example, the program passes the data to another program to actually do some work. We call this "work" program SOCKETINF in the example. The data is passed to the SOCKETINF program, along with a request for information, and it produces a parameter that contains the requested information.

For example, if you request information about account number X from the SOCKETINF program, that program does the file lookups and passes the account information back to the sockets program. The returned information is then translated from EBCDIC to ASCII and sent through the socket to the PC via the Write() API. Notice that this is exactly the opposite of the function performed with the Read() API. The parameters for Write() are described in Table 9.9

Table 9.9: Parameters for the Write Data API, Write()				
Parameter	**Description**	**Type**	**Attr**	**Size**
Returns	An integer indicating the following: • -1—An error occurred. • 0—The write was successful.	Output	Integer	10
1	The descriptor of the file.	Input	Integer	10
2	A pointer to the buffer that contains the data to be written.	Output	Pointer	16
3	The number of bytes to write into buffer.	Input	Integer	10

The entire process continues until the program is ended. As a general rule, the program ends when the PC sends a *STOPSRV command to the buffer, or when the AS/400 is shut down. Once the end-of-job is requested, the **Close()** API is called to clean up the resources used. The parameters for **Close()** are shown in Table 9.10.

Table 9.10: Parameters for the End Socket Connection API, Close()				
Parameter	Description	Type	Attr	Size
Returns	An integer indicating the following: • -1—An error occurred. • 0—The close was successful.	Output	Integer	10
1	The descriptor of the socket to close.	Input	Integer	10

There is one important fact to note when dealing with socket APIs. If you look at the documentation for these APIs, you will see that some parameters are defined to accept integers. When you look at the valid entries for these parameters, however, you will see character constants as valid entries! For instance, the first parameter of the **Socket()** API is the "address family," and is defined as an integer. If you look at the valid entries for this parameter, the first one you see is AF_INET, which is clearly not an integer!

Obviously, some type of translation is going on here. If you look at the program coding for the **Socket()** API, you can see that it passes a constant named AF_INET that is defined with the number 2. How did we know that when the documentation called for AF_INET, it really wanted the number 2? Once again, we turned to our good friend, library QSYSINC.

By now, you should be acutely aware that when dealing with APIs, you should use the definitions in the QRPGLESRC source file found in library QSYSINC. Up to this point, using the definitions in library QSYSINC has been optional. When dealing with the socket APIs, however, you cannot translate the documented APIs in the manuals into code without looking in source file SYS in library QSYSINC. There is a member named SOCKET that is very valuable when dealing with sockets. We have included the translations in the tables for each API that we have covered in our sample program.

You should also take note that, when compiling this program (or any program using socket APIs), you will need to use two special binding directories. In previous chapters, you saw the QC2LE binding directory for dealing with the C-type APIs. You also need this directory when compiling APIs dealing with sockets, if you want to code error-handling. Socket APIs use the C-type error-handling routines found in binding directory QC2LE. The APIs are accessed through the QUSAPIBD binding directory. Be sure to specify both of these binding directories when compiling the sample program.

When you submit the sample program to subsystem QINTER, it runs continually (usually sitting on the **Accept()** API statement) until a customer phones in a request for information.

Connecting the Dots

When you are dealing with sockets, you need to be aware of the Work with TCP/IP Network Status, or NETSTAT. You will use this command to check the status of your connection with the PC. If necessary, you can end the connection through this command.

When you first run the command, a screen similar to the one in Figure 9.3 appears.

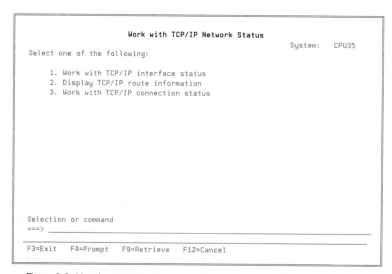

Figure 9.3: Use the NETSTAT command to test the connection status.

To test the status of your connection, select option 3, and a screen similar to the one shown in Figure 9.4 will appear. If you need to end the connection, find the local port number you are using (in our case, it was 2510) and use option 4 to terminate the connection.

```
                    Work with TCP/IP Connection Status
                                                   System:   CPU35
     Local internet address  . . . . . . . . . . :    *ALL


     Type options, press Enter.
       4=End   5=Display details


         Remote          Remote      Local
     Opt Address         Port        Port      Idle Time  State
       _    *              *         ftp-con >  020:33:33  Listen
       _    *              *         telnet     000:01:20  Listen
       _    *              *         bootps     000:02:57  *UDP
       _    *              *         tftp       020:30:41  *UDP
       _    *              *         www-http   010:43:55  Listen
       _    *              *         netbios >  020:32:27  Listen
       _    *              *         netbios >  000:00:44  *UDP
       _    *              *         netbios >  000:00:43  *UDP
       _    *              *         netbios >  020:32:27  Listen
       _    *              *         snmp       020:32:25  *UDP
       _    *              *         as-svrmap  000:01:21  Listen
                                                             More...
     F5=Refresh   F11=Display byte counts   F13=Sort by column
     F14=Display port numbers   F22=Display entire field   F24=More keys
```

Figure 9.4: The NETSTAT command gives you the option to monitor or end your connection with the PC.

Summary

Sockets are a powerful communications tool, and are the preferred method of communicating with PC programs. This chapter has covered only a tiny fraction of the APIs that deal with sockets communications, but you have seen enough of the basic steps to get a good start.

So go ahead, use what you learned here, read the manuals, and write a few programs. In no time, you will be able to say, "socket to me."

10

WEB APIs

The fact that the Internet has changed the world is old news. It has changed how we communicate, shop, bank, and even vacation. If you think that your AS/400 is immune to this ongoing revolution, you have not been paying attention. IBM has made no secret of the fact that it wants your AS/400 to be the server of choice. If you want to be gainfully employed in the years to come, you should be doing what you can to help IBM attain this lofty goal.

If you are one of the unfortunates still trying to clear your in-box from the Y2K hangover, you might not have had the opportunity to spend much time on education in the last year or two. You might be surprised at how much Internet capability your AS/400 has. You say that you want to serve Web pages from your AS/400? No problem! You need to create an Internet-based Frequently Asked Questions (FAQ) page on your AS/400? You can do it! You're ready to participate in the business-to-business (B-to-B) and business-to-consumer (B-to-C) e-commerce revolution? Your AS/400 is ready!

This chapter shows you how to write a secure application that will deliver AS/400 spooled files to the Internet. The application is password-protected and allows you to direct selective spooled output to the specific users you want. This means that spooled files can be made available to your Internet browser without a physical connection to your AS/400. Best of all, this chapter supplies the RPG IV code required to accomplish this!

You have spent nine chapters reading all about how to work with APIs in RPG IV. Now it's time to begin discussing the APIs that let you write programs to communicate with the Internet. Surprisingly, there are only a handful of them. These APIs enable you to write *Common Gateway Interface (CGI)* programs. CGI programs can be written in a number of different languages, on a number of different platforms, but this chapter concentrates on how to write them with APIs and RPG IV on your AS/400.

Some Internet Basics

The most common way to communicate over the Internet, of course, is via a browser like Microsoft's Internet Explorer or Netscape's Navigator. Devices running a browser are commonly referred to as *browser clients*, or just *clients*.

When communicating over the Internet, a navigational request is made through the browser by means of an Internet address, or *URL (Uniform Resource Locator)*. The URL is a little like a street address. It tells the Internet where you want your browser to go, and in some cases, what program you want to run on the server at the specified address.

You are probably familiar with this concept of entering a URL and having a Web page returned to your browser. The Web pages delivered to your browser are written in a simple language called *HTML*, which stands for *Hypertext Markup Language*.

HTML documents come in two flavors, *static* or *dynamic*. A static Web page is one that is sitting on a server somewhere and is delivered whenever its URL is requested. A dynamic Web page, on the other hand, is created "on-the-fly" by a program residing on a server. There are uses for both types of HTML documents, and your AS/400 is certainly qualified to serve both. This chapter, however, concentrates on how your AS/400 can be used to serve dynamic HTML documents to a browser over the Internet using the standard Internet protocol called Common Gateway Interface, or CGI.

CGI is really just a standardized protocol that enables programs to communicate via a browser like Internet Explorer or Navigator. A CGI program resides on the server and usually presents an HTML document that requires some sort of operator action. The operator might press selection buttons or complete entry boxes of some kind, and then press an HTML button to submit the information back to the CGI program. The CGI program on the server would then present a new HTML document (otherwise known as a dynamic Web page) based on the operator's action choices. These steps repeat themselves until the desired result is achieved.

You might have noticed that there is something a little inconsistent about using APIs and RPG IV on your AS/400 to write CGIs for the Internet. As you probably know, the AS/400 was designed to communicate primarily in EBCDIC. The Internet, on the other hand, is just like your PC, which communicates asynchronously, or in ASCII. So how, you might be asking, are you going to be able to resolve these fundamental differences? The answer, of course, is in the APIs! The APIs covered in this chapter act as "interpreters" to exchange the information between the two very different protocols.

Before you get too excited about writing AS/400 programs for the Internet, however, there are some prerequisites that you need to understand.

Prerequisites for Internet Connections

Communication is one of the many things that the AS/400 is really good at. This is one system that really *can* talk to anything. Before you can hook your AS/400 up to the Internet, however, you will need to get your ducks in a row. First, you will need to find yourself an *ISP*, or *Internet Service Provider*. The ISP will provide you with the means to physically connect your AS/400 to the Internet, and will help you register your *domain name*, which is the Internet equivalent of a postal address. But not so fast! If you are going to hook your AS/400 up to the Internet, you should seriously consider putting a top-of-the-line firewall in place.

A firewall can be thought of as a digital traffic cop, designed to manage and track the flow of information to and from your computer. It is designed to keep the bad guys out, while letting you and your customers pass information to and from your system as needed. For our own purposes, we chose an external firewall on a Windows/NT server. Our setup looks much like the diagram in Figure 10.1.

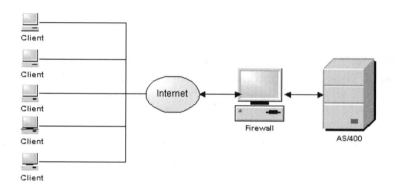

Figure 10.1: A typical AS/400-to-Internet connection includes a firewall.

When a request is made to our AS/400 server via the Internet, it comes in through our ISP and is delivered to our firewall, where the request is logged and either accepted or denied. If the request is deemed valid by the firewall, the request is then posted to the HTTP server on our AS/400. HTTP stands for *Hypertext Transport Protocol*, and it is the method you employ to serve HTML documents to the Web. (You will see more about the HTTP server later in this chapter.)

Next, make sure that your system security is configured for level 40 or above. Anything less, and you are exposing your system to potential disaster. There are numerous password policies that you should employ, as well. We strongly recommend that you visit IBM's *AS/400 Web Builder's Workshop* Web site:

```
www.as400.ibm.com/tstudio/workshop/webbuild.htm
```

Carefully review the security recommendations made there. Would you leave the front door to your house standing open all of the time? Of course not. For all practical purposes, that is what you are doing with your AS/400 if you do not put a proper security plan into place.

With your firewall in place and your system security tightened up, it's time to select a good ISP. Make sure you choose a solid and reputable company. There has been a tremendous amount of upheaval in the ISP arena in recent years, most of which has translated into downtime and lost revenue for customers who were left high and dry.

As mentioned earlier, your ISP will help you register your domain name, which will enable people to reach your AS/400 from the outside world. Keep the domain name short if possible. The shorter it is, the easier it will be for customers and prospects to get to your site. (Just in case you were wondering, *AS400.com* has been taken, so you will have to get a little more creative than that.)

Your ISP will also supply you with your *IP address*. *IP* stands for *Internet Protocol*. Essentially, it is your address on the Web. It will look something like 111.222.111.222, where each component of the address is a number between 0 and 256. Your system will automatically translate your domain name to the IP address, so outside parties will be able to get to your site using the domain name instead of your IP address. Obviously, it is easier to tell someone to "go to DougAndRon.com" than it is to say "go to 111.222.111.222."

Once you have accomplished these tasks, you are ready to configure your AS/400 for TCP/IP connections and set up the AS/400 HTTP server. You will need to have a PC that is connected to your AS/400. You will also need to have a sign-on user ID and password that gives you *IOSYSCFG and *ALLOBJ authority.

The steps required to configure TCP/IP and the HTTP server are beyond the scope of this book. Suffice it to say, though, that if you visit the IBM Web site mentioned earlier, you will find all of the information you need to get your AS/400 up and running on the Web.

Once you have your AS/400 attached to the Web, you are almost ready to begin serving dynamic Web pages from your RPG IV programs. First, however, you need to create an HTTP server instance for your CGI programs. You can setup a server instance through the administration Web pages on your AS/400, as described on IBM's *AS/400 Web Builder's Workshop* Web site, or you can do it the old "green-screen" way. From the green screen, you begin by running the Work with HTTP Configuration (WRKHTTPCFG) command. Figure 10.2 shows an example of the server instance named DOUGANDRON that we set up for our CGI programs.

```
                      Work with HTTP Configuration
                                                    System:    CPU35
      Configuration name . . . . . . . :    DOUGANDRON


    Type options, press Enter.
      1=Add    2=Change   3=Copy    4=Remove    5=Display    13=Insert


         Sequence
    Opt   Number    Entry
     __     ____
     __    00010     Enable GET
     __    00020     Enable POST
     __    00030     map /cgi-bin/* /QSYS.LIB/RON.LIB/*.PGM
     __    00040     Exec /QSYS.LIB/RON.LIB/*




                                                                Bottom
    F3=Exit    F5=Refresh   F6=Print List   F12=Cancel   F17=Top   F18=Bottom
    F19=Edit Sequence
```

Figure 10.2: You can use WRKHTTPCFG to set up an AS/400 HTTP server instance.

The references at the end of this chapter give you all the information you need about server instances and configurations. The important things to notice in Figure 10.2 though, are the *directives*, statements that tell the system what you are allowed to run within the server instance being configured.

The ENABLE directives in your HTTP configuration tell the system which operations are allowed. To write CGI programs, you need the ENABLE directives for GET and POST. These directives tell the system what will and what will not be allowed from a URL on a browser that is communicating with your AS/400. The EXEC directive tells the system where your executable code is located. In our example, the code is in library RON. The MAP directive tells the system where to go and what to do when a CGI request comes into it via a URL request made from a browser.

Once your HTTP configuration has been performed, you need to start your server instance using the Start TCP Server (STRTCPSVR) command. An example of this command is shown in Figure 10.3.

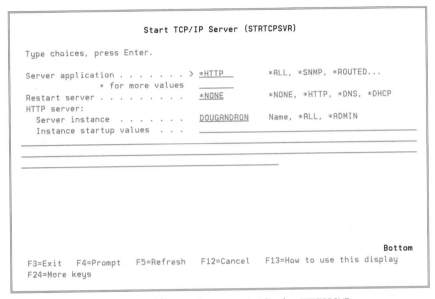

```
                    Start TCP/IP Server (STRTCPSVR)

 Type choices, press Enter.

 Server application . . . . . . . >  *HTTP        *ALL, *SNMP, *ROUTED...
            + for more values
 Restart server . . . . . . . . .   *NONE        *NONE, *HTTP, *DNS, *DHCP
 HTTP server:
   Server instance  . . . . . . .   DOUGANDRON   Name, *ALL, *ADMIN
   Instance startup values  . . .




                                                                    Bottom
 F3=Exit   F4=Prompt   F5=Refresh   F12=Cancel   F13=How to use this display
 F24=More keys
```

Figure 10.3: After setting up the server instance, start it using STRTCPSVR.

Once your server has been started, you are ready to intercept requests from the Internet. You can use the Work with Active Jobs (WRKACTJOB) command to check the status of your HTTP server instance. You should see it running under the QHTTPSVR subsystem. Now that the operational chores are finished, it's time to move on to writing CGI programs.

CGI Programming

IBM gave you a little gift when it shipped your AS/400, in the form of a service program named QTMHCGI in library QTCP. This service program has procedures that let you send and receive data from a client browser. Since library QTCP is probably not in your library list, however, you need to copy this program out to the library where your CGI programs will reside. Even if library QTP is in your system library list, failure to copy this service program could result in malfunctions in your program if IBM decides to change it later.

Obviously, you would not want programs to fail simply because you performed an operating system upgrade. The code in Figure 10.4, therefore, creates a duplicate copy of the program into library RON, which is where we elected to keep the CGI programs written for this book.

```
CRTDUPOBJ OBJ(QTMHCGI) FROMLIB(QTCP) OBJTYPE(*SRVPGM) TOLIB(RON)
```

Figure 10.4: Create a duplicate copy of the QTMHCGI service program.

The next step is to create a binding directory to make it easier to compile programs. In Figure 10.5, you can see how a binding directory named WEBBNDDIR is created in library RON. The QTMCGI service program is added to the binding directory using the command in Figure 10.6.

```
CRTBNDDIR BNDDIR(RON/WEBBNDDIR)
```

Figure 10.5: Create the binding directory.

```
ADDBNDDIRE BNDDIR(RON/WEBBNDDIR) OBJ((RON/QTMHCGI))
```

Figure 10.6: Populate the binding directory with the QTMHCGI service program.

You're not quite through with the binding directory, though. There's one more useful service program to add to it. You might remember the Create User Space Procedure (**CrtUsrSpc**) procedure from chapter 1. That procedure is used later in this chapter to create a user space to hold a list of spooled files.

The binder language code to put that procedure in a service program called WEBSRVPGM is shown in Figure 10.7.

```
STRPGMEXP
EXPORT      SYMBOL(CRTUSRSPC)
ENDPGMEXP
```

Figure 10.7: WEBSRVPGM is a service program.

Create the service program in Figure 10.7, and then add it to the WEBBNDDIR binding directory following the steps in Figure 10.6. When you are done, use the Display Binding Directory (DSPBNDDIR) command to check your results. They should look something like Figure 10.8.

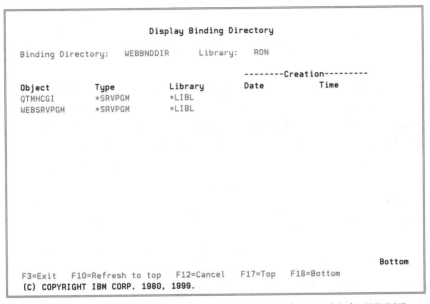

```
                          Display Binding Directory

    Binding Directory:   WEBBNDDIR      Library:   RON

                                         --------Creation---------
    Object          Type            Library     Date         Time
    QTMHCGI         *SRVPGM         *LIBL
    WEBSRVPGM       *SRVPGM         *LIBL




                                                                   Bottom
    F3=Exit    F10=Refresh to top    F12=Cancel   F17=Top   F18=Bottom
    (C) COPYRIGHT IBM CORP. 1980, 1999.
```

Figure 10.8: Using the DSPBNDDIR command, you can view the completed WEBBNDDIR binding directory.

The preliminary work has now been completed, and you are ready to write some code. The first sample program presents an HTML document that asks for the operator to sign onto the system. The Web page does this by prompting for a user ID and password.

This is not part of the standard AS/400 security. When you access an AS/400 using a CGI program, your default user ID will always be QTMHHTP1. If you were simply accessing objects via the HTTP server, your default user ID would be QTMHHTTP. There is a way to override these values using the HTTP configuration, but they are the standard defaults. You can see the security implications if everyone accessing your system through the HTTP server shares the same two user IDs.

Web pages served via the HTTP server do not get an AS/400 sign-on screen. If the information you are serving is of a potentially sensitive nature, you need to manage the security of the application yourself. You could write a simple validation program that stores user IDs and passwords in a database file, but this could hardly be considered secure. Remember the security APIs covered in chapter 7? One of the sample API programs in that chapter demonstrates how to work with and maintain validation lists. Coincidentally, that is exactly how IBM recommends you should deal with security issues when writing CGI programs.

The program shown in Figure 10.9 automatically generates the HTML required to serve the Web page shown in Figure 10.10. The program constructs the HTML code and then delivers it to the HTTP server by employing the Write Standard Out (**QtmhWrStout**) API . The parameters for this API are shown in Table 10.1.

```
****************************************************************
*   TO COMPILE:
*    CRTBNDRPG PGM(XXXLIB/WEBSIGNON) SRCMBR(FIG1009) DFTACTGRP(*NO)
****************************************************************

HKeywords++++++++++++++++++++++++++++++++++++++++++++++++++++++++
h bnddir('WEBBNDDIR')

DName+++++++++++ETDsFrom+++To/L+++IDc.Keywords+++++++++++++++++++++++
 * Prototype for Write Standard Out API
d StandardOut     PR                  EXTPROC('QtmhWrStout')
d                             1024
d                              9B 0
d                              116

 * Compile time array for HTML specifications
d HTML            s             80    dim(12) ctdata perrcd(1)

 * Standard Error Data Structure
d ErrorDs         DS            116    INZ
d  ErrBytPrv              1      4B 0 inz(116)
d  ErrBytAvl              5      8B 0 inz(0)
d  MessageId              9     15
d  ERR###                16     16
d  MessageDta            17    116

 * End-of-Line Character
d EOT             C                   CONST(X'15')
```

Figure 10.9: The WEBSIGNON CGI program automatically generates HTML (part 1 of 2).

```
d DoNumber          S              4 0
d Index             S              4 0
d Output            S             1024
d OutputLen         S               9B 0

CLON01Factor1+++++++Opcode&ExtFactor2+++++++Result++++++++Len++D+HiLoEq
 * Write HTTP Header and Heading
c                   Eval      Output = %Trim(HTML(1)) + EOT
c                   Exsr      WriteIt
c                   Eval      Output = %Trim(HTML(2)) + EOT + EOT
c                   Exsr      WriteIt

 * Write HTML
c                   Eval      DoNumber = %Elem(HTML) - 1
c        3          Do        DoNumber      Index
c                   Eval      Output = %Trim(HTML(Index))
c                   Exsr      WriteIt
c                   EndDo

 * Write HTTP Footer
c                   Eval      Output = %Trim(HTML(%Elem(HTML))) + EOT
c                   Exsr      WriteIt

c                   Eval      *INLR = *On

 *****    Subroutine: WriteIt   ****************************************
 ***   Write HTML Record ********************************************
csr  WriteIt        BEGSR
c                   Eval      OutputLen = %len(%trim(Output))
c                   Callp     StandardOut(Output:OutputLen:ErrorDs)
csr                 EndSR

** CTData HTML
Content-type: text/html
Pragma: no-cache
<html><head><title>Sign On Please</title></head><Body>
<h1><center>Sign On</h1><br />
<h2>Enter your login information:</h2><br><br />
<FORM action="WEBVALID8" method="POST">
<table><tr><td>Name:</td><td>
<INPUT type=text name=UserId size=10></td></tr>
<tr><td>Password:</td>
<td><INPUT type=Password name=Password size=10></td></tr></table>
<br><br><INPUT type=submit value="Submit">
</form></center></body></html>
```

Figure 10.9: The WEBSIGNON CGI program automatically generates HTML (part 2 of 2).

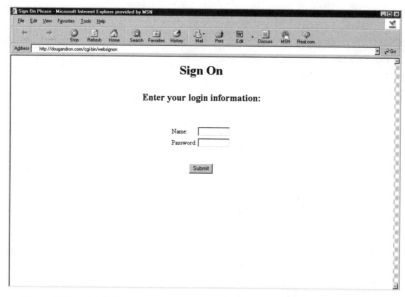

Figure 10.10: This Web page is dynamically served by WEBSIGNON.

We prototyped the API to make it a little easier to call. The procedure that employs this API is found in the service program copied in from the TCP library. By specifying the WEBBNDDIR binding directory in the header specification, as in Figure 10.9, you can access any of the procedures in the QTMHCGI and WEBSRVPGM service programs without having to implicitly specify the binding directory when compiling the program.

Table 10.1: Parameters for the Write to Stdout API (QtmhWrStout)				
Parameter	**Description**	**Type**	**Attr**	**Size**
1	Variable data; a field that will hold information returned by the API.	Input	Char	Varies
2	The length of parameter 1.	Input	Binary	4
3	A standard error data structure.	I/O	Char	Varies

After the WEBSIGNON program creates an HTML document and submits it to the browser, it turns on the Last Record indicator and is done with its work. What happens next depends on what the operator does with the HTML document that was served to the browser.

The HTML generated by WEBSIGNON is shown in Figure 10.11. It might seem a little confusing at first, but as you can see, it took very little HTML code to generate the Web page in Figure 10.10.

```
<html><head><title>Sign On Please</title></head><Body><h1><center>Sign
On</h1><br /><h2>Enter your login information:</h2><br><br /><FORM
action="WEBVALID8" method="POST"><table><tr><td>Name:</td><td><INPUT
type=text name=UserId size=10></td></tr><tr><td>Password:</td><td><INPUT
type=Password name=Password size=10></td></tr></table><br><br><INPUT
type=submit value="Submit"></form></center></body></html>
```

Figure 10.11: The WEBSIGNON CGI program generates HTML.

When an operator uses the Web page to enter a user ID and password, and then presses the SUBMIT button, the WEBVALID8 program in Figure 10.12 is automatically launched. The event that caused the WEBVALID8 program to be called was the pressing of the SUBMIT button. The FORM statement in the HTML tells the system to launch the WEBVALID8 program when SUBMIT is pressed.

The WEBVALID8 program in Figure 10.12 processes the initial Web page that the WEBSIGNON CGI program served to the browser. As you might have surmised, this program is the most complicated in this series. That is because WEBVALIB8 calls four different APIs, as well as one of the security programs from Chapter 7 (using the validation list APIs). It will serve one of two different Web pages, depending on the validity of the user ID and password entered. That is a lot of ground to cover for a single program.

```
*****************************************************************
*    TO COMPILE:
*      CRTBNDRPG PGM(XXXLIB/WEBVALID8) SRCMBR(FIG1012) DFTACTGRP(*NO)
*****************************************************************
```

Figure 10.12: The WEBVALID8 CGI program processes the initial Web page that the WEBSIGNON CGI program served to the browser (part 1 of 6).

```
HKeywords+++++++++++++++++++++++++++++++++++++++++++++++++++++++++++
H bnddir('WEBBNDDIR')

FFilename++IPEASFRlen+LKlen+AIDevice+.Keywords++++++++++++++++++++++++
fWebOutqs  if   e           k disk

DName+++++++++++ETDsFrom+++To/L+++IDc.Keywords+++++++++++++++++++++++++
d RcvDs           e ds                    extname(WEBSIGNPF)

 * Compile time HTML Array
d HTML            s              80    dim(18) ctdata perrcd(1)

 * Prototype for CharToNum procedure - converts numeric length
dCharToNum        PR             30p 9
d                                32    options(*varsize)

 * Prototype for Write Standard Out API
d StandardOut     PR                    EXTPROC('QtmhWrStout')
d                               1024
d                                 9B 0
d                                116

 * Standard API error data structure
d ErrorDs         DS                    INZ
d  ErrBytPrv              1      4B 0 inz(116)
d  ErrBytAvl              5      8B 0 inz(0)
d  MessageId              9     15
d  ERR###                16     16
d  MessageDta            17    116

 * End-of-line character
D EOT             C                     CONST(X'15')

d Action          s              1
d Index           S              4 0
d EnvRec          S           1024
d Description     s             50
d ErrorText       s             70
d RcvRec          S           1024
d Output          S           1024
d OutputLen       S              9B 0
d Rtncode         s              1
d FileDs          s             20    inz('WEBSIGNPF QGPL       ')
d EnvLen          S              9B 0
d EnvRecLen       S              9B 0 inz(%size(EnvRec))
d EnvName         S             14    inz('CONTENT_LENGTH')
d EnvNameLen      S              9B 0 inz(%size(EnvName))
d DoNumber        S              9  0 inz(%elem(HTML))
```

Figure 10.12: The WEBVALID8 CGI program processes the initial Web page that the WEBSIGNON CGI program served to the browser (part 2 of 6).

```
d RcvLen          S              9B 0
d RcvRecLen       S              9B 0
d CvtLen          S              9B 0 inz(%size(RcvDs))
d CvtLenAv        S              9B 0
d CvtStat         S              9B 0
d ShowMe          S              50

d Lower           C                     CONST('abcdefghijklmnopqrst-
d                                       uvwxyz')
d Upper           C                     CONST('ABCDEFGHIJKLMNOPQRST-
d                                       UVWXYZ')

CLON01Factor1+++++++Opcode&ExtFactor2+++++++Result++++++++Len++D+HiLoEq
 * Write HTTP Header and Heading
c                 Eval      Output = %Trim(HTML(1)) + EOT
c                 Exsr      WriteIt
c                 Eval      Output = %Trim(HTML(2)) + EOT + EOT
c                 Exsr      WriteIt

 * Write Opening HTML
c       3         Do        5              Index
c                 Eval      Output = %Trim(HTML(Index))
c                 Exsr      WriteIt
c                 EndDo

 * If invalid user/password
c                 If        RtnCode = 'N'
c       6         Do        7              Index
c                 Eval      Output = %Trim(HTML(Index))
c                 Exsr      WriteIt
c                 EndDo
c                 Else
 * Translate User ID keyed to upper case
c       Lower:Upper  XLATE(P) UserID         UserID

 * Go get Out Queue from the WEBOUTQ File
c       UserId    Chain     WebOutqs
c                 If        not %Found
 * If no record is found, bring up QPRINT as a default
c                 Eval      OOutq = 'QPRINT'
c                 Eval      OOutLib = 'QGPL'
c                 EndIf
c
c                 Eval      Output =
c                           'Congratulations ' + %Trim(UserID) +
c                           '!<H1></Color></Font><BR />' + EOT
c                 Exsr      WriteIt
```

Figure 10.12: The WEBVALID8 CGI program processes the initial Web page that the WEBSIGNON CGI program served to the browser (part 3 of 6).

```
c        8           Do        11              Index
c                    Eval      Output = %Trim(HTML(Index))
c                    If        Index = 10
c                    Eval      Output = %trim(Output) + %Trim(OOutLib) +
c                              '&OUTQ=' + %Trim(OOutQ) + '&' +
c                              '" Method="POST">'
c                    EndIf
c                    Exsr      WriteIt
c                    EndDo
c                    Endif

 * Write HTTP Footer
c                    Eval      Output = %Trim(HTML(%Elem(HTML))) + EOT
c                    Exsr      WriteIt

c                    eval      *INLR = *On

 *****    Subroutine: WriteIt  *****************************************
 ***   Write HTML Record ***********************************************
csr  WriteIt         BegSR
c                    Eval      OutputLen = %len(%trim(Output))
c                    Callp     StandardOut(Output:OutputLen:ErrorDs)
csr                  EndSr

 *****    Subroutine: ReadStdInp **************************************
 ***   Read Standard Input  ********************************************
csr  ReadStdInp      BEGSR
 * Obtain environment data
c                    CALLB     'QtmhGetEnv'
c                    PARM                    EnvRec
c                    PARM                    EnvRecLen
c                    PARM                    EnvLen
c                    PARM                    EnvName
c                    Parm                    EnvNameLen
c                    Parm                    ErrorDS
 * Calculate buffer length
c                    Eval      RcvLen=CharToNum(EnvRec)
 * Check for maximum buffer length
c    RcvLen          Ifgt      1024
c                    Z-add     1024            RcvLen
c                    EndIf
 * Execute "Read Standard Input" API
c                    CallB     'QtmhRdStin'
c                    Parm                    RcvRec
c                    Parm                    RcvLen
c                    Parm                    RcvRecLen
c                    Parm                    ErrorDs
csr                  EndSr
```

Figure 10.12: The WEBVALID8 CGI program processes the initial Web page that the WEBSIGNON CGI program served to the browser (part 4 of 6).

```
*****   Subroutine: ConvertDB  **************************************
***  Convert data using fields from the external data structure ****
csr   ConvertDB     BegSr
c                   Eval      RcvLen = %Len(%Trim(RcvRec))
c                   CallB     'QtmhCvtDb'
c                   Parm                    FileDs
c                   Parm                    RcvRec
c                   Parm                    RcvLen
c                   Parm                    RcvDs
c                   Parm                    CvtLen
c                   Parm                    CvtLenAv
c                   Parm                    CvtStat
c                   Parm                    ErrorDS
csr                 EndSr

 *****   Subroutine: *InzSR   *******************************************
 ***  Initialize Subroutine  *******************************************
csr   *InzSR        BegSr
c                   ExSr      ReadStdInp
c                   ExSr      ConvertDB
 * Validate Password
c                   Call      'FIG0710'
c                   parm      'V'           Action
c                   parm                    UserId
c                   parm                    PassWord
c                   parm      *blanks       RtnCode
c                   parm                    ErrorText
c                   parm                    Description
csr                 EndSR

 * Convert output length to numeric value
PName+++++++++++..T.................Keywords+++++++++++++++++++++++++
pCharToNum        B                  export
DName++++++++++ETDsFrom+++To/L+++IDc.Keywords++++++++++++++++++++++++
dCharToNum        PI            30p 9
dChar                           32  options(*varsize)

 * Overlay data structure
d                 ds
dAlphaChar                      1
dNumerChar                      1  0 overlay(AlphaChar) inz(0)

 * variables
dDecPos           s             3  0 inz(0)
dFndDecimal       s             1    inz('0')
dIndex            s             3  0
dNbr              s            30p 9
```

Figure 10.12: The WEBVALID8 CGI program processes the initial Web page that the WEBSIGNON CGI program served to the browser (part 5 of 6).

```
dSign              s              1  0 inz(1)
dUsed              s              3  0
dWkNbr             s             30p 0

CLON01Factor1+++++++Opcode&ExtFactor2+++++++Result++++++++Len++D+HiLoEq
 * Determine how many characters are used
c                     eval        Char = %triml(Char)
c        ' '          checkr      Char          Used
c        1            do          Used          Index
c                     eval        AlphaChar=%subst(Char:Index:1)
 * Look for numeric sign
c                     select
c                     when        AlphaChar='-'
c                     eval        sign= -1
 * Look for decimal position
c                     when        AlphaChar='.'
c                     eval        FndDecimal='1'
 * Place numeric digit
c                     when        AlphaChar >='0' and AlphaChar <= '9'
c                     eval        WkNbr  = WkNbr  * 10 + NumerChar
 * Increment decimal positions, once determination has been made
c                     if          FndDecimal = '1'
c                     eval        decpos = decpos + 1
c                     endif
c                     endsl
c                     enddo
 * Placement for sign and decimal positions
c                     eval        Nbr = WkNbr  * sign / 10 ** decpos
c                     return      Nbr
PName+++++++++++..T.................Keywords++++++++++++++++++++++++++++
PCharToNum         E


** CTData HTML
Content-type: text/html
Pragma: no-cache
<html><head><title>Spooled Files</title></head><Body>
<h1><center>Spooled Files</h1><br /><br /><br />
<Font Size = "7" Color="Red"><H1>
Invalid User ID or Password Entered!</h1><br /><br /></color></font>
<h2><strong>Press BACK on your Browser and try again!</strong></h2>
You have entered the Spooled File Distribution System</H2>
<BR />Please Press the button to continue...<BR /><BR /><BR />
<FORM action="WEBSPLLIST?LIB=
<INPUT type=submit value=" Press to Continue ">
</form></center></body></html>
```

Figure 10.12: The WEBVALID8 CGI program processes the initial Web page that the WEBSIGNON CGI program served to the browser (part 6 of 6).

One of the reasons WEBVALID8 is a little more complex is due to the way the user ID and password must be passed from the WEBINPUT program to the WEBVALID8 program. There are really two ways you can pass information from one CGI program to the next. The first is to pass the information as part of a query string through the URL. If you are familiar with using a browser on the Web, you have seen the query string method, whether you recognized it or not. (You'll see more about it later in this chapter.) Passing the user ID and password through the URL would obviously not be very secure, however, so the Read Standard In (**QtmhRdStin**) API method is used instead. This API lets you read information from a Web page without having to post it to the URL.

Since the WEBVALID8 program is so important, it's worth examining in detail. As you would expect, the processing begins with the initialization subroutine, *INZSR. The first function that is performed is to call the **ReadStdInp** subroutine, which in turn calls the Get Environment Variable (**QtmhGetEnv**) API. The parameters for this API are shown in Table 10.2. This API is designed to retrieve information about the environment within the browser session. Later in this chapter, you'll see how this API can be used to retrieve information from the URL. For the purposes of this program, however, the API is called to determine the size of the input variable that will be read in the Read Standard In (**QtmhRdStin**) API.

The Get Environment Variable API returns the size of the input variable on the Web page that was served in the WEBINPUT program. However, the size of the input variable is not returned to the program as a numeric value. To solve this little problem, we borrowed some code to make up the **CharToNum** procedure from the sample programs found in IBM's *Web Programming Guide* (see the references at the end of this chapter) to convert the field to a numeric value. Once the program has the numeric representation of the size of the input variable, it is ready to call the Read Standard In (**QtmhRdStin**) API.

The Read Standard In API reads information from a Web page that was served using the POST operation. If you take a minute to look back at the HTML code generated by the WEBSIGNON program (in Figure 10.11), you will see that POST is used with three different input values: user ID, password, and the SUBMIT button.

Table 10.2: Parameters for the Get Environment Variable API (QtmhGetEnv)

Parameter	Description	Type	Attr	Size
1	A variable receiver field that will hold information returned by the API	Output	Char	Varies
2	The length of parameter 1.	Input	Binary	4
3	The length of the data to be returned.	Output	Binary	4
4	The request variable; the environment variable's name.	Input	Char	Varies
5	The length of the environment variable's name.	Input	Binary	4
6	A standard error data structure.	I/O	Char	Varies

The value of the SUBMIT button doesn't really matter; it simply initiates the form post action required by the next step. The values of the user ID and password input fields are crucial, however, and that's where the Read Standard In (QtmhRdStin) API comes in.

The parameters for this API are shown in Table 10.3. As you can see, it is pretty simple. You tell it to go get the information, and it returns the data as one long string of data. In this case, the data would look something like "**UserID=Doug& Password=pass&...**," and the string would continue for as many input fields as were specified. The next step, therefore, is to parse the input string into distinctly different fields. That is where the Convert to DB (**QtmhCvtDB**) API comes in. The parameters for this API are shown in Table 10.4.

Table 10.3: Parameters for the Read from Standard In API (QtmhRdStin)

Parameter	Description	Type	Attr	Size
1	A variable receiver field that will hold information returned by the API.	Output	Char	Varies
2	The length of parameter 1.	Input	Binary	4
3	The length of the data to be returned.	Output	Binary	4
4	A standard error data structure.	I/O	Char	Varies

Table 10.4: Parameters for the Convert to DB API (QtmhCvtDB)

Parameter	Description	Type	Attr	Size
1	The qualified database name; a field that will hold information returned by the API.	Input	Char	20
2	The input variables to be parsed.	Input	Char	Varies
3	The length of the data parsed.	Input	Binary	4
4	Response variable; the converted data after matching the input string with the database file in parameter 1.	Output	Char	Varies
5	The length of the buffer where the response variable will be parsed,	Input	Binary	4
6	The length of the converted data.	Output	Binary	4
7	The response code, which is one of the following: • 0—The data is translated according to fields in the database file. • -1—The fields in the database file described more fields than were found in the input data. • -2—The input data includes one or more fields that were not defined in the database file. • -3—A combination of the two preceding errors was encountered. • -4—An error occurred during translation. The data may be unusable. • -5—The API is not valid unless the program is called by the HTTP server. No parsing was performed. • -6—Parsing is not valid when in %%BINARY%% mode.	Output	Binary	4
8	A standard error data structure.	I/O	Char	Varies

The Convert to DB API lets you specify a data structure that will define the data elements using the same DDS you use to describe a physical file. In the example program, a physical file named WEBSIGNPF is created (shown in Figure 10.13) and then used as an external data structure to describe the data elements. The API works by looking for data elements in the query string that match up fields in the

DDS. Therefore, any characters directly preceding the equal sign (=) would be considered a field element. The characters directly following the equals sign, but before to the next ampersand (&) would be considered to correspond with the aforementioned field element. After running this API, the data from the URL will be contained in the fields defined by the database file.

```
***********************************************************************
*   TO COMPILE:
*  CRTPF FILE(XXXLIB/WEBSIGNPF) SRCMBR(FIG1015)
***********************************************************************
AAN01N02N03T.Name++++++RLen++TDpBLinPosFunctions++++++++++++++++++++++++++++
A          R WEBREC
A            USERID        10              TEXT('User ID')
A            PASSWORD      10              TEXT('Password')
```

Figure 10.13: The WebSignPF physical file is used for translation with the QtmhCvtDB API.

Once the user ID and password read by the Read Standard In API have been deciphered, the Validation List Entry test (discussed in chapter 7) must be performed on them. The validation program (Figure 7.7 in chapter 7) is used to add, delete, and validate entries in the validation list. The WEBVALID8 program simply calls this program and passes it a *V*, telling the program to validate the user ID and password entries. If the user ID and password are not deemed valid, an *N* will be passed back in one of the parameters of the WEBVALID8 program. This will be important for the next step.

Now that the Initialize subroutine (*INZSR) has been completed, control is transferred to the main logic cycle of the program. The cycle begins by writing the opening HTML statements to the HTTP server. You might notice that a field named EOT is concatenated to the opening statements. This field is a "new line" character required when writing CGI programs for the HTTP server. Once the HTML header and heading information has been written, the logic of the program varies depending on whether the user ID and password are valid. If they are invalid, the HTML to produce the Web page shown in Figure 10.14 is written to the HTTP server. The operator is prompted to press the Back button on the browser and try entering the user ID and password again.

Figure 10.14: This Web page is served by the WEBVALID8 program if an invalid ID or password is entered.

On the other hand, if the user ID and password did pass the validation routine, the user ID is converted to uppercase and then chained out to the WEBOUTQ database file to see if this user ID has been assigned a specific output queue. (The DDS for this file is shown in Figure 10.15.) If not, the program defaults to the QPRINT output queue in library QGPL. The WEBOUTQ file lets you direct a user to a specific output queue. The user ID in the WEBOUTQ file must match both the user ID in the authorization list and the user ID entered on the Web page, if you are going to use this "output filter" feature.

```
****************************************************************
*  TO COMPILE:
*  CRTPF FILE(XXXLIB/WEBOUTQS) SRCMBR(FIG1016)
****************************************************************
AAN01N02N03T.Name++++++RLen++TDpBLinPosFunctions+++++++++++++++++++++++
A                                     UNIQUE
A           R WEBORECS
A             OUSERID        10        TEXT('User ID')
A             OOUTLIB        10        TEXT('OUTQUEUE LIBRARY')
A             OOUTQ          10        TEXT('OUTQUEUE')
A           K OUSERID
```

Figure 10.15: The WebOutQs physical file is used to determine the output queue that will be displayed.

Once the output queue has been determined, the remaining HTML produces the Web page shown in Figure 10.16. Once again, the POST method is used on the HTML FORM statement. This time, though, the query information required by the WEBSPLLST program is sent through the URL, where it will be dealt with in the subsequent operation.

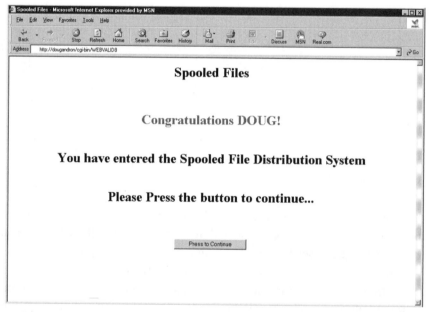

Figure 10.16: This Web page is served by the WEBVALID8 program if a valid ID and password is entered.

Finally, the closing HTML statements are written to the HTTP server, and the WEBVALID8 program is terminated. The bottom line of the WEBVALID8 program is that if the user ID and password are valid, the WEBSPLLST program will be the next program launched, as specified by the method used in the FORM statement of the HTML generated by WEBVALID8. If not, a Web page is served telling the operator to try again.

The WEBSPLLST program in Figure 10.17 was designed to process the Web page served in WEBVALID8. The WEBSPLLST program will read the query string from the browser URL and parse the information into fields that will be used to create a list of the spooled files in the designated output queue.

The list of the spooled files will then be presented on a Web page, where the individual spooled files may be selected for output. No new CGI APIs are used in this program, but there is a new API to extract the spooled files from the output queue.

```
*****************************************************************
*   TO COMPILE:
*     CRTBNDRPG PGM(XXXLIB/WEBSPLLST) SRCMBR(FIG1017) DFTACTGRP(*NO)
*****************************************************************

HKeywords+++++++++++++++++++++++++++++++++++++++++++++++++++++++
h bnddir('WEBBNDDIR')

* Compile time HTML Array
DName+++++++++++ETDsFrom+++To/L+++IDc.Keywords++++++++++++++++++++
d HTML            s              80    dim(18) ctdata perrcd(1)

* Prototype for Creating a User Space
d CrtUsrSpc       PR                    *
d   CrtSpcName                    20    const

* Prototype for Write Standard Out API
d StandardOut     PR                    EXTPROC('QtmhWrStout')
d                              1024
d                                9B 0
d                               116

* Common header information
d GenHeadDs       DS                    based(FilePtr)
d ListOffset            125      128B 0
d NumberList            133      136B 0
d EntrySize             137      140B 0

* Returned data from QUSLSPL SPLF0200 format
dQUSF0200         DS             200    based(FileLstPtr)
d QUSNBRFR00                       9B 0

* The information represented by each key is returned in this format
d KeyStructure    DS
```

Figure 10.17: The WEBSPLLST program processes the Web page served by the WEBVALID8 program (part 1 of 6).

```
 d  LenRtn                          9B 0
 d  Key                             9B 0
 d  type                            1
 d  Rsvd                            3
 d  Len                             9B 0
 d  Data                            10

  * Name and location of the Output Queue
 d OutQName        DS
 d  QName                           10
 d  QLibrary                        10

 d DataBin         DS
 d  DataAlpha                       10
 d  bin4                            9B 0 overlay(DataAlpha:1)

  * Key data structure to indicate what information to return
 d Keys            DS
 d  Key201                          9B 0 inz(201)
 d  Key202                          9B 0 inz(202)
 d  Key203                          9B 0 inz(203)
 d  Key204                          9B 0 inz(204)
 d  Key205                          9B 0 inz(205)
 d  Key209                          9B 0 inz(209)
 d  Key211                          9B 0 inz(211)

  * Standard API error data structure
 d ErrorDs         DS                    INZ
 d  BytesProvd              1      4B 0 inz(116)
 d  BytesAvail              5      8B 0
 d  MessageId               9     15
 d  Err###                 16     16
 d  Message                17    116

 d EnvRec          s             1024
 d EnvLen          s               9B 0
 d EnvRecLen       s               9B 0 Inz(%Size(EnvRec))
 d EnvName         s              12    Inz('QUERY_STRING')
 d EnvNameLen      s               9B 0 Inz(%Size(EnvName))
 d FmtName         s               8
 d FormType        s              10    inz('*ALL')
 d Index           s               4  0
 d JobName         s              10
 d JobNameF        s              26
 d JobNumber       s               6
```

Figure 10.17: The WEBSPLLST program processes the Web page served by the WEBVALID8 program (part 2 of 6).

314

```
d NbrOfKeys        s              9B 0 inz(7)
d Output           s            1024
d OutputLen        s              9B 0
d Pos              s               4 0
d SpoolName        s              10
d Spool#           s               4 0
d TotPages         s               7 0
d UserName         s              10
d UserData         s              10
d UserDataR        s              10
d UserSpace        s              20    inz('HTMLSPOOL QTEMP')

 * End-of-line character
d EOT              C                    CONST(X'15')

 * Create user space for list of files
CLON01Factor1+++++++Opcode&ExtFactor2+++++++Result++++++++Len++D+HiLoEq
c                   Eval      FilePtr = CrtUsrSpc(UserSpace)
 * List spooled files to user space
c                   Call      'QUSLSPL'
c                   Parm                     UserSpace
c                   Parm      'SPLF0200'     FmtName
c                   Parm      '*ALL'         UserName
c                   Parm                     OutqName
c                   Parm      '*ALL'         FormType
c                   Parm      '*ALL'         UserData
c                   Parm                     ErrorDs
c                   Parm      *blanks        JobNameF
c                   parm                     Keys
c                   parm                     NbrOfKeys

 * Load the QUSF0200 data structure
c                   eval      FileLstPtr =  (FilePtr + ListOffset)

 * Retrieve each spooled file
c                   DO        NumberList
c                   Eval      Index = 5
 * For each spooled file, get the detail information
c                   DO        QusNbrFr00
c                   Eval      KeyStructure = %subst(QusF0200 :
c                             Index : %len(Keystructure))

 * Load the individual fields represented by each key
c                   Select
c                   When      Key = 201
```

Figure 10.17: The WEBSPLLST program processes the Web page served by the WEBVALID8 program (part 3 of 6).

```
C                     Eval      SpoolName = Data
C                     When      Key = 202
C                     Eval      JobName = Data
C                     When      Key = 203
C                     Eval      UserName = Data
C                     When      Key = 204
C                     movel     Data           JobNumber
C                     When      Key = 205
C                     movel     Data           DataAlpha
C                     z-add     Bin4           Spool#
C                     When      Key = 209
C                     movel     Data           UserDataR
C                     When      Key = 211
C                     movel     Data           DataAlpha
C                     z-add     Bin4           TotPages
C                     Endsl
 * Get the next key
C                     eval      Index = Index + LenRtn
C                     ENDDO

 * Format infomation into HTML and write table record
C                     EXSR      FormatIt

 * Get next spooled file
C                     eval      FileLstPtr = (FileLstPtr + EntrySize)
C                     ENDDO

 * Write the bottom of the web page
C                     Eval      Output = %Trim(HTML(10)) + EOT
C                     Exsr      WriteIt
C                     Eval      *InLr = *ON

 *****    Subroutine: FormatIt  ****************************************
 ***    Format HTML detail table record  ***************************
Csr   FormatIt        BEGSR
C                     Eval      Output = '<tr><td>' + %Trim(HTML(9)) +
C                               'User=' + %Trim(UserName) +
C                               '&Job=' + %Trim(JobName) +
C                               '&File=' + %Trim(SpoolName) +
C                               '&Nbr=' + %Trim(JobNumber) +
C                               '&SNbr=' + %Char(Spool#) +
C                               '&UsrDta=' + %Trim(UserDataR) +
C                               '&Pages=' + %Trim(%Char(TotPages)) + '">' +
C                               %Trim(SpoolName) + '</a></td>' +
C                               '<td>' + %Trim(JobName) + '</td>' +
```

Figure 10.17: The WEBSPLLST program processes the Web page served by the WEBVALID8 program (part 4 of 6).

```
c                              '<td>' + %Trim(JobNumber) + '</td>' +
c                              '<td>' + %Trim(UserName) + '</td>' +
c                              '<td><Center>' + %Char(Spool#) + '</TD>' +
c                              '<td>' + %Trim(UserDataR) + '</td>' +
c                              '<td><Center>' + %Char(TotPages) + '</TD>' +
c                              '</tr>'
c               Exsr          WriteIt
csr             EndSr

 *****    Subroutine: WriteIt ****************************************
 ***   Write HTML Record ********************************************
csr   WriteIt   BegSr
c               Eval          OutputLen = %len(%trim(Output))
c               Callp         StandardOut(Output:OutputLen:ErrorDs)
csr             EndSr

 *****    Subroutine: *InzSR  ***************************************
 ***   Initialize Subroutine  **************************************
csr   *InzSR    BegSr
 * Get the query string from the browser
c               CallB         'QtmhGetEnv'
c               Parm                        EnvRec
c               Parm                        EnvRecLen
c               Parm                        EnvLen
c               Parm                        EnvName
c               Parm                        EnvNameLen
c               Parm                        ErrorDS

 * Parse out the query string to get Library
c               Eval          Pos = %Scan('?LIB' : EnvRec)
c               Eval          QLibrary = %Subst(Envrec: Pos + 5)
c               Eval          Pos = %Scan('&' : QLibrary)
c               If            Pos > 0
c               Eval          QLibrary = %Subst(QLibrary: 1 : Pos - 1)
c               EndIf

 * Parse out the Out Queue Name
c               Eval          Pos = %Scan('&OUTQ' : EnvRec)
c               Eval          QName = %Subst(Envrec: Pos + 6)
c               Eval          Pos = %Scan('&' : QName)
c               If            Pos > 0
c               Eval          QName = %Subst(QName: 1 : Pos - 1)
c               EndIf

 * Write Web Page Header
```

Figure 10.17: The WEBSPLLST program processes the Web page served by the WEBVALID8 program (part 5 of 6).

```
C                        eval       Output = %trim(HTML(1)) + EOT
C                        ExSr       WriteIt
C                        eval       Output = %trim(HTML(2)) + EOT + EOT
C                        ExSr       WriteIt

 * Write Web Page Heading
C                        eval       Output = %Trim(HTML(3)) + %Trim(Qname) +
C                                   ' in Library ' + %Trim(QLibrary) + EOT
C                        ExSr       WriteIt

 * Write table heading
C          4             Do         8              Index
C                        Eval       Output = %Trim(HTML(Index))
C                        ExSr       WriteIt
C                        EndDo
Csr                      Endsr

** CTData HTML
Content-type: text/html
Pragma: no-cache
<html><head><title>Spooled Files from Out Queue
</title></head><br /><Body><Center><Font Color="blue"><h2>
Select a spooled file to be displayed:</font><br /></h2><Form>
<Table Border="1" Cellpadding="10" Cellspacing="10">
<tr bgcolor="silver"><th>Name</th><th>Job</th><th>Job Nbr</th>
<th>User ID</th><th>Spool Nbr</th><th>User Data</th><th>Pages</th></tr>
<A Href="WEBSPOOL?
</table></form></center></body></html>
```

Figure 10.17: The WEBSPLLST program processes the Web page served by the WEBVALID8 program (part 6 of 6).

The WEBSPLLST program begins in the initialization subroutine (*INZSR), where the first thing it does is call the Get Environment (**QtmhGetEnv**) API. This time, though, the API is used to retrieve the query string from the URL on the Web page.

The HTML header, heading, and table heading code are then written out to the HTTP server. Next, control is turned over to the mainline code, which begins by creating a user space named HTMLSPOOL in library QTEMP. The user space is created using the **CrtUsrSpc** procedure, which was placed in the WEBSRVPGM service program earlier in this chapter.

Take a look at the query string on the URL of the Web page in Figure 10.18. Do you see the question mark in the middle of it? That is where the data begins. We could have simply used the Convert to DB API (**QtmhCvtDB**) to parse the data passed, but we wanted to demonstrate another way to perform this function. Therefore, we used a combination of the %SCAN and %SUBST built-in-functions to parse out the name of the out queue and library. This information will be used later in the program.

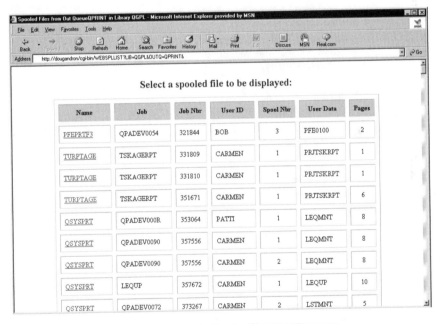

Figure 10.18: This is the output generated by the WEBSPLLST program.

The user space is created in library QTEMP because QTEMP is a temporary library that is unique to every job. Next, the List Spooled Files to User Space (QUSLSPL) API creates a list of all spooled files in the newly created user space. This API lists all spooled files that are found in the output queue identified in the initialize subroutine. The parameters for this API are listed in Table 10.5. (For more information on list APIs, see chapter 2.)

Table 10.5: Parameters for List Spooled Files to User Space API (QUSLSPL) (part 1 of 2)

Parameter	Description	Type	Attr	Size
1	A qualified user space name, where the first 10 bytes are the name, and the second 10 are the library. The library also accepts *LIBL and *CURLIB.	Input	Char	20
2	The format name, which is one of the following: • SPLF0100—Internal identifiers for the spooled file and job. • SPLF0200—Information that is shown in the Work with Spooled Files Command.	Input	Char	8
3	The name of the user whose spool files are to be retrieved. *ALL and *CURRENT are also accepted.	Input	Char	10
4	The qualified output queue name, where the first 10 bytes are the output queue name, and the second 10 are the library. This parameter also accepts *ALL (all output queues), *LIBL (output queues in the library list), and *CURLIB (output queue in the current library).	Input	Char	20
5	The form type of spooled files to be retrieved. This parameter also accepts *ALL and *STD (standard form type).	Input	Char	10
6	User-specified data to be included in the list. This parameter also accepts *ALL.	Input	Char	10
7	A standard error data structure.	I/O	Char	Varies
Optional Parameters				
8	The qualified job name. Leave this blank to include all jobs.	Input	Char	26
9	The list of the fields to be returned in the SPLF0200 format. When keys are specified, only fields with the matching keys will be included on the list.	Input	Binary	Varies

Table 10.5: Parameters for List Spooled Files to User Space API (QUSLSPL) (part 2 of 2)

Parameter	Description	Type	Attr	Size
10	The number of fields to be returned in the SPLF0200 format.	Input	Binary	4
11	The auxiliary storage pool, an optional parameter that reflects the storage pool where spool files should be retrieved.	Input	Binary	4

As the program builds the list of spooled files in the user space, it executes the **FormatIt** subroutine, which formats the HTML and writes it out to the HTTP server. The **FormatIt** subroutine creates an HTML link using the HREF tag (which stands for *hypertext reference*). HREF enables a line in the output table to incorporate a link to another Web page. These kinds of links are generally displayed in blue and underlined, so that the operator recognizes them as hypertext. These links are shown in the name column of the table in Figure 10.18. Clicking on the name of the spooled file launches the WEBSPOOL program, which automatically turns that spooled file into a Web page to be displayed in the browser.

A hypertext link is enabled in the **FormatIt** subroutine through a special address that looks like this:

```
<A HREF="WEBSPOOL?User=DOUG&JOB=JBNAME&FILE=FILE&Nbr=123456&SNbr=1234…>
```

The **<A** that begins this link is referred to as an *anchor character*. The link is closed with the closing anchor, or > character. The HREF= indicates the hypertext reference, and the WEBSPOOL indicates the name of the program that should be launched from the URL. By now, you probably recognize that the data following the question mark indicates the beginning of a query string, which will be posted in the URL as well. This query string includes the user ID, job name, file name, job number, spool number, user data, and total number of pages for the spooled file in question. All of this information is passed to the WEBSPOOL program via the query string in the URL, where the string will be decoded and the spooled file will be converted to HTML.

The rest of the **FormatIt** subroutine holds the HTML required to complete the table entries in Figure 10.18. This process repeats until there are no more spooled files in the designated output queue to be displayed. At that point, the WEBSPLLST program is terminated and control is turned over to the browser.When the WEBSPLLST program terminates, the result is a Web page with a list of spooled files from the output queue determined back in the WEBVALID8 program. The Web page looks like the one in Figure 10.18. When the operator selects one of the spooled files by clicking on the hyperlink spooled file name, the HREF HTML tag ends up completing the link to the WEBSPOOL program, shown in Figure 10.19. The query string that is sent as part of the URL through the HTTP server allows the WEBSPOOL program to serve yet another Web page.

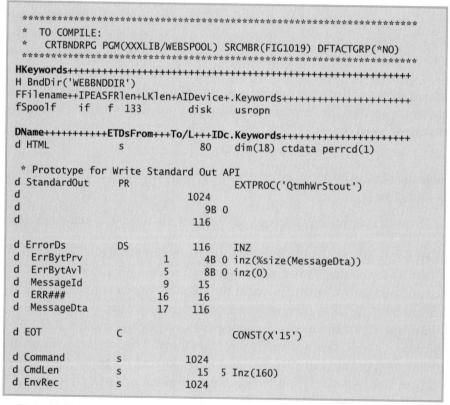

```
 ********************************************************************
 *   TO COMPILE:
 *    CRTBNDRPG PGM(XXXLIB/WEBSPOOL) SRCMBR(FIG1019) DFTACTGRP(*NO)
 ********************************************************************
HKeywords+++++++++++++++++++++++++++++++++++++++++++++++++++++++++++++
H BndDir('WEBBNDDIR')
FFilename++IPEASFRlen+LKlen+AIDevice+.Keywords+++++++++++++++++++++++++
fSpoolf    if   f 133        disk   usropn


DName++++++++++++ETDsFrom+++To/L+++IDc.Keywords+++++++++++++++++++++++++
d HTML           s               80    dim(18) ctdata perrcd(1)

  * Prototype for Write Standard Out API
d StandardOut    PR                     EXTPROC('QtmhWrStout')
d                              1024
d                                9B 0
d                               116

d ErrorDs        DS             116    INZ
d  ErrBytPrv             1       4B 0 inz(%size(MessageDta))
d  ErrBytAvl             5       8B 0 inz(0)
d  MessageId             9      15
d  ERR###               16      16
d  MessageDta           17     116

d EOT            C                      CONST(X'15')

d Command        s             1024
d CmdLen         s               15   5 Inz(160)
d EnvRec         s             1024
```

Figure 10.19: The WEBSPOOL program displays the spooled file to the browser (part 1 of 5).

```
d EnvLen          s              9B 0
d EnvRecLen       s              9B 0 Inz(%Size(EnvRec))
d EnvName         s             12    Inz('QUERY_STRING')
d EnvNameLen      s              9B 0 Inz(%Size(EnvName))
d FileName        s             10
d JobNbr          s              6
d JobName         s             10
d Output          s           1024
d OutputLen       s              9B 0
d Pos             s              5 0
d SpoolNbr        s              4
d Totpages        s              7
d UserData        s             10
d UserId          s             10
 *

IFilename++SqNORiPos1+NCCPos2+NCCPos3+NCC.............................
iSpoolf    NS
i                                    1    1  Control
i                                    2  133  Record

 * Once housekeeping has been performed, loop through spooled file
CL0N01Factor1+++++++Opcode&ExtFactor2+++++++Result+++++++Len++D+HiLoEq
c                   Dou       %Eof
c                   Read      Spoolf
c                   If        %Eof(Spoolf)
c                   Leave
c                   EndIf

 * If print control characters require extra spacing, send blank lines
c                   If        Control = '0' or
c                               Control = '-' or
c                               Control = '1'
c                   Eval      Output = '</Pre><BR /><Pre>'
c                   If        Control = '-' or
c                               Control = '1'
c                   Eval      Output = %Trim(Output) +
c                               '</Pre><BR /><Pre>'
c                   EndIf
c                   EXSR      WriteIt
c                   EndIf

 * Output spool file record
c                   Eval      Output = '<Big>' + Record + '</Big><Br />'
c                   EXSR      WriteIt
c                   EndDo

 * End of web page
c                   Eval      Output = %Trim(HTML(%Elem(HTML))) + EOT
```

Figure 10.19: The WEBSPOOL program displays the spooled file to the browser (part 2 of 5).

```
C                      EXSR        WriteIt
C                      eval        *INLR = *On

*****    Subroutine: WriteIt  *******************************************
***   Write HTML Record *********************************************
csr   WriteIt          BEGSR
C                      Eval        OutputLen = %len(%trim(Output))
C                      Callp       StandardOut(Output:OutputLen:ErrorDs)
csr                    EndSR

*****    Subroutine: *InzSR  *******************************************
***   Initialize Subroutine   *****************************************
csr   *InzSR           BegSr
* Get the query string from the browser
C                      CallB       'QtmhGetEnv'
C                      Parm                    EnvRec
C                      Parm                    EnvRecLen
C                      Parm                    EnvLen
C                      Parm                    EnvName
C                      Parm                    EnvNameLen
C                      Parm                    ErrorDS

* Parse out the query string to get User ID
C                      Eval        Pos = %Scan('?User' : EnvRec)
C                      Eval        UserID = %Subst(Envrec: Pos + 6)
C                      Eval        Pos = %Scan('&' : UserID)
C                      If          Pos > 0
C                      Eval        UserID = %Subst(UserID: 1 : Pos - 1)
C                      EndIf

* Get the job name
C                      Eval        Pos = %Scan('&Job' : EnvRec)
C                      Eval        JobName = %Subst(Envrec: Pos + 5)
C                      Eval        Pos = %Scan('&' : JobName)
C                      If          Pos > 0
C                      Eval        JobName = %Subst(JobName: 1 : Pos - 1)
C                      EndIf

* Get the spool file name
C                      Eval        Pos = %Scan('&File' : EnvRec)
C                      Eval        FileName = %Subst(Envrec: Pos + 6)
C                      Eval        Pos = %Scan('&' : Filename)
C                      If          Pos > 0
C                      Eval        FileName = %Subst(FileName: 1 : Pos - 1)
C                      EndIf

* Get the job number
C                      Eval        Pos = %Scan('&Nbr' : EnvRec)
C                      Eval        JobNbr = %Subst(Envrec: Pos + 5)
```

Figure 10.19: The WEBSPOOL program displays the spooled file to the browser (part 3 of 5).

```
C                   Eval      Pos = %Scan('&' : JobNbr)
C                   If        Pos > 0
C                   Eval      JobNbr = %Subst(JobNbr: 1 : Pos - 1)
C                   EndIf

 * Get the spooled file number
C                   Eval      Pos = %Scan('&SNbr' : EnvRec)
C                   Eval      SpoolNbr = %Subst(Envrec: Pos + 6)
C                   Eval      Pos = %Scan('&' : SpoolNbr)
C                   If        Pos > 0
C                   Eval      SpoolNbr = %Subst(SpoolNbr: 1 : Pos - 1)
C                   EndIf

 * Get the User Data
C                   Eval      Pos = %Scan('&UsrDta' : EnvRec)
C                   Eval      UserData = %Subst(Envrec: Pos + 8)
C                   Eval      Pos = %Scan('&' : UserData)
C                   If        Pos > 0
C                   Eval      UserData = %Subst(UserData: 1 : Pos - 1)
C                   EndIf

 * Get the spooled file number
C                   Eval      Pos = %Scan('&Pages' : EnvRec)
C                   Eval      TotPages = %Subst(Envrec: Pos + 7)
C                   Eval      Pos = %Scan('&' : TotPages)
C                   If        Pos > 0
C                   Eval      TotPages = %Subst(TotPages: 1 : Pos - 1)
C                   EndIf

 * Delete Preceding Overrides
C                   Eval      Command =
C                             'DLTF (QTEMP/S' + JobNbr + ')'
C                   Call      'QCMDEXC'                            68
C                   Parm                Command
C                   Parm                CmdLen

 * Create the SPOOLF file in library QTEMP
C                   Eval      Command =
C                             'CRTPF FILE(QTEMP/S' + JobNbr +
C                             ') RCDLEN(133)'
C                   Call      'QCMDEXC'
C                   Parm                Command
C                   Parm                CmdLen

 * Go out and copy the requested spooled file
C                   Eval      Command = 'CPYSPLF FILE(' +
C                             %Trim(Filename) +
C                             ') TOFILE(QTEMP/S' + JobNbr +
C                             ') JOB(' +
```

Figure 10.19: The WEBSPOOL program displays the spooled file to the browser (part 4 of 5).

```
C                             %Trim(JobNbr) + '/' +
C                             %Trim(UserID) + '/' +
C                             %Trim(JobName) +
C                             ') SPLNBR(' + %Trim(SpoolNbr) + ') ' +
C                             'CTLCHAR(*FCFC)'
C              Call          'QCMDEXC'
C              Parm                            Command
C              Parm                            CmdLen

 * Override to SPOOLF file in library QTEMP
C              Eval          Command =
C                            'OVRDBF FILE(SPOOLF) TOFILE(QTEMP/S' +
C                            JobNbr + ')'
C              Call          'QCMDEXC'
C              Parm                            Command
C              Parm                            CmdLen

C              Open          Spoolf

 * Write web page header
C              eval          Output = %trim(HTML(1)) + EOT + EOT
C              EXSR          WriteIt

 * Write web page heading
C              eval          Output = %trim(HTML(2)) +
C                             %trim(HTML(3)) + EOT
C              EXSR          WriteIt

C              eval          Output = %trim(HTML(4)) +
C                            'File Name:</B>' + FileName +
C                            '</td><td><b>User ID:</b>' + UserID +
C                            '</td><td><b>Job Name:</b>' + JobName +
C                            '</td><td><b>Spool ID:</b>' + SpoolNbr +
C                            '</td></tr></table></center></h1>'
C              Eval          Output = %Trim(Output) + EOT
C              EXSR          WriteIt

 * Set the font to courier new
C              Eval          Output = '<Font Face="Courier New">+
C                             <Font Size="3" Color="Blue"><Pre>'
C              EXSR          WriteIt
csr            Endsr

** CTData HTML
Content-type: text/html
<html><head><title>Spooled Output</title></head><Body>
<h1><center>Spooled File Output</center><hr />
<Center><Table border="1" bgcolor="lightgrey" cellspacing="10"><tr><td>
</color></font></pre></body></html>
```

Figure 10.19: The WEBSPOOL program displays the spooled file to the browser (part 5 of 5).

The WEBSPOOL program was designed to take the query information posted in the URL (by the WEBSPLLST program), break out the information for an individual spooled file, and display that file to the browser, as shown in Figure 10.20.

Just like in the preceding examples, the WEBSPOOL program begins with the initialize subroutine (*INZSR). The first thing the subroutine does is retrieve the information from the URL by running the Retrieve Environment (**QtmhGetEnv**) API . The retrieved query information is then parsed out into individual fields, just like in the WEBSPLLST program. It is easy to see what information was passed to the WEBSPLLST program if you look at the URL on the browser in Figure 10.20.

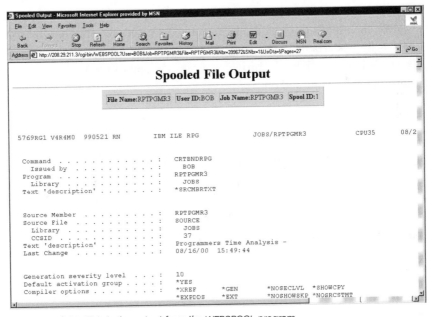

Figure 10.20: This is the output from the WEBSPOOL program.

With the spooled file information identified, the WEBSPOOL program retrieves the spooled file so that it can be posted to the Web page. It then uses the QCMDEXC API to create a work file in library QTEMP, and runs the Copy Spooled File (CPYSPLF) command to copy the spooled file into the newly created work file. Before creating the work file, the QCMDEXC API runs the Delete File (DLTF) command to delete any work files of the same name that happen to be hanging around in library QTEMP.

Next, the work file is created, the Copy Spooled File (CPYSPLF) command is performed, the file is overridden, and then the file is opened. Notice that the User Controlled keyword is used on the file definition specification for SPOOLF file. The file-open process had to be user-controlled because the file obviously could not be read before it was created and the override was performed.

Once the spooled file is retrieved, the program writes the Web page header and heading to the HTTP server. Some additional HTML code is used to format the spooled file into the desired "look and feel."

The program then loops through the work file, converting the spooled file records to HTML as it goes. The HTML is written out to the HTTP server as it processes the records. When complete, the program writes the end of the Web page, and the last-record indicator is turned on.

Summary

We hope that the application presented in this chapter gets you excited about the prospect of using your AS/400 as a portal to the Web. Because this book's focus is on APIs, this chapter only scratches the surface of the Web capabilities of the AS/400. We are confident, though, that our talented and creative readers will help take the AS/400's Web capabilities to a whole new level. The following references will help get you started:

IBM Manuals

HTTP Server for AS/400 Webmaster's Guide, QB3AEO04 (GC41-5434)

HTTP Server for AS/400 Web Programming Guide, QB3AEQ03 (GC41-5435)

IBM General Resources on the Web

http://publib.boulder.ibm.com/html/as400/infocenter.html

IBM AS/400 Web Builder's Workshop:

`http://www.as400.ibm.com/tsudio/workshop/webbuild.htm`

Other Sources

Stone, Bradley V. *e-RPG: Building AS/400 Web Applications with RPG*. Carlsbad, CA: Midrange Computing, 2000.

APPENDIX

ABOUT THE CD-ROM

The CD-ROM that accompanies this book contains the source code for most of the figures found within the text. Table A.1 is a cross-reference for the figures and the files found on the CD-ROM.

Table A.1: CD-ROM Cross-Reference Information (part 1 of 3)

File Name	Figure	Description
FIG0104	1.4	Different data types used by APIs.
FIG0105	1.5	A technique for determining the proper size of the receiver variable.
FIG0106	1.6	Using the Create User Space (QUSCRTUS) API to create a user space.
FIG0107	1.7	Using the Retrieve User Space Pointer (QUSPTRUS) API to get a pointer to a user space.
FIG0108	1.8	Using the Retrieve User Space (QUSRTVUS) API to retrieve data from a user space.

Table A.1: CD-ROM Cross-Reference Information (part 2 of 3)

File Name	Figure	Description
FIG0109	1.9	Using the Change User Space Attribute (QUSCUSAT) API to change the attributes of a user space.
FIG01010	1.10	How to make a "receiver variable API" send data to a user space.
FIG0111	1.11	The "ultimate user space procedure," CrtUsrSpc.
FIG0112	1.12	Using the CrtUsrSpc procedure.
FIG0113	1.13	Using the "optional" error data structure with an API.
FIG0202	2.2	The General Header data structure.
FIG0204	2.4	How to list and reorganize files with deleted records using the QUSPTRUS API.
FIG0205	2.5	The General Header data structure.
FIG0206	2.6	How to open the List Control data structure format.
FIG0207	2.7	An RPG IV program to display spooled files for multiple users using open list APIs.
FIG0208	2.8	A display file for RPG IV code to display spooled files for multiple users using open list APIs.
FIG0302	3.2	The DDS for the Display File Description.
FIG0303	3.3	A better Display File Description using QDBRTVFD.
FIG0304	3.4	How to list fields in a display file using QDFRTVFD.
FIG0403	4.3	Using QCMDEXC to override printer attributes.
FIG0404	4.4	The customer-list prompt-screen display file.
FIG0406	4.6	Prototyping the QCMDEXC command to submit jobs from within an RPG program.
FIG0408	4.8	Using the QCAPCMD API to prompt commands from within an ILE RPG program.
FIG0501	5.1	A program to edit a data area using the Retrieve Data Area (QWCRDTAA) API.
FIG0502	5.2	A display file for the Edit Data Area program in Figure 5.1.
FIG0504	5.4	A program using the QUSLJOBS API to list jobs.
FIG0505	5.5	The DDS for the List Jobs with QUSLJOBS program.
FIG0507	5.7	A program using the Retrieve Job Information (QUSRJOBI) API.
FIG0508	5.8	A program using the Retrieve Job Status (QWCRJBST) API.
FIG0509	5.9	A program using the Retrieve Job Queue Information (QSPRJOBQ) API.

Table A.1: CD-ROM Cross-Reference Information (part 3 of 3)

File Name	Figure	Description
FIG0510	5.10	A program using the Retrieve System Values API (QWCRSVAL).
FIG0601	6.1	The SndErrMsg procedure.
FIG0602	6.2	The RmvErrMsg procedure.
FIG0603	6.3	An example of using the SndErrMsg and RmvErrMsg procedures.
FIG0604	6.4	The GetTrgPgm procedure.
FIG0701	7.1	A procedure using the Retrieve Encrypted Password (QSYRUPWD) API.
FIG0702	7.2	A procedure using the Set Encrypted Password (QSYSUPWD) API.
FIG0703	7.3	The Retrieve User Information (QSYRUSRI) API.
FIG0705	7.5	A program to retrieve user profile information and send it to a remote data queue.
FIG0706	7.6	A program to create a duplicate user profile with password.
FIG077	7.7	A program using validation list APIs.
FIG0801	8.1	An "exists" procedure.
FIG0803	8.3	The display file for the LIBDSP program.
FIG0804	8.4	A display-library-description program.
FIG0807	8.7	A job-monitoring program using QRCVDTAQ.
FIG0808	8.8	A program to end job-monitoring using QSNDDTAQ.
FIG0809	8.9	A program to list programs by last-used date using user indexes.
FIG0902	9.2	The sockets program.
FIG1007	10.7	The WEBSRVPGM service program.
FIG1009	10.9	The WEBSIGNON CGI program.
FIG1012	10.12	The WEBVALID8 CGI program.
FIG1015	10.15	The WebSignPF physical file used for translation with the QtmhCvtDB API.
FIG1017	10.17	The WebOutQs physical file used to determine the output queue that will be displayed.
FIG1017	10.17	The WEBSPLLST program.
FIG1019	10.19	The WEBSPOOL program.

Transferring the Source Code

The CD-ROM includes source code for the sample programs and code snippets listed in Table A.1. You will need a PC and IBM's Client Access or some other file-transfer utility software to transfer the source to your AS/400. In addition, your system will need the RPG compiler. Your system will also need to be on Version 4, Release 4 of the IBM Operating System, OS/400.

To transfer the source, follow these steps:

1. Sign on to the AS/400 with a user profile that has the authority level of QPGMR or above.

2. If you want, create a library to contain the software on the CD-ROM. For example, you could call it APIBOOK for ease of identification:

   ```
   CRTLIB LIB(APIBOOK)
   ```

3. Create a source physical file called SOURCE in the library just created:

   ```
   CRTSRCPF APIBOOK/SOURCE RCDLEN(112) TEXT('API Book Source Code')
   ```

4. Transfer all of the source code on the CD-ROM to the source file you just created. Table A.1 lets you match the figures in the book to the source code.

Compiling the Source Code

Many of the source code examples on this CD-ROM are not meant to be compiled. They have been supplied for reference only. In those cases where the source was meant to be compiled, you will find instructions on compiling it in the first few lines of the source member itself.

As a general rule, the following examples may be used as guidelines for compiling the source members on the CD-ROM:

- For display files:

   ```
   CRTDSPF FILE(APIBOOK/XXX) SRCFILE(APIBOOK/SOURCE)
   ```

- For ILE RPG IV source members:

   ```
   CRTBNDRPG PGM(APIBOOK/XXX) SRCFILE(SOURCE/SOURCE
   ```

Index

A
Accept( ) API and parameters, 283, 283*t*, 286
Add Exit Program (ADDEXITPGM), 249
Add User Index (QUSADDUI), 232, 266-268,
   267*t*
ALLOC keyword, 12
Allow User Domain (QALWUSRDMN) system
   value, 27
anchor characters, in Web APIs and Web
   applications, 321
API Work Management Manual, 132
application program interfaces (APIs), xi
AS/400 System API Reference, 3
AS/400 Web Builder's Workshop Web site, 292
AS/400, xi-xii
ASCII
   Translate (QDCXLATE) API for, 283-284, 284*t*
   Web APIs and Web applications and, 291
asynchronous processing of open list APIs in,
   33-34, 57
attaching data queues to jobs using
   QRCVDTAQ, 245-252

data queue creation for, 249-250, **249**
job-notification exit points in, 248-249, **249**
parameters for, 248-250
authorities, 211-220

B
batch jobs, 133
BINARY data types, 7
Bind( ) API and parameters, 281-282, 282*t*
binding directory, 226
   CGI programs in, 296, 296, **296**
   Display Binding Directory (DSPBNDDIR)
     for, 297, **297**
   QC2LE, 226, 286
   socket APIs and, 286
   WEBBNDDIR, 300
browsers, 290

C
C language, 5
CALL statements, 6

Note: boldface numbers indicate illustrations or code listings; italic t indicates a table.

F

G

H

I

Note: boldface numbers indicate illustrations or code listings; italic t indicates a table.

Note: boldface numbers indicate illustrations or code listings; italic t indicates a table.